# Kickback

## Exposing the Global Corporate Bribery Network

## David Montero

VIKING

VIKING

An imprint of Penguin Random House LLC
375 Hudson Street
New York, New York 10014
penguin.com

[If applicable, insert the photo/text credits or the page reference to the credits here.]

ISBN 9780670016471 (hardcover)
ISBN 9780698139589 (ebook)

Printed in the United States of America
<FLUSH LEFT>10 9 8 7 6 5 4 3 2 1
<CENTERED>1 3 5 7 9 10 8 6 4 2
<FLUSH RIGHT>1 2 3 4 5 6 7 8 9 10

Set in [FONT NAME]
Designed by [NAME]

# Kickback

In Loving Memory of Patrica Ann Montero

# Contents

## Part I
### Encounters

## PART II
### The Kickback System

# PART III
## Impact

# PART IV
## Redress

# Part I

# Encounters

# Chapter 1

# **Introduction**

During Watergate, the appointment of a special prosecutor to investigate President Nixon's alleged tampering with elections was intended to mark the close of a sordid chapter of American history. Instead, that effort, culminating in Nixon's resignation, would prove to be only the beginning of a deeper political morass that America would face for decades to come. Congressional investigations would uncover for the first time that multinational corporations, through slush funds and bribes, were not only secretly funding political organizations at home, like Nixon's reelection campaign, but corrupting foreign officials abroad. This new perspective on the corporate abuse of power and its impact overseas would result in the Foreign Corrupt Practices Act (FCPA)—groundbreaking legislation that, by prohibiting commercial bribery for the first time in history, sought to change how capitalism and political affairs were conducted around the world.

Now, more than forty years later, we are experiencing a kind of déjà vu, as a special counsel investigates whether the president allegedly abused his power, again by obstructing an inquiry into a possible manipulation of the country's elections. Just as was the case in Watergate, whatever Special Counsel Robert Mueller uncovers will likely mark the beginning, rather than the end, of a reassessment of how power actually operates in this country. And just as in Watergate, there is the possibility that Mueller's far-reaching probe may reveal how tightly political corruption and corporate corruption are linked through bribery, just under the surface of American political life.

Nixon was the recipient of secret corporate donations, which were considered illegal because they should have been disclosed. But the payments, while unlawful, did not compromise the presidential election itself. Mueller's Russian inquiry is directed at a potentially far more serious crime: whether Donald Trump, the head of a sprawling business empire, colluded with a foreign power to deliberately sway the American electorate, committing the very crime that the FCPA has been trying to eradicate since Watergate—the offer of a foreign bribe, a kickback.

That law specifically states that a corporate bribe need not involve an actual exchange of money; an offer of anything of value, such as a promise, to a foreign government official is sufficient to violate its terms. This is precisely what Mueller is trying to ascertain: whether Trump, his company, his associates, or his family—or some combination of them—offered a promise to Russian government officials, a quid pro quo, that if they helped Trump by manipulating the elections, Trump, if victorious, would ease U.S. sanctions against Russia. Doing so would allow greater U.S. investment in Russia and would benefit Russian officials and oligarchs, the Trump business organization, the corporate interests of Trump's family, and former members of his senior staff, including Paul Manafort, his onetime campaign chairman, and Michael Flynn, his disgraced national security adviser. If the Trump Organization or anyone connected with it did make such a promise, and depending on how that promise was conveyed to Russian officials, the Justice Department would have strong grounds for pursuing an FCPA charge (among others). An FCPA violation is within Mueller's mandate to investigate "any matters that arose or may arise directly from the investigation." As has been widely observed, Mueller has hired two former federal law enforcement officials with extensive experience in investigating fraud, money laundering and overseas bribery—Andrew Weissmann, who ran the Justice Department's Fraud Section, which enforces the FCPA, and Greg Andres, who helped oversee FCPA policy in the Criminal Division.

The drama playing out in Washington starkly highlights the fact that "foreign corporate bribery" can be a deeply misleading term. We have come to regard it, when we think of it at all, as something that unscrupulous companies do in distant countries, so that any impact it has must be contained overseas. If a corporation pays kickbacks to a greedy government official abroad, why should we be concerned? But in a highly interconnected world, bound together by a global market, a global financial system, and the constant migration of people, goods, and capital, corruption rarely stays "out there." Bribes eventually harm Americans, American society, American values, and American interests, both domestically and around the world, in ways that are difficult to gauge.

Why do firms resort to bribery? The obvious reason is to gain an advantage over their competitors. But illicit payments also buy the illusion of growth in the short term, of increased market share and inflated firm value. It does not take into account the harm that this practice causes to companies themselves: sinking employee morale, diminished profit margins, and the possibility of hundreds of millions of dollars in fines and penalties—not to mention a reputation that will be associated with corruption and deceit. They also effectively steal the public's money because the majority of bribery cases involve capital-intensive development and infrastructure projects—such as roads, dams, defense systems, oil extraction, or mining—that are publicly funded. To recoup the bribes involved in winning such contracts, companies conspire with foreign officials to inflate the costs, sometimes by tens or even hundreds of millions of dollars. While the companies and the officials win out, tax payers are left shouldering the burden.

Corporate bribes involve a remarkable amount of money: The World Bank has estimated $1 trillion a year, though this may represent the high end; others have placed the amount at 10 percent of the $4 trillion spent annually on global public procurement.[1] Bribery is never just a matter of money, however; it almost always involves power as well. The actual payments are the manifestation of a secretly collusive system that, for most of modern history, corporations have been forging with foreign government officials around the globe. "These bribes are not just a way of doing business. They tell a much deeper tale: the officials receiving bribes are selling the natural resources of their own country. They're essentially destroying that country. Companies are complicit in that," says Michael Won, who retired from the FBI's FCPA squad in 2016.[2]

Corporate bribery is not a rogue act. IBM, Hewlett-Packard, Alcoa, Halliburton, Chevron, Pfizer, and Johnson & Johnson are only a few of the most prestigious corporations in America that have paid extraordinary fines to avoid prosecution on bribery charges. Many more are under criminal investigation, including, notably, Walmart. The companies that pay kickbacks are not being exploited or extorted; for many businesses in America and Europe, bribery is an active core strategy, a highly organized and sophisticated process, and one that is often approved by the CEO. In a 2011 survey of eleven thousand global businesses, one of the largest studies ever conducted, corporate managers reported that 32 percent of firms similar to theirs paid bribes for contracts.[3]

The officials whom corporations bribe are often heads of state, not merely low-level tax collectors or customs guards, though bribery at this level also appears to be widespread. Recently settled cases involve American and European corporations allegedly bribing several successive presidents of Nigeria and the former presidents of Panama, Costa Rica, Argentina, and Kazakhstan, to name just a few. Dozens of high-level government officials—ministers of oil or defense, parliamentarians, and vice presidents—detailed in these cases also received kickbacks. Large multinationals have also made payments to political parties in Greece, Nigeria, and Benin, among others, thereby effectively manipulating elections in those countries.

"Bribery" itself can be a misleading term, as we generally think of it as meaning a simple exchange of money, cash placed in the hand of a corrupt official. Millions of dollars in kickbacks are certainly made in that fashion. But because bribery is perpetrated by very sophisticated operators who seek to cover their tracks, the transactions are rarely that straightforward. These schemes can just as often involve the currency of power, with bribes paid out in favors, or some combination of favors and cash. These arrangements are almost always intricately layered affairs, engineered to be confusing in order to stymie law enforcement. ("If you're confused by this, that is exactly the idea," a British prosecutor once remarked to a jury, as she laid out the convoluted structure of a bribe.)[4] The people perpetrating the schemes often achieve opacity by hiding them behind an innocuous facade, whether a meeting at Trump Tower to discuss child adoptions in Russia, a consulting agreement with the U.S. president's lawyer for health-care policy advice, or an innocent-looking contract to hire houseboats in the swamps of Nigeria.

Because foreign kickbacks are widely perceived to be strictly a business issue, the public has also come to view them as causing no real harm beyond the "market." American prosecutors, likewise, treat foreign bribery as little more than a market transgression. As one example, Siemens Corporation, the German engineering giant, was criminally fined by the Justice Department and German authorities for running one of largest bribery operations in history—in less than a decade, the company paid more than $1 billion in kickbacks in dozens of countries, including some of the poorest, most unstable places on earth. It eventually paid $1.6 billion in fines to avoid being prosecuted, the largest such penalty in history.[5] But Siemens was fined for failing only to keep accurate financial records and for cheating its competitors, not for any impact its corruption may have had in foreign countries. In fact, Siemens paid most of its fines to the U.S. and German governments, and nothing to many of the foreign governments and citizens actually affected by the kickbacks. Since then, the company has avoided acknowledging that its bribes may have caused harm in those countries. Meanwhile, more than three thousand news reports have been published about the Siemens matter, making it one of the most visible and well-documented corruption cases. Yet not a single article in the English language press has attempted to follow the Siemens money trail and its consequences in the countries where the bribes were paid.

Part of the reason for this misconception is that bribery, unlike other crimes, often plays out slowly, with secret payments flowing between a company and a government over the course of years, if not decades, so its impact is not obvious until long after money or power has changed hands. The result is a slow-motion disaster, leaving economic, political, and social damage that cannot be detected unless someone begins to look for it.

Once we do become aware of it, though, we begin to recognize that bribery is widespread, and is implicated in major political events and news stories, as well as histories we thought we knew— like the origins of the United States, like Watergate, like the war in Iraq. Perhaps the Trump presidency may yet compel Americans, in particular, to understand the ramifications of bribes. The unnerving sense of violation we now feel is a way of life in many nations of the world. In Greece, Nigeria, Costa Rica, and Panama, to name just a few, citizens have become outraged that foreign corporations have succeeded in interfering with and manipulating their political systems. In this regard, the United States can no longer lay claim to exceptionalism.

Under the FCPA, the Justice Department cannot bring charges against foreign officials who receive bribes, and therefore cannot openly name them. In court documents, these individuals are designated by references like "High-level Official 1," with their period in office usually detailed as well. Through investigation and reporting, however, it is possible to identify the perpetrators and the regimes they have served. A critical part of understanding the danger of overseas bribery is uncovering just whom corporations are bribing and following the money on the ground, in the foreign country where it was paid. Unpacking the story of the afterlife of a bribe is the subject of this book.

As I will detail in the coming pages, kickbacks have directly supported some of the most dangerous individuals on earth—men who are directly working against democracy, freedom, and equality. Through bribes, corporations become participants in their repression and violence.

Assessing the extent of this damage will help explain why the fight to eradicate corporate bribery is so vital. Many important steps have already been taken in this regard. For the first thirty years of its existence, the FCPA was virtually never enforced, enabling the culture of corporate kickbacks to flourish. But in the early 2000s, a host of factors—greater international legal cooperation, the terrorist attacks of September 11, the passage of the Sarbanes-Oxley Act, and the war in Iraq—galvanized the Justice Department to launch the first-ever global crackdown against corporate graft. Although it does not often come to the public's attention, the antibribery effort is second only to fighting terrorism as a priority for U.S. law enforcement.

This campaign, which has led to more than two hundred bribery-related investigations in the United States alone, has produced thousands of pages of court documents, including internal company emails, memos, and banking information, as well as testimony from dozens of witnesses, corporate-executive defendants, and law enforcement agencies. Thanks to this treasure trove of information, we now know more than ever how the system operates, particularly which companies are involved; how much they are paying in bribes and for what contracts; how these companies use middlemen and criminals to gain access; and how companies route and hide the payments through a complex system of fake contracts, altered receipts, hidden shell companies, and offshore bank accounts. In the last ten years alone, two dozen prosecutors at the Justice Department's Fraud Section in Washington, D.C., have brought a record number of FCPA prosecutions, ramped up the stakes for offenses, and placed long-overdue pressure on companies to reform from within.

Even as President Trump refuses to discuss his own questionable relationship with Russia, he has been an outspoken critic of efforts to stop bribery. In a 2012 interview with CNBC he said: "Now every other country goes into these places and they do what they have to do. It's a horrible law and it should be changed," adding, "I mean, we are like the policemen for the world. It's ridiculous."[6] Trump's views do not seem to have changed since entering the White House. According to a 2017 article in the *New Yorker*, he complained to then Secretary of State Rex Tillerson that the FCPA unfairly penalized American companies for paying bribes.[7]

The Trump administration is already endeavoring to turn this position into policy, appointing an outspoken critic of the FCPA, Jay Clayton, to chair the Securities and Exchange Commission, the regulatory body that is responsible for enforcing the FCPA in conjunction with the Justice Department.[8] The administration has also revised FCPA enforcement policy to be more "business friendly," making it much easier for companies to cut deals to avoid prosecution, in the eyes of many critics. This comes in conjunction with a rollback of the Cardin-Lugar provision of the Dodd-Frank Act, which required energy companies listed on U.S. stock exchanges to disclose when they make payments to foreign government officials—legislation that was considered a key point of progress in U.S. efforts to combat corporate kickbacks overseas. The Republican-led Congress voted to repeal Cardin-Lugar shortly after Trump entered the White House, and the president signed it into law in February 2017.[9] (It should be noted that, should Special Counsel Mueller recommend an FCPA-related charge against the Trump Organization, it might well benefit from the lessening of FCPA enforcement that Trump himself is promoting.)

With their numerous questionable deals and even more questionable links to Russian oligarchs and a hostile Putin regime,

Trump and Manafort are emblematic figures of the global culture of corporate kickbacks. The men who profit from bribery in business often move from business into politics. But when they rise to the level of the White House and begin bending the will of the American government to minimize their liability for corruption, and make it possible for their family and associates to further profit from conflicts of interest, a line has been crossed from which there may be no turning back. If the United States, a nation whose very existence was in part a principled stand against corruption, becomes an enabler of corruption, it would constitute a betrayal of its own history.

Western civilization has, throughout its history, confronted a number of corporate bribery scandals. Exposing them has not only revealed their wide scope, but given rise to a powerful discourse about democracy and the limits of corporate power. We can examine this by tracing the thread of bribery back to the emergence of modern corporations, and an eighteenth-century scandal involving India and Great Britain that would reverberate for centuries and figure into the origins of the United States.

# Chapter 2

# "Foul Corruption"

Clouds threatened rain by the time Robert Clive, a cunning and ambitious director of the British East India Company, arrived at the grove of mango trees known as Laksha Bagh with some three thousand soldiers under his command. It was the morning of June 23, 1757, and they had come to the small village of Plassey, on the banks of the Hughli River in West Bengal.[1] With its rich agricultural lands and abundant textile production, Bengal was the seat of industrial power in eighteenth-century India, which made it a coveted prize in the company's fierce competition with the Dutch and the French. Standing in the way was Siraj-ud-Daulah, the country's twenty-four-year-old prince and a fierce opponent of British interests. As Clive's soldiers formed into three divisions, Siraj-ud-Daulah's forces, numbering some fifty thousand, were dug into entrenchments a mile away. The prince was equipped with war elephants and more than fifty cannons, not to mention home-field advantage. But Clive had an advantage of his own: He had paid off the enemy with a bribe. When storms erupted at noon and the prince's cannons opened fire, Clive retired to a hunting lodge in a wood—and slept. The battle, he had ensured, had already been won.[2]

The British East India Company, founded in London in 1601, was the first modern corporation in history—the first to issue joint-stock ownership, the first to offer limited liability to shareholders, and the first to use bribery as a tool of political and economic manipulation in the developing world. The company's officers were well versed in the art of graft, having bribed dignitaries and officials, both at home and abroad, since at least the late 1600s.[3] In 1695, the British House of Commons investigated allegations that Sir Thomas Cooke, one of the company's governors, paid a bribe to the Duke of Leeds, hoping to favorably influence the renewal of the company's charter. He was jailed in the Tower of London and later impeached.[4] In 1717, the company used bribes to secure the largest trade concession ever granted to a foreign company in India. They lavished gifts upon the feeble-minded Mughal emperor Farrukhsiyar and promised him three thousand rupees a year.[5] In return Farrukhsiyar bartered away the economic sovereignty of Bengal by granting the company permission to conduct tax-free trade there—giving them a virtual monopoly.

If bribing Farrukhsiyar marked the opening move in the company's eventual dominion over India, Clive's bribe in 1757 was the closer. Clive had arranged a series of secret meetings with Mir Jafar, the commander in chief of Siraj-ud-Daulah's army, promising to make Jafar the new prince if he agreed to stand aside when Clive's private militia invaded Bengal. Though grossly outnumbered at Plassey, the British prevailed. After the prince's cannons were fired, Jafar's forces abandoned the battlefield, and Siraj-ud-Daulah fled, only to be later captured and killed. Clive's act of treachery would effectively inaugurate the ascendancy of the British Empire in India, and the colonial subjugation of millions of South Asians for two centuries. Speaking years later before the House of Commons, he unapologetically affirmed: "When the very existence of the Company was at stake . . . it was a matter of true policy and of justice to deceive so great a villain."[6]

The Plassey agreement was the prototypical corporate kickback deal: a bribe secretly offered to a foreign official to secure a business advantage in an emerging market. The elements of the Plassey bribe, however, were more sharply pronounced than is typical of such deals today. Plassey featured not only deceit, but betrayal. Most contemporary bribes do not result in a corporation's winning control of an entire country. And corporations, of course, no longer wield private armies as the instrument of empire. Still, these are differences in degree, not kind. Just as Mir Jafar betrayed his countrymen and his prince, so too do foreign officials betray the citizens they serve now. Often what is bartered away today is, if not a country, then a large percentage of its national wealth.

After Plassey, Bengal, once India's most fertile bed of industry, was plunged into devastating famine and economic ruin. The British Parliament would open an inquiry in 1772 to probe the issue, which would eventually focus on Clive, his private fortune, and his personal integrity.

This would not be the last investigation of the East India Company's corrupt practices. In fact, the British Crown and its citizens—including such pillars of the Enlightenment as Thomas Paine—would publicly grapple with the moral and political consequences of the company's overseas corruption for several years. This new form of crime, involving illicit acts committed by citizens of one country in the territories of another, led to a public discourse, one of the earliest of its kind, about corporate responsibility, about bribery's toll overseas, about the morality of profit gained by corruption.

Their Indian adventure made Clive and his cohorts rich beyond their dreams. On their return to England, they used the proceeds of their deception to buy off politicians and bribe their way into office. The historian William Dalrymple quotes the great orator Edmund Burke, who railed against them: "To-day the Commons of Great Britain prosecutes the delinquents of India. Tomorrow these delinquents of India may be the Commons of Great Britain."[7]

\* \* \*

In April 1774, Thomas Paine, then thirty-eight years old, left England a dejected and broken man, terminated from his job as an excise collector and divorced from his second wife. Seeking a fresh start, he boarded a ship for the New World, carrying in his pocket letters of introduction from Benjamin Franklin, whom he had chanced to meet in London the year before. Paine settled in Philadelphia that November and took a job editing the *Pennsylvania Magazine*, an abolitionist publication, and soon reinvented himself as a journalist.

With distance from England, Paine could see his former home more clearly, and began publishing ferocious diatribes against what he viewed as its many evils: its tyranny in the American colonies, its slave trading in Africa, the growing shadow of its empire around the world. These writings would, of course, become the inspiration for *Common Sense* and *The Rights of Man,* the foundational treatises that helped inspire the American Revolution and the American Constitution.

But what originally agitated Paine was the corruption and plunder of the East India Company. While in London, he had followed the condemnation of the company then playing out in parliamentary hearings between 1772 and 1773—hearings that "made the public generally acquainted for the first time with many startling facts," as one historical account relays. Rumors about the extent of Robert Clive's personal fortune, meanwhile, were legion, to the point of scandal. Clive himself lamented that "the public papers . . . teem with scurrility and abuse against me."[8]

In the summer of 1772, John Burgoyne, a parliamentarian from Preston, made an urgent plea before the House of Commons to establish a special committee to probe the governance and corruption of the East India Company and determine measures for its reform. For Burgoyne, the question of how to regulate the company was not merely a matter of business; presciently, he associated the regulation of corporate conduct overseas with a much greater issue: "The fate of a great portion of the globe . . . the rights of humanity are involved in this question. Good God! what a call!" he thundered.[9] The House, swayed by Burgoyne's oratory, approved the formation of the committee, and the inquiry began. With Burgoyne serving as its head, its hearings soon focused on Clive.

The company had committed countless atrocities in the course of expanding its dominion, not only in India, but also in China, Africa, and the Americas. But what particularly incensed Burgoyne—in fact, what he harped upon for several days of heated discourse in the summer of 1772—was Clive's treachery at the Battle of Plassey: "The famous revolution which removed Surah al Dowla from the Throne was brought about by means which have left a lasting infamy on the English name,"[10] Burgoyne said.

The precise details of the Plassey affair are murky. But one point in particular is worth noting: The East India Company drew up a thirteen-article treaty with Mir Jafar. Its final article stated that the company would assist "Meer Jaffier Khan Behauder with all our force, to obtain the Soubahship [rulership] of the Provinces of Bengal, Behar, and Orissa."[11] As submitted to the company's official records, however, the treaty omitted this article, and therefore any reference to the bribe. (A copy containing the article turned up later among other treaties.) Burgoyne interrogated witness after witness in an attempt to uncover why the thirteenth article had been removed, but failed to do so. Clive testified that he had forgotten that such an article had ever existed. The closest Burgoyne came to the truth was when Clive's secretary, John Walsh, surmised that there were likely two copies of the treaty: Mir Jafar was given one that included the thirteenth article, while a second copy, omitting it, was deposited in the company's accounts. Walsh attributed the omission to a clerical error, or, as he put it: "great irregulation in the office, there being few servants."[12] Nonetheless, Burgoyne's investigation revealed how, among its many other transgressions, the East India Company kept lax, and possibly dubious, internal books and records—one of the earliest examples of such violations being examined.

Burgoyne and his committee went on to discover that the greatest crime of Plassey was not the bribe itself, but its aftermath. The company drained Bengal's ample treasury, loading more than a hundred boats with gold and silver, worth almost $300 million in today's currency, and shipping them off to England. Much of that wealth flowed directly into the accounts of Clive, now appointed governor of Bengal. Overnight he became one of the richest men in England (according to Dalrymple, Clive profited to the tune of £23 million in today's currency[13]). Even as Bengal's wealth was depleted, Clive's administration decreased wages for weavers while increasing their land taxes. When the country was devastated by floods and droughts, the company refused to provide public aid. Famine spread, and a third of Bengal's population is believed to have perished between 1769 and 1773. (Estimates range from 1 million to 10 million people.) In reporting these "accounts shocking to human nature" to the House, Burgoyne, paraphrasing from *Hamlet*, charged that the Company's "foul corruption mining all beneath/Infects unseen."[14]

With so many dead and dying, land revenues plummeted. The company faced a mounting debt of £1.5 million, as its stock price began to plunge. By 1772 it was in full-blown crisis. In a foreshadowing of our own times, the world's most powerful corporation needed a government bailout and asked the Bank of England for a loan of £1 million. Directors like Clive, meanwhile, lived opulently, buying property throughout England. In 1773, with bankruptcy looming, the East India Company raised the price of tea in America—prompting a chain of events that began with the Boston Tea Party and eventually led to the American Revolution.

Burgoyne had promised that his inquiry would "hold up the mirror of truth to the Company, wherein they may see themselves and their affairs as they are."[15] In examining how the company comported itself abroad, he also turned a mirror to the character of British society of the time. It is still fascinating to read in the transcripts of these debates learned men of the eighteenth century commiserating with the subjugated victims of the Subcontinent. The committee members often debated until dawn. Sir William Meredith, a Rockingham Whig representing Wigan, observed, "[B]elieving there is a God above us, I believe also, that acquisitions made by shedding the blood of innocent princes, and by wringing from an innocent people their substance, can never prosper."[16]

For the most part, however, Burgoyne failed in his objective. Outraged at the manner in which Clive had personally enriched himself, Burgoyne believed the prodigious sums that Clive and his officers had amassed from Bengal's treasury belonged to the British government. "Robert Lord Clive abused the power with which he was entrusted, to the evil example of the servants of the public,"[17] Burgoyne said on May 3, 1773. He wanted a vote to censure Clive and strip him of his wealth.

But Clive had by then achieved the status of a national war hero. He was also a member of Parliament (MP), had been knighted, been made a baron, and had conferred on him countless other titles. The parliamentary committee not only exonerated him but added another honor to Clive's glory: It voted unanimously to pass a resolution stating that Clive "rendered great and meritorious services to his country."[18]

The revelations of Burgoyne's committee did, however, lead to the passage of the Regulating Act of 1773, the first attempt by the British government to control the East India Company. Salient among the act's provisions was a requirement that the company furnish all its correspondence regarding revenue in Bengal to the British Treasury, and all correspondence regarding civil and military matters to the Secretary of State.[19] Another forbade the company's employees from accepting gifts or bribes, though it did not prohibit them from *offering* gifts or bribes. (England would not specifically criminalize corporate overseas bribery until 2010.) Still, the act was, among other things, a prototypical attempt by government to introduce internal corporate compliance and anti-corruption measures. In return for accepting these strictures, the company received its government bailout of £1 million.

Robert Clive, paragon of the empire, had been acquitted of corruption charges, but ultimately he could not acquit himself. On November 22, 1774, he was found dead in his home, apparently by his own hand. Clive was said to have been both a manic depressive (he had twice in his life attempted suicide) and an opium addict, having taken the drug for chronic abdominal pains. Some accounts claim he took his life with an overdose of drugs; others, with a penknife to the throat. Historians concur that Clive, a mentally unstable parvenu, never recovered from having his name being so publicly tarnished.

One week later, Thomas Paine's ship reached American shores. In March 1775, he published a short but powerful pamphlet entitled "Reflections on the Life and Death of Robert Clive," in which he attacked Clive's moral bankruptcy, as well as that of the company. "Lord Clive is himself a treatise upon vanity, printed in a golden type," Paine wrote. "The British sword is set up for sale; the heads of contending Nabobs [princes] are offered at a price, and the bribe taken from both sides."[20]As historian Daniel O'Neill has argued, "The atrocities in India were a fundamental impetus for Paine's argument, in *Common Sense* (1776), on behalf of American independence."[21]

In "A Serious Thought," published the following October, Paine wrote, "When I reflect on the horrid cruelties exercised by Britain in the East Indies—How thousands perished by artificial famine . . . I hesitate not for a moment to believe that the Almighty will finally separate America from Britain."[22] This was one of the earliest publications to prefigure the Declaration of Independence.

During the Revolutionary War, when Paine promoted the cause of American independence, he again cited Clive. In *The Crisis,* published in 1778, he wrote: "[Britain's] late reduction of India, under Clive and his successors, was not so properly a conquest as an extermination of mankind. . . . For the domestic happiness of Britain and the peace of the world, I wish she had not a foot of land but what is circumscribed within her own island."[23]

America, the colony of a monarchy and subject to the economic hegemony of the East India Company, was uniquely attuned to the idea that freedom from corruption was a human right, and one that could legitimately be gained through sedition. America was conceived as a tabula rasa, a place that would stand apart from and in direct opposition to such practices. Perhaps it is fitting, then, that a nation founded on such principles should also be the first to explicitly prohibit corporations from paying bribes overseas—though it would take more than two hundred years to do so.

*  *  *

In 1975, Peter Clark was a young attorney in the Enforcement Division of the U.S. Securities and Exchange Commission. Founded three years earlier, the Enforcement Division was tasked with investigating possible violations of federal securities laws. One morning, Clark was in his office when the division's director, Stanley Sporkin, appeared, greatly vexed.[24] Sporkin, tall and corpulent with deep-set eyes, was waving a newspaper, Clark recalled. "How the 'bleep' could a publicly held company have a slush fund?" Sporkin asked.

Two years had passed since the Watergate scandal broke, and less than a year since President Nixon had resigned, but the reverberations of the scandal were still rocking Washington. Its revelation that multinational corporations, including some of the most prestigious brands in the United States, had been making illegal contributions to political parties not only at home but in foreign countries around the world would later be described by Ray Garrett, the chairman of the SEC, as "the second half of Watergate, and by far the larger half."[25]

By 1975, Frank Church of Idaho had convened a Senate Subcommittee on Multinational Corporations to examine, as one of his colleagues said, "U.S. corporate business practices abroad" and to "ascertain the impact of these practices on U.S. foreign policy."[26] Each night Sporkin would return home from work and watch the hearings on television. One evening in mid-May he listened to Robert Dorsey, the chairman of the board of Gulf Oil, testify before the committee. Dorsey admitted that between 1966 and 1970 Gulf Oil had paid $4 million in bribes to the Democratic Republican Party of South Korea, funds principally intended to support the party's reelection campaign in 1971. Dorsey went on to explain how Gulf funneled the money: "Although each of the contributions came from company funds in the United States, the transfers were recorded as an advance to Bahamas Exploration Co. Ltd., where they reflected on the books and records of Bahamas Exploration Co., as an expense."[27] (In January 1976, Dorsey and three other officers of Gulf Oil resigned.)[28]

Sporkin was beside himself. In addition to being an attorney, he had also been trained as a certified public accountant and wanted to know more about how Gulf's slush fund worked. He got a member of his staff, Robert Ryan, on the phone, and told him, "I want you to go to the company and find out what happened here, how they did it."[29] Gulf Oil executives candidly explained to Ryan that they had moved the money by transferring it from Gulf to the bank account in the Bahamas in amounts small enough to avoid suspicion from the IRS and external auditors. Most important, they confirmed Dorsey's testimony that they had falsely recorded the payments as capital contributions.

At the time, there was no law that specifically prohibited a U.S. corporation from bribing a foreign government official, although several existing statutes, including the Bank Secrecy Act, the RICO laws, and provisions of the IRS's criminal code were applicable to how a bribe was paid and how it might be covered up. But what really struck Sporkin was that whereas businesses had to keep books, there was no federal law requiring publicly traded companies to keep *honest* books and records. "It was inconceivable to me," he recalled, "that companies could be bribing all over the world, and the shareholders not know how they're making their money."[30]

The SEC filed an injunctive order against Gulf Oil on the grounds that their bribes were material information that should have been disclosed to investors, and that by failing to disclose them, it violated existing federal securities laws. The SEC soon investigated other large corporations and discovered that many had established subsidiaries, often domiciled in distant countries, and opened accounts in which hundreds of millions of dollars were hidden.[31] In many cases, these funds were withdrawn as cash and delivered directly to foreign officials or transferred to their bank accounts in Switzerland or Singapore.

This was, in fact, standard procedure for some of the largest corporations in America. Lockheed, the aircraft manufacturer, used a company called Triad to bribe Saudi generals, while Northrop, an aerospace giant, paid off various foreign officials through a company called the Economic and Development Corporation (EDC).[32] The template for modern-day bribery had been established by multinational corporations sometime after the end of the Second World War. In the case of Gulf Oil, its chairman, William K. Whiteford, had set up Bahamas Exploration Co. in 1959 to "serve as a conduit for illegal and questionable payments."[33] By 1976, Sporkin and the Enforcement Division had filed injunctive orders against sixty-five large corporations.

As the investigations unfolded, Northrop revealed that it had paid $30 million in just two years to foreign agents to win business deals.[34] Exxon admitted to paying $46 million to political parties in Italy,[35] while Lockheed had paid $200 million to foreign agents and officials around the world, including the prime minister of Japan and Prince Bernhard in the Netherlands.[36] As Senator Charles Percy of Illinois observed, "I am convinced that creative minds in the name of greed can concoct schemes faster than we can get legislation against them."[37]

These discoveries convulsed both Washington and Wall Street. At eight o'clock on the morning of February 3, 1975, Eli M. Black, the founder and CEO of United Brands, the multinational fruit company, went to his offices on the Forty-fourth floor of the Pan Am Building in Manhattan. Black had built United, and its Chiquita brand was responsible for nearly one third of all bananas brought into the United States. The SEC had discovered that United Brands had offered $2.5 million in bribes to foreign officials, including the president of Honduras, Oswaldo López Arellano.[38] Using his briefcase, Black smashed out the windows facing Park Avenue and, still holding the case, leaped out the window, plunging to his death.

"We kept bringing these cases. The companies would not contest them. We would get consent decrees," Sporkin recalled. "And the reason they would not contest them is they didn't want to have to lay out the facts of the bribery."[39] Eventually the SEC's inquiry into overseas bribery encompassed more than 200 U.S. companies. While this represented only a fraction of American concerns doing business overseas, the list included 117 members of the Fortune 500, the biggest and best of American industry. "None of us dreamed there were the millions, the tens of millions, the hundreds of millions, that we have found," Ray Garrett told *Newsweek* at the time. "This is bribery, influence-peddling and corruption on a scale I had never dreamed existed."[40]

Sporkin's team did not have the resources to investigate all the implicated companies. "It was a task force, really like a pickup baseball team—ten sharp people," Peter Clark explained. Sporkin discussed the matter with Garrett and others, and the team devised a plan. In early 1976, the Enforcement Division announced a voluntary disclosure program. The SEC stipulated that if multinationals wanted to settle injunctive actions, they would have to agree to certain terms: They would have to publicly disclose any possible bribe payments they had made; they would have to set up, at their own expense, an independent committee to fully investigate the bribes; and they would have to demonstrate that they had taken the steps to ensure that such activity would never happen again.[41] This system of credit for cooperating is a bargain that has defined corporate overseas bribery settlements to this day. "It promised nothing— you weren't guaranteed immunity. It didn't say you would not be charged civilly or criminally," Clark, who helped oversee the program, noted.

"I don't think anyone was prepared for the number of disclosures that came forward," Clark added. [42] The official number reported at the time was between three hundred to four hundred companies, but Clark believes it was closer to six hundred. The companies admitted to having paid the combined equivalent in today's currency of more than $1 billion in bribes to officials overseas, in many cases, top management was aware of the payments.[43] "The bribes and payoffs associated with doing business abroad represent a pattern of crookedness that would make, in terms of its scope and magnitude, crookedness in politics look like a Sunday school picnic by comparison," Senator Church observed.[44] The problem was, even when Sporkin's team identified solid evidence of egregious corruption, there was no law under which to bring the charges. "We could prove bribery, but we couldn't prosecute it as bribery," Clark explained.

Senator William Proxmire of Wisconsin, chairman of the Senate Banking Committee, had led the investigation into Lockheed's alleged bribery in Japan and the Netherlands, and so was certainly aware of the existence of corporate bribery. But the magnitude of payments uncovered by Sporkin and the SEC shocked him. "This bloodletting, unfortunately, is continuing. It is the disgrace of our free enterprise system," he said in public remarks at the time.[45]

Proxmire believed that although the SEC had done all it could under the disclosure program, what was really needed was a law specifically prohibiting foreign bribery. The existing laws were not sufficient, as they addressed only the means through which a bribe might be paid, but not the act of paying a bribe itself. Proxmire was encouraged in part by Robert Dorsey, Gulf's chairman, who told the Senate subcommittee that such a law would be welcomed by the companies themselves: "Such a statute on our books would make it easier to resist the very intense pressures which are placed upon us from time to time. If we could cite our law which says that we just may not do it, we would be in better position to resist these pressures and to refuse requests," he observed.[46]

Proxmire had his staff contact Sporkin and asked how he could help the team's efforts. "And I said to him," Sporkin recalled, "'Well, we're doing pretty well with what we have, but we could use a law.' He says, 'What kind of law?' And I had been thinking about it. I said we need a law that requires a public company trading in the United States to keep accurate books and records." That alone would not go far enough, Proxmire replied. "He wanted to have a bribery provision. It would be against the law for a public company that makes filings with the SEC to bribe a foreign official to obtain business," Sporkin explained. "I wasn't keen on bribery because I thought it would be too hard to prove bribery overseas. That was his choice."

In December 1977, after a hard-fought battle, Proxmire got the law he wanted: The Foreign Corrupt Practices Act was approved by the House of Representatives by a vote of 349–0, approved by the Senate, and then signed into law by President Jimmy Carter on December 19.

Today, nearly forty years later, enforcement of the FCPA has become a critical focus of the Justice Department, the SEC, and the FBI. It is one of the largest white-collar crime concerns of the private bar; it has resulted in veritable upheaval and dramatic reform in corporate culture, not to mention international law; it has yielded billions of dollars in corporate fines and penalties. It has, in short, fundamentally changed what it means to *do* business around the world—and what it means to *be* a business in the world.

The question is: What exactly did this curious piece of law stand for? What did it originally hope to accomplish? And is modern enforcement of the law living up to its original intent?

\* \* \*

Why did it take modern societies so long to outlaw these practices? The early history of corporate activity abroad, particularly with regard to corruption, is spotty at best, but given that the East India Company indulged in the practice, many other companies probably did as well, especially since no laws in any land prevented them from doing so. The law proscribing corporations from bribing officials overseas was a peculiarly American response, one that came at an especially dark and unstable moment in the nation's history.

Not only had corruption had been exposed in the White House, but corruption overseas was undermining the image of America and what it hoped to achieve in the world. To understand why this was the case, it is instructive to recall the period of reckoning that gave rise to the Foreign Corrupt Practices Act.

Two years of congressional hearings preceded the passage of the FCPA in 1977. Never before—or since—had Congress and the American public looked so deeply and unflinchingly into the most alarming aspect of commercial bribery: its destructive impact overseas. Throughout the congressional deliberations, senators, speakers, and expert witnesses all stressed that bribery was not just a business transaction or an economic matter. Joe Biden, then a young senator from Delaware, captured its greater significance: "I get really very upset and concerned about not just the bribery, but how it directly flies in the face of our foreign policy and the best interest of our government."[47]

As investigations by the SEC and the Senate revealed in minute detail, Lockheed had not just bribed officials in Japan, but paid tens of millions of dollars to democratic political parties in Italy. In both cases, the company was negotiating sales of military aircraft. When these payments were exposed, the two governments involved were shaken and nearly toppled. The Japanese prime minister, who had allegedly received $1.7 million in bribes, eventually resigned, while in Italy, the communist party won spectacularly during elections in 1976 on the grounds that they were less corrupt than the democratic parties that had received bribes from Lockheed.[48] The repercussions in Japan led Representative Stephen Solarz of New York to conclude: "A relationship which is at the very heart of our foreign policy was potentially jeopardized." He added, regarding Italy: "It is not inconceivable that as a result of these disclosures, our whole foreign policy in both the Mediterranean as well as the southern flank of NATO will be ultimately undermined."[49]

The hearings conducted between 1975 and 1977 opened another dimension in this discourse: The greatest fallout from the bribery cases was borne by the foreign countries where the payments were made. In a Senate hearing in 1975, in an exchange between Senator Church and William Cowden, the chief international salesman of Lockheed, Church pointed out that Lockheed's C-130 plane had no direct competition, yet Lockheed had paid bribes to government officials in Indonesia in order to sell it. "Why do you even pay commissions or kickbacks or bribes when you don't even have a competitor for this plane?" he asked. Cowden replied, "Because we are frequently competing not necessarily with another airplane just like ours but we are competing for the sales dollars that would be spent on something else"—effectively acknowledging that the company had bribed foreign officials to buy military equipment that Indonesia might not even need and could have spent on something else, like schools. "That is an extraordinary argument," Church responded, adding, "If you base your sales on payoffs to government officials and make them rich, then you force these governments in the direction of military sales purchases when other purchases might be far more beneficial to them and to their people." He concluded: "The bigger the bribe then the bigger the profit for the company and the greater the diversion of resources from poor countries to the purchase of this kind of stuff."[50]

The cases examined by Congress exposed the profound power of bribes to affect political development overseas—even the course of history. For example, after Gulf Oil bribed South Korea's Democratic Republican Party, it won by only 51 percent. Senator Dick Clark of Iowa asked Bob Dorsey: "It is conceivable, it seems to me, that your contribution may have made the difference. Do you think that is possible?" "Statistically," Dorsey replied, "I would have to admit you are right."[51] Congressman John E. Moss then counseled: "Surely the public expects more than to have foreign policy made in the boardrooms of United Brands or Lockheed."[52]

Senator Percy, who, with his keen and articulate observations, often served in these deliberations as the voice of the American conscience, admonished: "The means we use to achieve our objectives in this world define the type of world we are going to live in."[53]

The adoption of the Foreign Corrupt Practices Act thus represented a response to bribery's impact on American foreign policy and security goals, and on the democratic and economic development of foreign nations. Its emphasis on transparency in business transactions and on safeguarding free markets was not its ultimate goal: "At its inception, Congress understood the FCPA as an instrument for promoting democratic values in developing countries," Andrew Spalding, an assistant professor of law at the University of Virginia, has written.[54] The framers of the FCPA, working during the height of the Cold War, worried that bribery would play into the hands of Communists, as it had in Italy. The fight to eradicate corporate kickbacks was a key policy concern, for if something was not done to address them, "this country and its major allies are going to wake up one morning and find that the basis of stable democratic government has been eaten away," Senator Church observed.[55]

Spalding describes how unprecedented an effort the FCPA was: It was not just that the statute criminalized the bribing of an official—many existing laws did that—but it forbade bribing a foreign official in another country, and as such represented an assertion of jurisdiction never before attempted in the fight against bribery. The law effectively sought to punish an extraterritorial crime, committed by both American and foreign companies, whose ultimate victims were the citizens of a foreign nation. "Congress enacted a statute in which U.S. taxpayers would pay to protect non-taxpayers from the harms of bribery," Spalding wrote.[56]

"For the first time in the history of the world, a measure for bribery was introduced into law that was universal as far as those subjected to the law were concerned. For the first time, a country made it criminal to corrupt the officials of another country," John T. Noonan writes in his exhaustive work on the subject, *Bribe: The Intellectual History of a Moral Idea.*"[57] Noonan's point is that, for more than three hundred years, corporate bribery was endured as an inevitable global evil. It was no small feat the United States took it upon itself to prohibit it, at a time when other governments essentially looked the other way regarding kickbacks and their impact.

\* \* \*

The Foreign Corrupt Practices Act is a deceptively simple statute, comprised of two parts. The first, which owes its existence to Stanley Sporkin, requires that any corporation that trades on a U.S. stock exchange keep accurate books and records, and implement a system of internal accounting controls. In other words, it addresses the issue of how bribes can be hidden through falsified financial accounting. The law applies not only to American corporations, or corporations headquartered in the United States, but to any foreign publicly traded corporation that issues stock on an American stock exchange. The United States had effectively granted itself the power to police foreign corporations, even though the home countries of those entities did not outlaw bribery themselves, and in some cases tacitly encouraged it. (Until the early 2000s, corporate bribes in Germany were actually tax deductible.) These extraterritoriality provisions gave the FCPA controversial authority, which would later be reinterpreted and then extended to dramatic effect. Private corporations headquartered in the United States are also subject to the law.

The second part of the FCPA, which owes its existence to William Proxmire, criminalizes the actual paying of bribes to officials of a foreign country. The law states that a company needn't actually pay a bribe to a foreign official to fall afoul of the law—the promise of a payment or "anything of value" is enough to trigger a violation. The statute also ensures that corporate entities do not avoid culpability by using the financial chicanery that Gulf, Lockheed, and others had employed in using a middleman, agent, or hidden subsidiary to pay a bribe. The law makes clear that corporations are liable for the bribery of their subsidiaries and their agents.

Proxmire had to fight for this provision, as many of his senatorial colleagues did not believe it necessary or feasible to criminalize bribery. Some argued that requiring corporations to disclose their bribes would be sufficient—that multinationals could be counted on to police themselves, to turn up evidence of their wrongdoing, and to implement the necessary changes. "Certainly, there are subtleties and complexities in the foreign bribery issue," Proxmire said, "but we should be able to agree after more than a year of investigation the time has come to provide a remedy for an act as simple and outrageous as bribery."[58]

However profound the FCPA's ratification, the subsequent history of its enforcement has been disappointing. During the congressional hearings, Senator Proxmire and others made clear their preference that the SEC be in charge of enforcing any new anti-bribery law. This was not only a practical decision, given the SEC's history of securities regulation and its investigation of corporate bribery after Watergate, but also one driven by a deep skepticism, held by Congress and the public alike, of the U.S. Justice Department at that time. "If we learned anything in the Watergate affair, we learned that the Department of Justice is not a department we can always rely on, especially when you have top influential corporate officials that are involved," Proxmire said. "They prosecute the hoodlums. They haven't got such a good record on white-collar crime."[59]

The problem was that the SEC did not want the job. The commission's chairman, Roderick M. Hills, testified before Congress in 1976 that it "would prefer not to be involved even in the civil enforcement of such prohibitions."[60] The SEC recognized that enforcing a foreign bribery law, ipso facto, would necessarily involve it in matters of U.S. foreign policy and national interests—an expertise far beyond its official mandate "to protect investors, maintain fair, orderly, and efficient markets, and facilitate capital formation," as Barbara Black, a professor of law at the University of Cincinnati College of Law, has pointed out.[61]

In the end, the solution was a division of responsibility: Roughly speaking, the SEC was tasked with enforcing the books and records provision of the FCPA, and bringing civil cases when and where necessary, and the Department of Justice was tasked with the enforcing the criminal prohibition against bribery, and bringing charges when and where necessary. In truth, neither entity was adequately prepared, from either the perspective of resources or proficiency, to prosecute large corporations. It is perhaps not surprising then, that between 1977 and 2005, the Justice Department brought only sixty-seven FCPA cases—an average of less than three a year.[62]

* * *

By 1999, the leading industrialized countries of the world, following the United States' example, finally banded together to outlaw commercial bribery. This was achieved through the Organisation for Economic Cooperation and Development. The OECD, an intergovernmental economic organization, was formed in 1961 to help administer the Marshall Plan for the reconstruction of Europe. Its members—which today comprise thirty-five countries, including the United States, Germany, Canada, and Japan—collectively account for 70 percent of the world's exports and 90 percent of foreign direct investment. Many of these countries had continued turning a blind eye to bribery long after the United States had outlawed it, but following a decade of intensive negotiations, each of them pledged to reform their respective laws so as to outlaw commercial bribery, and to empower their law enforcement agencies to cooperate on international corruption investigations, including by sharing evidence. The agreement was known as the Convention on Combating Bribery of Foreign Public Officials in International Business Transactions.

The OECD convention was a political and economic victory for the United States, which had been lobbying its major trading partners to implement the law. "We put all our eggs in the OECD basket, and it paid off over time. The U.S. really got what it wanted," Peter Clark, who traveled countless times to the OECD headquarters in Paris, said.

Ironically, by the time the industrialized world committed

itself to outlawing bribery, communism had collapsed, and with it the FCPA's major motivation to protect democracy and citizen overseas. In Spalding's reading: "With the collapse of the Soviet Union . . . the foreign policy implications of antibribery law gradually grew obscure."[63] In 1998, when Congress held new hearings on the FCPA to amend the statute to better conform with the OECD Convention, almost no mention was made of communism's destructive impact. Instead, the rhetoric was reframed to focus on how the bribery being carried out by other countries was undercutting American competitiveness.

The perceived victim was no longer poor citizens overseas, or democracy, but American business itself. Throughout the 1990s, under a pro-export Clinton administration, corporate bribery had effectively become a trade and commerce issue, not a foreign policy matter, and the FCPA, an instrument for protecting American corporate power. Andrew Pincus, then general counsel for the Department of Commerce, told Congress that, according to estimates, U.S businesses had lost out on $30 billion worth of international contracts because their foreign competitors were still resorting to bribes.[64] The new mind-set of "leveling the playing field" meant assigning the FCPA to monitor the market system. A disconnect between the spirit of the FCPA and the DOJ's actual enforcement began to harden into a misguided policy.

Corporations, meanwhile, simply ignored the new law, evading law enforcement while paying lip service to tighter accounting controls and antibribery measures. They succeeded in bribing one of the most dangerous dictators on earth, directly under the scrutiny of the United Nations, despite one of the most comprehensive and seemingly effective sanctions regimes in history. Iraq was a wake-up call, as it revealed that corruption remained rampant despite the

FCPA and the OECD Convention, that merely having a law on the books was not a sufficient deterrent, and that bribery remained a critical foreign policy concern.

Chapter 3

# Money Boxes

Staff Sergeant Kenneth Buff and Sergeant First Class Daniel Van Ess took a deep breath before crossing the darkened threshold of a small building, its facade carefully hidden behind trees. It was April 18, 2003, and their unit, the 3rd Infantry Division (Mechanized), had just captured Baghdad in a quick and dizzying blitz. They had taken up camp in one of Saddam Hussein's old palaces, a sumptuous estate containing dozens of luxury cottages just outside the capital.

During the period after the Americans launched the invasion on March 19, the entire defense and intelligence apparatus of the U. S. government had been searching for Saddam's purported weapons of mass destruction, which they believed could be hidden anywhere. Buff and Van Ess were therefore cautious when, as they walked the grounds that morning, they came upon an odd-looking cottage, its front doors and windows sealed with concrete cinder blocks.

*It doesn't look right*, Buff thought. "There was a block sticking out of the window,"Buff recalled.[1] "I put a crowbar behind it and the block just fell down." Light poured into the darkened space, spilling over a tangle of objects on the floor. As their eyes adjusted, the men saw dozens of small boxes placed in neat rows on the ground, stretching back into the darkness.

*We've got to go inside*, Buff reasoned. They broke down the concrete barrier at the front and then kicked in a wooden door to the inner rooms. There was no explosion, as they feared, or blast of toxic gas, only silence. As they stepped closer they could make out that the boxes were made of galvanized aluminum and were riveted shut. "We were real careful opening the boxes. We didn't know what was inside," said Buff, who retired from the military in 2006 and now works as a security officer at a nuclear power plant.

The men did not find weapons of mass destruction, but what they discovered was equally unsettling. It would soon be linked to the disgrace of the United Nations, the deaths of thousands of U.S. and coalition soldiers, and a host of destructive consequences the United States, Iraq, and the world community are struggling to deal with to this day.

After prying open one of the boxes and angling it toward the light, Buff saw stacks of crisp $100 bills inside, each sealed with blue strapping tape. He quickly counted the money: this one box held $4 million. Stunned, he and Van Ess then counted the boxes and calculated that there was $160 million in cash in the building. Following Buff and Van Ess's lead, the men of the 3rd began to break into several other cottages on the estate. By the end of the day, they had uncovered $760 million—one of the greatest hauls of enemy plunder in U.S. military history.[2]

For a decade, the United Nations had imposed a punishing regime of trade sanctions to starve Saddam of foreign cash reserves, but the 3rd Infantry Division had turned up such massive amounts of hidden money that a C-130 Hercules plane—normally used to transport tanks—had to be requisitioned to fly it to a secure location. "We learned later that Saddam had withdrawn $1 billion from the bank of Jordan two days before the invasion," says Buff.

How had the Iraqi leader, under one of the most stringent sanctions programs ever implemented, amassed at least a $1 billion in secret cash?

*   *   *

In January 2001, Oscar S. Wyatt boarded his company's private plane for an overseas voyage. Balding and rotund, Wyatt was a pillar of Houston society, a self-made oil billionaire who often jetted between his lavish homes and country clubs. But now he was headed for Baghdad International Airport. Wyatt's wealth came, in large part, from Saddam's oil: Throughout the 1970s, his company, the Coastal Corporation, had imported almost 75 percent of its oil—equivalent to 250,000 barrels of a day—from Iraq—making it one of Saddam's best customers.[3] After Saddam invaded Kuwait in 1990, sanctions imposed by the United Nations had cut into Wyatt's business. But since 1996, when the United Nations allowed Saddam to resume sales under a program known as Oil-for-Food, Coastal had been doing a brisk trade in Iraq.

Wyatt was on his way to Baghdad for a meeting at the headquarters of Iraq's State Oil Marketing Organization (SOMO), a department that played a crucial role in the Oil-for-Food Program. Under the terms of the program, SOMO was allowed to sell a regulated amount of oil on the international market to approved buyers like Wyatt. But instead of paying Iraq directly for the oil, Wyatt and other customers were required to deposit money into an escrow account that the UN administered in New York. With these funds, the UN purchased food, medicine, and infrastructure supplies intended for the Iraqi people. The purpose of this arrangement was twofold: to soften the blow of punishing sanctions, and to prevent Saddam from having direct access to the money.

The UN had actually granted Saddam ultimate authority to choose which companies and individuals got access to his oil. In fact, as investigators would later learn, he kept a secret list of his approved customers, and Oscar Wyatt's name was always on the top of that list. Since the Oil-for-Food Program had begun, he'd purchased hundreds of millions of dollars of oil through the formal protocol.

As he always did when he visited Iraq, Wyatt stayed at Baghdad's once lavish centerpiece hotel, the Al Rasheed, later to become famous as the hotel from which journalists reported the American invasion and occupation of the country. From there he drove the four miles to SOMO headquarters, a route that took him past the Iraqi Parliament and through a shattered landscape of crumbling buildings and pervasive ruin, the result of U.S. sanctions.

Although a Texas oilman like then president George W. Bush, Wyatt had vociferously opposed the administration's sanctions program. Iraq sat on the second-largest deposits of oil in the world, and Wyatt, believing that effectively robbing the world of its oil made no economic sense, defied the Bush administration and maintained relations with Saddam. "Somebody has got to keep the contact with these huge oil producers when these sanctions come off," Wyatt once told a reporter.[4]

On his arrival at SOMO headquarters, an imposing, Soviet-style building, Wyatt was warmly received by its officials, who ushered him to the building's central conference room. SOMO had always been a hive of activity, the center of Saddam's oil industry, but on this visit there seemed to be more energy than usual. As Wyatt was seeing firsthand, it was the headquarters of a massive secret corporate bribery scheme that Saddam had personally initiated.

Wyatt had first learned of its existence a year earlier, when Iraqi officials had informed representatives of the Coastal Corporation that they were instituting a new way of doing business: Every foreign company that wanted to buy Iraqi oil would now have to pay a "surcharge" of between ten and fifty cents on each barrel of oil. The Iraqis insisted that the fee was necessary to cover their administrative costs, which the UN had refused to reimburse. There was an important provision attached: The surcharges had to be paid not to the UN escrow account in New York, but to a separate bank account controlled by Iraq and housed in either Lebanon or Jordan. To anyone familiar with the Oil-for-Food Program, the implications of such an arrangement would be clear: Although the UN might control the majority of Iraq's oil revenues, Saddam was now demanding a bribe for access to them. Oscar Wyatt's son Steve, who visited Iraq dozens of times as an oil consultant, remembers being told about the surcharge. "I had a meeting with SOMO. They said, 'Now Steve, we're going to do a change of policy.' I said what? They said the change was that the money was going to come directly to a Jordanian bank account. I knew that was against the policy. I said, whoa, no thanks. I bowed out."[5]

Steve's father, however, did not. The senior Wyatt, whom *Texas Monthly* once called "meaner than a junkyard dog," was not someone who shrunk from a challenge. With one of his most important sources of oil in jeopardy, he had come to SOMO himself.[6] This was not a matter he would leave to his subordinates to resolve. Receiving him that day was Amir Rashid, the Iraqi oil minister, who would later become famous to the world as the Six of Spades in the U.S. military's card deck of the most wanted members of Saddam's government.[7] (His wife was a chemical weapons specialist known as Dr. Germ.)[8] Today, though, he was Wyatt's enthusiastic partner in an audacious scheme to provide an illicit revenue stream that would put hundreds of millions of dollars from Western corporations directly into the pockets of the ruler of Iraq.

*   *   *

Not long after Wyatt touched down, Dr. Rehan Mullick sat at his computer at the UN's Multidisciplinary Observation Unit in Baghdad, puzzling over a vexing question.

Originally from Lahore, Pakistan, Mullick had completed a PhD in sociology and statistics at Iowa State University in 1999. He liked the city of Ames so much that he stayed on after receiving his degree, taking a job as a surveyor for the Department of Agriculture. In the daytime, he surveyed small rural farms, returning home in the evening to his wife, their baby daughter, and a comfortable apartment. It was a pleasant routine.

But in the summer of 2000, Mullick received a phone call that changed his life: a friend from the university asked him if he would be interested in working with the United Nations as a data analyst in a program called Oil-for-Food. After a decade of crushing sanctions that had left the Iraqi people destitute, the UN hoped to engineer the largest humanitarian effort in its history, worth $100 billion. By helping to monitor the flow of goods coming into Iraq, Mullick had a chance to be part of it. "Going to Iraq, to work for the UN, for someone who just finished their studies, it was a very exciting idea," Mullick says.[9] He accepted the job.

In September 2000, the young PhD boarded a plane to Amman, Jordan, and from there drove five hundred miles overland to Iraq. En route he could see the effects of sanctions everywhere: on the very road he traveled, which turned from newly paved in Jordan to broken and rutted once he entered Iraq; in shops, where medicine and food were alarmingly scarce; in the houses, which had critical shortages of electricity and running water;[10] He saw it, too, in the eyes of children, who wandered the streets in search of food. Child mortality had skyrocketed; nearly five thousand Iraqi children were dying each month, according to one estimate.[11]

When he agreed to work with the UN, Mullick hoped to put his skills to good use, to make some money, and then to leave Iraq. But once he settled into the Baghdad office, Mullick began to wonder what was actually happening to all the aid that was coming into Iraq. While pursuing his doctorate in sociology, he had become accustomed to making graphs to chart complex numerical operations, and set out to plot one to chart the shipments coming in and the aid being distributed to the population. The more he looked at the result, the less sense it made: as much as $1 billion in aid funds had simply vanished. "I started realizing there was something wrong with the program. The whole program was a lie," he says.

\* \* \*

Charles A. Duelfer and his team entered the detention area of U.S. military base Camp Cropper, just outside Baghdad. Sometimes called central booking, Camp Cropper was noisy and chaotic. The air thumped with the constant roaring of planes taking off at nearby Baghdad International Airport, while hundreds of prisoners screamed and struggled as they were brought in for processing.

Duelfer's group made its way to a quieter part of the camp, where the Americans kept their most highly valued detainees, including Saddam Hussein himself—an area known by the camp's inhabitants as the petting zoo[12]. They entered a row of low-slung buildings and proceeded to the cell of Muhammad Mahdi al-Salih, Iraq's former minister of trade—the Six of Hearts in the military's deck.

By now ten months had passed since Sergeants Buff and Van Ess had found Saddam's hidden money stashes. Investigations had begun in both Iraq and Washington about where the money had come from and how it had been used to finance Saddam's weapons of mass destruction. With most of Saddam's inner circle in custody, Duelfer, the chief weapons inspector of the Central Intelligence Agency, was determined to get the prisoners to reveal how Saddam's regime financed the weapons program.

"I knew going in that somehow getting at the numbers and looking at how they were using the resources they had as a tool was going to tell a tale about the intentions of the regime, particularly as referred to WMD," Duelfer recalled.[13] The numbers, when he found them, told a much different tale than he had expected.

Salih was at first a recalcitrant detainee, but finally agreed to speak, although not about biological agents or nuclear components. He talked about trucks—trucks that his ministry had obtained legitimately through the Oil-for-Food Program, and then, in clear violation of the program, had handed over to the Ministry of Defense and Iraq's intelligence service.

It was not the information Duelfer was looking for, but it was obviously important. Many other detainees confirmed Salih's account. One senior trade official not only verified it, but told Duelfer that beginning in August 2000, Iraq's Ministry of Trade, under the express orders of Saddam, had begun extracting a 10 percent bribe from every company doing business with Iraq through the UN.

Soon afterward, Duelfer found evidence corroborating the

kickback scheme. Iraq's vice president, Taha Yasin Ramadan, had personally sent a memo, on Saddam's orders, to all Iraqi ministries that August. Outlining "additional revenues for commercial activities," it instructed the ministries to impose a mandatory kickback from suppliers providing humanitarian aid on behalf of the UN. These suppliers numbered in the thousands and included companies like Johnson & Johnson, Volvo, and DaimlerChrysler. The document was remarkable both for being so transparent and so brazen in describing the percentage of contracts to be paid to Saddam as bribes: "From 2 to5 percent for food and medication . . . From 5 to10 percent for everything but food and medication."[14] It also made it clear that the vendors doing business with Saddam would have been explicitly aware that kickbacks were being demanded. Hundreds, if not thousands, of companies chose to pay them. Duelfer's team also learned that during the same period Saddam had been levying a kickback on every barrel of oil he sold.

"I was amazed at the level of sophistication, the different revenue streams that they created," Steven Zidek, one of Duelfer's team leaders, recalled.[15]

All told, between 1996 and 2003, Iraq had sold $64 billion worth of oil on the world market, and with that money had purchased $36 billion in aid. Through bribes, the Iraqi dictator had not only reaped billions in cash but had stolen hundreds of millions of dollars worth of the aid itself.

In practice, the intricate system of pilferage might have worked as follows: In a given year, the Coastal Corporation might purchase 10 million barrels of oil for $250 million, depositing the payment in the UN's escrow account in New York. But on the side, Iraqi officials also required Coastal to deposit an additional $5 million kickback—at fifty cents per barrel—in a separate, hidden account controlled by Saddam. Likewise, Volvo might sell the Iraqi Ministry of Trade $250 million worth of vehicles, purportedly for food distribution to the Iraqi people, and would be paid by the UN out of the New York escrow account. But once again, on the side, it would also pay the 10 percent fee, or $2.5 million, to a separate bank account controlled by Saddam. In addition to receiving the monetary kickback, Saddam could pilfer the vehicles for his military.

CIA director George Tenet had instructed Duelfer to "find the truth" about Saddam's purported weapons program.[16] In interview after interview, detainees insisted that Saddam had never had them, a fact increasingly corroborated by inspection teams on the ground. Although corporate bribery was not what Duelfer had come to investigate, he decided to follow the money trail to its end.

By the time he left Iraq, Duelfer's fourteen-hundred-member Iraq Survey Group had completed one of the most exhaustive examinations of Saddam's fallen regime undertaken by any branch of the American government. It would discover that the largest looming danger in Iraq was not WMDs, but the fact that, by amassing billions in the largest scheme of corporate bribery the world had ever seen, Saddam had succeeded in secretly reconstituting his military and intelligence services, laying the foundation for a devastating postwar insurgency.

* * *

The largest humanitarian effort in world history ultimately failed due to a simple yet glaring design flaw: Saddam Hussein was given control over all contractors—both those to whom Iraq sold oil, and those from whom it purchased humanitarian supplies. "This meant people and companies had to compete for Saddam's approval. And that just opened the whole system up to people paying bribes," says Victor Comras, who worked on Iraq sanctions at the State Department in the early 2000s.[17] This not only enabled Saddam to favor certain companies and countries over others—for example, Russia and France, both of whom had seats on the UN Security Council and shared Iraqi opposition to sanctions—but to benefit certain individuals as well.

Charles Duelfer had obtained Saddam's secret list of oil beneficiaries from captured documents. Among the purchasers of Iraqi oil were three American corporate giants: Chevron, ExxonMobil, and El Paso Corporation. Even more often than these companies, though, one name kept appearing: Oscar S. Wyatt. The UN's Oil-for-Food Program was structured into six-month phases during which Saddam was permitted to sell oil. In thirteen out of thirteen of those phases, Wyatt had received the largest individual concession of oil, totaling 74 million barrels. In fact, the first tanker of oil ever to leave Iraq under Oil-for-Food had been Wyatt's. There was nothing technically unlawful about Wyatt's buying oil from Iraq. What was illegal, though, as Iraqi Oil Ministry documents procured by Duelfer revealed, was that Wyatt had paid $7 million in bribes to Saddam in order to obtain it.[18]

Although it was not surprising that Wyatt, who had long been close to the Iraqi regime, would receive so many oil concessions, what was shocking was the fact that Benon Sevan, the director of the entire Oil-for-Food Program, was also on the secret voucher list.

Sevan, a citizen of Cyprus, had been handpicked in 1997 by Kofi Annan, the UN secretary-general, to lead the Oil-for-Food Program. Sevan had begun at the organization in 1968 and spent most of his professional life there, assisting missions in some of the world's most dangerous places, including Somalia, Iran, and Afghanistan.[19] Nearing the age of seventy, he was considered a paragon of UN efficiency and rectitude.

Sometime after 1996, though, Hussein placed Sevan on his secret oil list. Sevan would personally recommend to the Iraqi Oil Ministry companies that should be allowed to buy its oil allocations, and they would then be listed on Oil Ministry documents with Sevan's name in parentheses. During his investigations, Duelfer found that Vice President Ramadan would automatically issue an order for a company to be given oil concessions whenever he saw that it had received Sevan's approval. Iraqi records would ultimately show that companies associated with Sevan had purchased 7.291 million barrels of oil and sold them at a profit of $1.5 million.[20]

"Sevan was a guy who started off honest, who intended to make the system work, but he saw it falling apart all around him. He saw that everyone was making money, and he thought, dammit, why the hell shouldn't I?" says Victor Comras.

*   *   *

While Sevan had been busy cutting deals, Rehan Mullick's sleuthing was taking ever more disquieting turns, as he had discovered that Saddam's intelligence agents and party loyalists had infiltrated the very heart of the Oil-for-Food Program. These individuals were working in his office, right beside him: the son-in-law of Saddam's deputy foreign minister, the son of a former ambassador, the son of a retired intelligence official, relatives of other Ba'ath party members, and also the daughter of a top official. They all had access to the sensitive lists used to carry out surprise inspections of government warehouses, which meant they could tip off their Baathist allies, signaling them either to conceal illicitly acquired goods before inspectors arrived, or to make sure that stolen goods were on hand for inspections but pilfered immediately afterward.

Mullick could already see that supplies were going missing, and not just pencils and bottles of Advil, but generators, batteries, motor parts, and most alarmingly, cars, pickup trucks, and 4x4s—thousands of them. Through Iraqi contacts and sources at the UN, he was able to track where the vehicles were being diverted: They were being stockpiled and handed over to Saddam's military and his intelligence service, the Mukhabarat, as well as to Baath party loyalists. Some models of the pickup trucks that had been sent to Iraq to deliver food were also well designed for either pulling artillery or mounting heavy guns. The Iraqi military, in the very sight of the international community, was using the resources of the Oil-for-Food Program to rebuild its military logistics train—the very thing the program had been intended to prevent.

After restless deliberations, weighing the consequences for his own career and the implications for the UN and for the Iraqi people, Mullick wrote a report of his findings and waited for a response. But no response ever came. "Here I was, a nobody with a bunch of numbers, crying foul," Mullick described. Instead he suddenly found that his duties at work began to change. He was pulled off database analysis and assigned to edit reports that had nothing to do with his actual job or to operate projectors at meetings.

In 2002, a young Iraqi soldier who for years had guarded Mullick and his team killed himself within sight of the UN compound. To Mullick, it was a devastating sign that the program he had been working for was an utter failure, as the humanitarian relief it had purportedly been offering had failed to improve the Iraqi soldier's lot in life. "It was really heart wrenching. You can't justify the whole thing. You're stealing from people who are deprived of their basic needs," Mullick says. He had had enough. He secretly packed a bag full of UN documents, bought a plane ticket out of Baghdad, and headed to UN headquarters in New York.

* * *

Duelfer's 918-page report, released in October 2004, unleashed a political whirlwind. The U.S. Justice Department, the Treasury Department, and six congressional committees launched an unprecedented series of investigations, building on the mass of leads Duelfer had uncovered. With the reputation of its highest officials in the crosshairs, the UN appointed a commission of its own, headed by former Federal Reserve chairman Paul Volcker. When the Iraqi insurgency exploded into full view, broader questions would be raised about the role American and Western bribery had played in fomenting the violence. But for now, the various inquiries focused on two subjects: Benon Sevan and Oscar Wyatt.

Investigators working with the Volcker Commission eventually discovered $160,000 in cash payments that Sevan had received from a company called African Middle East Petroleum (AMEP).[21] The funds arrived after the company sold Iraqi oil obtained through Sevan's oil allocations from Saddam. Sevan allowed others to profit as well, the Volcker Commission found. Reports of kickbacks were brought to his attention several times, and one such notice in 2000 was specific enough to contain the names and bank accounts of several companies involved, yet Sevan did nothing to follow up. Instead, he did not include the kickback allegations in his regular reports to the UN Security Council.

In early July 2005, Sevan fled the United States for Cyprus while still under investigation. One month later the Volcker Commission formally charged him with bribery, and he was stripped of his diplomatic immunity, exposing him to criminal prosecution.

The Volcker Report also revealed that Sevan was not alone in his dereliction. Many of the UN's highest officials, including Secretary-General Annan and his deputy, Louise Fréchette, had not only failed to halt bribery and corruption, even when specific information was available for them to do so, but hid the details of this corruption behind a wall of silence. Representative Edward R. Royce would later comment: "The withholding of that information is a scandal which rivals the Oil-for-Food scandal."[22]

When the Oil-for-Food hearings began, Rehan Mullick became a key witness, providing some of the most damaging testimony. On March 17, 2005, Mullick described how several attempts he had made to contact the UN about corruption were met with silence. On October 1 2002, he managed to arrange a meeting with higher-level officials at the Office of Internal Oversight at UN headquarters in New York. There he described, as he had several times already in written reports, the massive discrepancies he had noted over the course of two years. Mullick was certain the officials would follow up on his findings, but once again, they never contacted him. When Mullick did finally hear back from the UN, it was to inform him that he was fired.

Mullick, who had struggled for years to support his family after losing his job, hoped that the public furor would result in sweeping reforms at his old employer. "The age-old Mafia-style management where well-meaning employees are humiliated into falling in line or fired must yield to a more open, transparent and democratic

UN, so that ordinary people like myself could go back to honest work under the UN," he told a congressional committee.[23]

"I look back and I always think that I did the right thing," Mullick recalls. "Had I stayed at the UN I'd be a senior official by now. But you don't want to earn your rank by stepping on starving people. I'm glad that I moved on."

* * *

The Oil-for-Food fiasco not only tarnished the reputation of the United Nations but also brought to light a public spectacle of Western corporate greed unprecedented in scale. Transparency International called the bribery at the heart of Oil-for-Food "one of the largest corruption scandals of our time, involving thousands of companies."[24]

On October 21, 2005, Federal agents surrounded Wyatt's mansion in the most exclusive residential district of Houston and took the eighty-one-year-old billionaire into custody. The following day a federal court in New York indicted him on charges of wire fraud for using U.S. banks to transfer bribes to the Iraqi regime. Wyatt would spend the next two years battling the allegations, in one of the only cases in the UN scandal that would ever to go to trial.

Oscar Wyatt's son Steve says his father was unfairly singled out for prosecution. "It's not like my dad was the only one. He was the only one who was *indicted*," Wyatt said. All told, 2,253 companies from 66 nations collectively paid Saddam Hussein $1.7 billion in kickbacks, according to figures tallied by Duelfer, Volcker, and others. This constituted half of all the companies contracted under Oil-for-Food.[25] Although American business represented a small fraction of the total amount—perhaps as much as $35 million— some of those involved were Fortune 500 companies, including Johnson & Johnson, General Electric, and Chevron.

Companies doing business with Saddam should have known they were paying a bribe, as evidence collected by Duelfer, the Volcker Commission, and subsequent investigations by the Justice Department and the Securities Exchange Commission would show. The Iraqis were explicit that if a company wanted to receive a contract, it had first to inflate the price of the contract—in order to accommodate the additional amount for a bribe—and then had to deposit the funds in a secret account. The congressional hearings provided an explicit example showing how one company—a large, publicly traded Scottish engineering concern called the Weir Group—complied. Steven Groves, counsel to the U.S. Senate Permanent Subcommittee on Investigations, said at the Senate hearing: "[Weir] could have refused to inflate its contracts. It could have refused to pay back any money to the government of Iraq. It could have decided to take its business elsewhere. Unfortunately, Weir agreed to comply with the new Iraqi demands, and for the remainder of the Oil-for-Food Program, Weir inflated each of its fifteen contracts by between 11 and 14 percent and deposited that inflated amount into a bank account in Geneva in the name of Corsin Financial Limited, a company that appears to have no existence other than being the holder of that particular bank account."[26]

Steve Wyatt said his father knew that paying bribes to the Hussein regime was illegal, but that he did it anyway to remain competitive in a market where bribery was the norm. "It's like steroids: everybody's doing it. And if you don't do it, you fall behind. The thinking was: 'If Exxon and Chevron are doing it, why can't we?' It was rampant."

Minnesota Republican senator Norm Coleman, upon learning about the scope of the bribery in Iraq, asked: "Weren't there folks who complained that they had to pay kickbacks? I mean, somewhere within the corporate world out there, there has got to be some sense of morality that says, hey, this is not the right thing to do. Did anybody raise a red flag?" Steven Groves replied: "We haven't found a single complaint where kickbacks were demanded, mainly because they don't appear to have been refused that often."

American companies were shown to have paid bribes to Iraqi officials not only to curry favor with Saddam but to prevent their competition from winning contracts. Corruption also resulted in Iraq's being flooded with thousands of products of substandard quality, which were either defective or out of date. As Groves testified:"You must understand that for every dollar that was kicked back to Saddam on a contract was a dollar that did not go to buy humanitarian goods, food or medicine or anything else, for the Iraqi people." [27]

By far the most devastating outcome, as Duelfer later testified before Congress, was that Saddam himself was able to regain what sanctions had attempted to prevent: billions in hard currency, popular support for his regime, and most important, influence around the world.

By 1996, the Iraqi economy was in shambles, and Saddam was in a fight for survival. But the spigot of black money flowed new funding into his regime and his depleted military forces. Saddam's Ministry of Defense alone managed to steal $1.4 billion worth of vital equipment from the UN, Duelfer found. Corporate bribes also provided Saddam's military with vital hard cash. Duelfer calculated that the budget for Iraq's Military Industrialization Commission alone exploded from just $7.8 million in 1996 to $500 million in 2003.[28] As would soon be learned, Saddam used this black money to exact revenge on invading U.S. and coalition forces.

* * *

During his time in Baghdad, making the rounds of detainee cells at Camp Cropper, Duelfer had begun to hear about the stirrings of a plot in the course of frank conversations about the mind-set of the Iraqi dictator in the run-up to the U.S. invasion. In 2003, even as he prepared for the inevitability of the incursion, Saddam was not alarmed, Abd-al-Tawab Abdallah Al-Mullah Huwaysh, the former minister of Military Industrialization, told Duelfer from his darkened cell.

In fact, at Saddam's final ministers' meeting, convened in late March 2003, the beleaguered dictator said something that struck Huwaysh: "Resist one week, and after that I will take over."[29] Iraqi officials took his assertion to mean that he indeed had the weapons of mass destruction the Americans so feared—and that he planned to use them.

But as Duelfer sought to corroborate the information, he came to see that Saddam's plan didn't, in fact, consist of bombing invading American forces with chemical weapons, because he didn't have any. Instead, he planned to pin the Americans down and pick them off slowly, by way of a carefully planned uprising. "Saddam believed that the Iraqi people would not stand to be occupied or conquered by the United States and would resist—leading to an insurgency," Duelfer later wrote in his report. Their plan was called the Challenge Project, and Duelfer learned from former Iraqi intelligence officials (whose identities he concealed) that it was led by a special cell within Iraq's intelligence service called M14, or the Directorate of Special Operations.

In the fall of 2002, Saddam Hussein ordered twelve hundred of his intelligence officers to undergo special guerrilla training with M14 at two facilities located at Salman Pak and Bismayah, near Baghdad, according to a Defense Intelligence Agency report. The officers, "young and talented" men from the Directorate of Military Intelligence and the Iraqi Intelligence Service, were each assigned a number and an alias, and were "told to prepare themselves for re-contact following the collapse of the regime," the report stated.[30]

Just weeks before the American invasion began, Saddam ordered the newly trained guerrillas to scatter "to key cities to assist local authorities in defending those cities and to carry out attacks." The men were told to begin planning bombing attacks. The explosives section of M14 spent their days constructing hundreds of suicide vests and belts. In May 2004, Deputy Secretary of Defense Paul Wolfowitz spoke publicly for the first time about the Challenge Project, highlighting its deadly effect: "M14 are responsible for planning roadway improvised explosive devices and some of the larger car bombs that have killed Iraqis, Americans, and other foreigners."[31]

In May 2003, at the onset of the U.S. incursion, only 54 American soldiers were wounded. By November 2004, shortly after Duelfer's report was released, IEDs had caused the monthly tally of wounded to rise to 1,214—one of the worst months, in terms of casualties, for American forces during the entire war. "Let's be clear," Wolfowitz stated, "[the] enemy includes Saddam Hussein, who was out there funding attacks on coalition forces right up until he was captured in December [2003]."[32]

* * *

In November 2004, Norm Coleman, then chairman of the Senate's Permanent Subcommittee on Investigations, began to express grave concerns about Saddam's black money. During a hearing into the Oil-for-Food Program, he said that credible sources—he did not name them—had brought the committee allegations that money had been diverted from the program to the Hussein regime. "The question must be raised as to what happened to Saddam's billions, and are they being used today to fuel an insurgency that has taken the lives of over one thousand American and Coalition servicemen and women and thousands of our Iraqi allies?"[33]

Millions in Western corporate bribes to Saddam had likely helped finance this violence. Saddam's money had to be traced, Coleman and others argued, and to that end, the Bush administration's chief financial investigators, including from the Treasury Department and the Internal Revenue Service, were asked to testify before Congress. Investigators on the ground in Iraq found that front companies controlled by Saddam had used bribes from the Oil-for-Food Program to procure weapons that had likely ended up in the hands of insurgents. Juan Zarate, Treasury's assistant secretary for Terrorist Financing and Financial Crimes, testified about a front company called Al-Bashair, which had used corporate kickbacks to secure missile components and surveillance equipment. "It is likely that some of these funds ended up in the coffers that are now available to fuel the Iraqi insurgency and terrorism inside and outside of Iraq," Zarate concluded about the UN kickbacks.[34]

One incident in particular added to suspicions that Saddam's bribe funds were fueling the attacks against Americans. At 4:00

A.M. on March 18, 2003, just hours before the American bombing campaign began, Saddam's thirty-seven-year-old son, Qusay,
arrived at the Central Bank of Iraq in Baghdad, accompanied by
Saddam's personal assistant, Abid al-Hamid Mahmood. Qusay,
who later became an important leader of the insurgency, had also
brought with him fifty helpers, three flatbed trucks, and a handwrit-
ten letter from his father instructing the head of the Central Bank,
Isam Rashid al-Huwaysh, to hand over to Qusay $920 million and
€90 million from the bank's vault. The money, which included
$100 bills organized into two hundred fifty metal boxes, was then
loaded onto the trucks,[35] a transfer that required several hours for
the workers to complete. Qusay then disappeared with the cash in
what the *New York Times* called "perhaps the greatest bank robbery
in history."[36]

    U.S. intelligence officials later learned that the nearly $1 billion
was part of Saddam's hidden pool of black money. In early March
2003, in an effort to protect his assets, Saddam had ordered all government ministries with accounts overseas to transfer their money
back to the Central Bank of Iraq. How much was actually moved
is not clear, but these sums were drawn from the same accounts,
at banks like Rafidain and Rasheed in Jordan and Lebanon respec-
tively, that had been secretly holding deposits of kickbacks on
behalf of the regime. Once the money was aggregated in Iraq, Saddam then ordered $920 million and €90 million of it to be removed
from the bank altogether to prevent its being destroyed or seized
when the Americans arrived. Saddam's assistant, Mahmood, had
personally witnessed Saddam writing the bank order.[37] What
became of Qusay's haul became known only when two sergeants
broke through the front door of the cottage on the grounds of one
of the Iraqi leader's former palaces and seized $760 million.[38] It is

unclear what happened to the remaining $160 million and €90 million that Qusay stole, though American officials believed he used the money to begin funding insurgent activity.[39]

*  *  *

How much of the hundreds of millions that Saddam Hussein received in corporate bribes, the majority of which was never seized, was actually funneled to the Iraqi insurgency? The answer has never been clear. The UN Oil-for-Food episode raised far more troubling questions than it could ever answer and was soon forgotten in the wake of the public furor over the growing debacle in Iraq. Although the Volcker Commission's report appeared to be laying the groundwork for sweeping prosecutions, a full reckoning never came.

After he lost his diplomatic immunity, more trouble followed Benon Sevan. In January 2007, federal prosecutors unsealed an indictment in Manhattan charging him with seven counts of bribery related to the kickbacks he received. To date he has successfully avoided prosecution, because Cyprus has no extradition treaty with the United States. Sevan has barely spoken a word publicly since. A reporter who once tracked him down in Cyprus found him openly living a quiet, comfortable life, and continuing to deny his central role in the one of the greatest corporate bribery scandals in modern history.[40]

Oscar Wyatt had vehemently fought the charges against him, even hiring a defense attorney who had once represented the mobster John Gotti. But his undoing came at the hands of star witnesses brought to testify at a federal trial in Manhattan in September 2007, including several Iraqi officials who had worked at SOMO's headquarters. Their testimony was the first time Iraqi officials had ever spoken publicly about the massive, hidden system of graft at the heart of the oil kickbacks.

During his trial testimony, Yacoub Y. A former finance official at SOMO, Yacoub described that, by 2000, Iraq's system of graft had become so extensive and institutionalized that SOMO had created an entire department dedicated to tracking, analyzing, and managing it. This kickback department not only had a dedicated staff but a searchable database of all the companies paying millions to Saddam's regime, including Wyatt's Coastal Corporation. As Baghdad fell and chaos swept across the city, Yacoub had taken care to back up the database. (The smuggling of its contents, coupled with his testimony, essentially rendered Yacoub a marked man, a traitor who turned against the regime and therefore could never return to Iraq. While on the stand, in fact, Yacoub and another witness, Mubdir al-Khudhair, had revealed that U.S. prosecutors had flown them out of Baghdad, provided them with green cards, and paid for their permanent relocation in the United States.)

While Yacoub was on the witness stand, prosecutors handed him a laptop that included a copy of the Iraq bribe database. He input Coastal's name for the jury to see. Up came the various front companies that Wyatt had used to funnel bribes. All in all, Yacoub testified, Wyatt had submitted $7 million in bribes to Saddam and his regime.[41]

Wyatt was facing seventy years in prison if convicted on all five counts, which included conducting business with an enemy of the United States and violating an embargo placed on Iraq. On October 1, 2007, the fourteenth day of his trial, he reversed his plea to guilty. Standing before U.S. District Court judge Denny Chin, he told the court:

On or about December of 2001, I agreed with others to
cause a surcharge payment of 220,000 euros . . . to be
deposited in a bank account controlled by Iraqi SOMO
officials at the Jordanian National Bank. . . . This payment was in violation of the United Nations Oil-for-Food
Program, because the program required that all payments
be made directly to the United States escrow account in
New York, and no money was to be paid directly to the
Iraqi government.[42]

In the end, Wyatt never admitted to paying the full $7 million
in bribes uncovered by Charles Duelfer. He pleaded guilty only
to committing wire fraud, agreed to forfeit $11 million, and was
sentenced to a prison term of one year.[43] That was six months
less than the lower limit suggested by federal sentencing guidelines, but Judge Chin said he was persuaded to be lenient because
of the outpouring of "amazing letters" he received in support of
Wyatt. Wyatt, who was then eighty-three, served out his term at a
minimum-security facility in Beaumont, Texas, near his home. He
became emblematic of a fading era, when businessmen could liberally pay kickbacks with no fear of reprisal, because the FCPA was
a dormant law. Wyatt's incarceration intimated a new regime of
antibribery enforcement that, starting in the United States, would
begin spreading globally. As his son Steve said: "He was a big test
case." Wyatt was released in November 2008 and has never spoken
of the Oil-for-Food episode since.

*   *   *

The war in Iraq was a battle of conflicting versions of the truth. In discovering one truth—that Iraq was not a story about weapons of mass destruction—Charles Duelfer and his team uncovered a different one—that it was in fact a story about "the largest bribery scheme in the history of the world," as the *Wall Street Journal* described it.[44] This was a defining political moment for the United States, not only because of the era's most disastrous war, but because it forced the nation to contemplate the power of corporations to shape world events with bribery. By subverting a system of successful sanctions, Western businesses effectively aided Saddam Hussein in gaining the destructive power he might otherwise not have been able to reclaim.

Would an insurgency have arisen had the Oil-for-Food program not been subverted by bribery? The evidence suggests that the leadership of the insurgency—particularly Saddam Hussein's sons, his relatives, and his trusted intelligence and military officials—later formed part of the leadership of the Islamic State in Syria (ISIS). It remains a mystery where ISIS derived its first sources of funding; but if the Iraqi insurgency was underwritten in part by Western bribes, then some of that money may also have funded the inception of ISIS. Duelfer has considered this possibility: "The ground was fertile for the next generation that became ISIS. Whatever funding structure existed for them before probably has evolved now and provided the start-up capital for the ISIS group." He added, "Izzat Ibrahim al-Douri has been funding himself somehow."[45] Al-Douri—the King of Clubs and one of Saddam's top military officials—is infamous for escaping the U.S. invasion and forming an insurgency based in Syria. Al-Douri's militia is now considered an ally of ISIS and helped the group sweep across western and northern Iraq in 2014.[46]

Western corporations might argue that they simply paid bribes as part of doing business, but after such money was paid out, the key question remains: Where did it go? In the most benign scenario, the Oil-for-Food bribes were secreted out of Iraq, enabling former Saddam loyalists to live lives of luxury in the West. At worst, the money funded suicide bombers who killed Americans. The money boxes in Iraq underscored the fact that paying a bribe was seldom merely a commercial transaction. The impact of these payments was far greater than the companies paying them would prefer to acknowledge. As Duelfer observed of the companies that bribed Saddam: "They make their own little microdecisions, then you put them all together and you have a macro outcome."

The macro consequences of corporate bribery in Iraq went beyond empowering a dictator and possibly funding an insurgency. The ultimate consequence was that corporate actors undermined the foundations of global democracy itself. The fact that 2,253 of the world's corporations chose to flout the rule of law was a subversion not only of the ideals, legal principles, and human values espoused by democracies everywhere, but the very foundations of the free market system. It became clear that the FCPA and the OECD Convention, which had been formulated to prevent exactly this type of scandal, were more relevant than ever before—but that they had not worked.

In the Oil-for-Food scandal, the OECD Convention made little difference at all in constraining bribery, as the scholar Yujin Jeong, who studies corporate corruption at American University, found. Jeong analyzed a sample set of companies that did business in Iraq, dividing them into those whose home countries were a signatory to the OECD convention, and those whose were not. She found that 71 percent of the companies from the group whose home countries were not a signatory to the OECD Convention paid bribes for contracts. This perhaps is not surprising. What is surprising is that even in the group of companies whose home countries were signatories—such as the United States, France, Germany, and the United Kingdom—58 percent of them paid bribes.[47] The deterrence effect of the OECD Convention, at least by the early 2000s, was meager at best.

While the OECD Convention had gone into effect only a few years earlier, the FCPA had been on the books for more than two decades when the Oil-for-Food program began. Among the scandal's many disturbing elements was what a sleeping law the FCPA had become—and not because there was no corporate bribery to indict. Prosecuting it was simply not a priority the U.S. government was willing to back up with resources.

Since 1977, just a single desk within the Justice Department had been dedicated to FCPA cases, headed by the veteran attorney Peter Clark, who had originally helped implement the FCPA. Clark was essentially a one-man FCPA team, launching a trickle of cases with the help of one or two dedicated prosecutors. In a testament to his drive, the number of FCPA cases started to tick up in the early 2000s, but Clark was stretched thin. It became clear to DOJ's upper management that if FCPA enforcement was going to be effective, as the Oil-for-Food scandal showed it needed to be, it had to grow beyond one man.

"Peter Clark was an institution," Paul Pelletier, who joined the Justice Department's Fraud Section in 2002, recalls. "He provided the FCPA Unit with credibility because of his depth of experience in that area, but there wasn't a lot of viability. Because he had only one prosecutor who was dedicated to it, and it was catch as catch can."[48]

In 2005, Clark was transitioned out of Justice and took a job as an attorney in private practice, and the Fraud Section brought in new management. Steven Tyrrell, a former Miami prosecutor who was part of that ramp-up, was surprised to find that despite having a number of potential FCPA cases, DOJ had no dedicated FCPA attorneys. "When I started as chief of the Section, it seemed like the attorneys sort of worked on whatever struck their fancy at any given moment," he said.[49] Tyrrell put attorneys to work full time on FCPA and pushed them to be more aggressive in bringing indictments. In the process, DOJ formed stronger links with the Securities and Exchange Commission, which was also looking more seriously at international bribery cases. As early as 2004, the SEC had begun issuing subpoenas to many of the companies identified as having paid bribes to Saddam Hussein. Those investigations would increase as the Justice Department and the SEC cooperated, and also began reaching out to the FBI. The sharing of resources enabled federal law enforcement to pursue the more serious and complex allegations unearthed by the Volcker Commission.

As more countries ratified the OECD Convention, its evidence-sharing protocols, called Mutual Legal Assistance Treaties (MLATs), began to bear fruit. In the past, sovereign states had been reluctant to share critical evidence in bribery investigations or simply lacked a legal mechanism through which to do so. "There was no voluntary disclosure," Peter Clark said, recalling a typical example. "We traced bribe money to the door of a bank in Switzerland. The Swiss told us, 'We would very much like to help you,'" but their laws prevented them from doing so.[50] Now, with MLATs, the evidence began flowing freely across borders.

Within a short amount of time, the Justice Department would collect billions of dollars in fines and secure guilty pleas on bribery charges against some of the largest corporations in the world, including BAE Systems, a British-American aerospace giant; Kellogg Brown & Root, a subsidiary of Halliburton; and Siemens, the German industrial giant. The Siemens settlement in particular, which resulted in a record $1.8 billion fine, would set a new standard for how FCPA prosecutions were conducted. It also gave rise to the birth of a new unit within the FBI. "We were struggling to get our resources together for national corruption—let alone international corruption," Joseph Persichini, then the assistant director of the FBI's Washington field office, recalls. "All of a sudden, you got Justice coming over and saying now we have to do international corruption." The magnitude of the Siemens case—involving payoffs to high level government officials in dozens of countries—was too large to ignore. International bribery would become one of the FBI's most important priorities. "We looked at it and said, 'Let's staff this. This is important.' FBI added a whole squad, ten to fifteen agents to deal with this."[51]

The new era of FCPA prosecutions exposed in minute detail—thanks to thousands of pages of court documents in hundreds of new investigations—the workings of the modern-day corporate bribery system and its various interconnecting parts: the Western companies that pay the bribes, why they pay them, and how they hide them; the middlemen these companies often hire to broker large-scale bribery deals abroad; and the corporate, legal, and financial architecture that foreign officials use to receive, launder, and make use of their bribes. A closer look at how this system actually works underscores the great disconnect between the nature of this crime and how it is prosecuted—and how its insidious damage to the foreign victims is often overlooked.

The first piece of the bribery system—the companies themselves—is dramatically illustrated in the story of the world's leading pharmaceutical companies. In a feverish race to drive sales and outcompete one another, they paid bribes on an extraordinary scale, and took extraordinary measures to hide them, in the world's largest drug market: China.

# PART II

# The Kickback System

# Chapter 4

# **Happy Fools**

On a side street in Hangzhou, a city in eastern China, Lijuan stood waiting outside a fashionable coffee shop. With a population of 21 million, Hangzhou is rich and flourishing, with an abundance of skyscrapers, and Maseratis and Teslas roaming its streets. As incomes rise in large Chinese cities, their citizens are spending more than ever before on health care. In 2015, the country spent $115 billion on drugs alone, second only to the United States. With profit margins soaring, the world's top drug companies are all battling for a bigger piece of the pie. Merck, Sanofi, Pfizer, and most of Big Pharma maintain a sales force of drug reps in Hangzhou, who go from hospital to hospital, doctor to doctor, pushing foreign-made products. Lijuan is one of them. On a recent fall afternoon, she agreed to speak about a secret aspect of her industry: bribery. But she would speak only if her real name and that of her employer not be revealed. Based in Europe, that company generated more than $1 billion in sales in China in 2014, and nearly $15 billion globally.

It is a cliché that Chinese drug reps are always young, pretty women, but in this case it turned out to be true. Lijuan is attractive, in her early thirties, and wore a stylish leather jacket, black pants, and high-heeled shoes. Her shoulder-length hair was blow-dried and styled, and she looked more like a model than a foot soldier in China's pharmaceutical wars. Though friendly and gracious, she would not stay long, as she had come to talk about bribery at a time when bribery had become a very dangerous issue to discuss in China.

For more than a decade, the world's leading pharmaceutical companies, including Bristol-Myers Squibb, Eli Lilly, Novartis, AstraZeneca, GlaxoSmithKline, and SciClone, have all resorted to the crudest means imaginable to generate billions in China: paying off thousands of Chinese doctors to prescribe their products instead of the competition's.

Corporate bribery schemes typically involve a corporation's paying a very large sum to a very high-ranking official in order to win a contract—millions to a Bahraini prime minister, for example, or a Nigerian governor, as the next two chapters will demonstrate. But bribery is also often carried out on a much smaller scale. In China, many companies have been making micropayments to low-level doctors. At times, the drug companies have not even paid cash but dealt in cigarettes, visits to strip clubs, or trips to Disneyland. Armies of drug reps like Lijuan, spanning the breadth of China, handle the payoffs. Bribery of this kind is certainly not as dramatic as grand-scale graft, but because so many companies have been doing it for so long, and compromising so many doctors throughout China, its impact has been just as acute. As Charles Duelfer had warned about bribes: seemingly minor microdecisions add up to a macro outcome.

With the Chinese drug industry now in turmoil because of this practice, both the U.S. and Chinese governments, after ignoring it for years, have gone to war with the drug companies. In 2010, U.S. law enforcement launched a sweeping crackdown, bringing charges against industry leaders like Pfizer and Eli Lilly, levying hundreds of millions in fines, and exposing in public filings the sordid details of the industry's bribery for the first time. Kickbacks to doctors have contributed to rising expenditures for the Chinese government, which has spent billions a year subsidizing basic health-care coverage to offset the crushing pharmaceutical expenses of ordinary citizens.[1] Public anger over high drug and medical costs, and the corruption linked to them, has exploded in thousands of violent attacks against doctors. As part of President Xi Jinping's larger offensive against corruption, foreign drug executives, local sales reps, and doctors have been arrested.

Yet for all the efforts to combat it, the bribery continues, though it has been forced underground, as Lijuan explained.

Bribing doctors in China may seem an easy process, and relatively speaking a harmless one. But managing thousands of illegal payments every year, and covering them up with lies to investors and regulators in the drug companies' home countries, is an incredibly complex operation. And although drug companies are ostensibly in the business of healing, their bribes have long undermined China's health-care system by compromising doctors' decision-making and potentially jeopardizing patient health.

With a pained smile and the slightest trace of embarrassment, Lijuan sat back and explained how and why Big Pharma uses this grossly inefficient, destructive system rather than an innovative strategy to sell the world's most advanced drugs in the world's most dynamic pharmaceutical market.

\* \* \*

As much as millions of Chinese patients are desperate for better quality Western medicine, Western drug companies have also desperately needed the Chinese market to grow their profits. Throughout most of the twentieth century, blue-chip drug manufacturers hardly gave a thought to China. The companies were making enormous profits selling patented drugs, and their most lucrative markets were North America and Europe. When drugs are patented, a company can charge virtually any price it likes, reaping huge rewards. Viagra, for example, generated sales of $1 billion for Pfizer in 1998, its first year.[2] In this scenario, growth is a given.

But that began to change by the mid-2000s. As many blockbuster drugs lost their exclusive patents, they began to face fierce competition from cheap generics. To keep profits up, pharmaceutical companies needed to get new patented drugs out of their pipelines and into the market. Stricter regulatory hurdles in the United States and Europe, however, spurred in part by accidental deaths and harmful side effects, slowed the introduction of new products. In the meantime, research and development costs crept ever higher, becoming virtually unsustainable.

For Novartis, the Swiss-based manufacturer of medications for cancer and high blood pressure, net sales in Europe grew by only 7 percent in 2005.[3] By 2008, growth in Europe had fallen to 1 percent.[4] For Bristol-Myers Squibb, based in Warsaw, Indiana, sales in the United States—where the patent for its popular blood thinner, Plavix, was about to expire—actually decreased by 1 percent in 2005 and by 7 percent the following year.[5] Falling margins panicked Wall Street and investors. As their stock prices and profits tumbled, drug companies began to cut their staffs. In 2007, GlaxoSmithKline (GSK), based in London, announced that it was eliminating thousands of jobs after its profits dipped by 2 percent. Pfizer said it would lay off 10,000 people, and AstraZeneca, 7,600.[6]

For drug companies to survive, they had to expand into emerging markets in the developing world. And no emerging market presented as much potential as China, which has the world's largest elderly population and faces increasing incidences of chronic disease; the largest diabetes epidemic in the world, with 100 million people affected; and more than 130 million cases of hepatitis B.[7] International drug companies have had a presence in China since the 1980s, but the market remained virtually untapped. As incomes rose there, however, and the middle class expanded, Big Pharma bet that the Chinese population would be more willing and able to pay for expensive Western drugs, and began investing billions in the country. Sir Andrew Witty, the CEO of GlaxoSmithKline, captured the prevailing sentiment when he announced in 2008: "For GSK, the center of gravity is moving to the east."[8]

China's health-care system itself can seem like a paradoxical maze: state controlled yet market driven, with Communist bureaucracy and cut-throat competition intertwined. For nearly thirty years under Chairman Mao Zedong, the Communist Party subsidized roughly 60 percent of all hospital expenses with the hospitals themselves making up the rest through the low-cost medical services they provided. But after Mao died in 1976, his successor, Deng Xiaoping, introduced a market-based economy, and the government began slashing hospital subsidies year after year.

Today, the state pays only about 10 percent of public hospital expenses. To offset the deficit, the government allows the nation's 13,500 public hospitals to sell drugs to patients at a 15 percent markup. Hospitals are basically the only place the Chinese can buy drugs, and drug sales account for up to 50 percent of hospitals' revenue and often 90 percent of their profit.[9] China's hospitals, though operating in a socialist health-care system, are essentially in the business of maximizing sales—a phenomenon the Chinese call *yi yao yang yi:* feeding hospitals by selling medicine.

Because public hospitals have a virtual monopoly on drug sales, competition among foreign drug companies for their business is frenetic—an ideal situation for foreign corporate bribery to flourish.

China's 2 million doctors each see as many as a hundred patients a day. Because they have scarcely any time to spend with them, their priority is often to prescribe drugs. In fact, their livelihood depends on it. State policy dictates that hospital physicians receive a low base salary, with bonuses paid out of a common pool. Those bonuses depend on how much revenue their respective hospitals generate—and the revenue, of course, is linked to drug sales. The doctors therefore have an incentive to overprescribe, particularly new and expensive foreign medicine, as a vast body of literature attests. According to one study, Chinese physicians must prescribe seven dollars' worth of drugs for every dollar in income they hope to make.[10]

But in a market where foreign companies are all fiercely competing for market share, which drug will a doctor choose? "Doctors have many options for antibiotics," Ping (not his real name), a sales rep who works for a leading U.S.-based pharmaceutical firm, explained. "And to be fair, is there any product that is much stronger than any other product, that is much safer? It's hard to say. So the only thing that can drive your sales growth is the money."[11] Bribes ensure that a doctor will prescribe *your* expensive antibiotic, not a competitor's.

The low base salary is an additional incentive to take corporate bribes. Official state salaries for most doctors are meager: $150 a month for entry-level physicians, and $400 a month for doctors with a few years of experience; even upper-level hospital directors earn only about $1,500 a month. Doctors can double this amount by taking kickbacks. The Chinese government is well aware of this practice but turns a blind eye to it. As long as the bribes keep flowing, the state can avoid raising doctors' salaries, saving billions a year.

Because of the expense of drugs, including the foreign drugs that doctors are bribed to push, most Chinese patients have enormously high medical bills (government medical insurance plans often do not cover many foreign drugs, meaning patients pay out of pocket). The average inpatient pharmaceutical bill per visit in urban areas is equivalent to 16 percent of annual per capital income. (In the United States, the equivalent would be a patient making fifty thousand dollars a year paying eight thousand dollars for drugs per visit to the hospital.) In rural areas, pharmaceutical bills are equivalent to 53 percent of annual per capital income—enough to send most Chinese into bankruptcy. [12] As one doctor described, "In China we say that if you become sick you become dirt poor."

\* \* \*

Even as their headquarters cut staff in other parts of the world, the China CEOs of Western pharmaceutical brands began building armies of drug representatives, thousands of new sales recruits eager to penetrate the Chinese market. [13] Yin Xudong, then the China CEO of AstraZeneca, a British-based drug maker, told a journalist in 2008 that his company was rapidly growing its sales force because it was preparing for an "arms race" with other companies. AstraZeneca hoped to make its heart drug Betaloc, whose sales were dropping in the West, into a blockbuster in China. [14] In 2008, Eli Lilly, headquartered in Indianapolis, Indiana, had a sales force in China of about 850 reps; [15] that number doubled over the next two years. Reps began surging into new frontiers, out of first- and second-tier cities into rural areas, pushing the company's diabetes and cancer drugs. All the major drug companies followed suit. Between 2006 and 2011 alone, the number of representatives in China working for the top ten drug multinationals more than quadrupled, from six thousand to twenty-five thousand.[16]

Lijuan was part of the pharmaceutical ramp-up. She explained that she had worked for her company for five years, specializing in three high-blood-pressure drugs. "Every month you have orders from your company about how much you need to sell," she said in a quiet voice. "And the more you sell, the larger your bonus." The compensation package at Lijuan's company thus contains two incentives for her to use bribes—to make her sales quota so she doesn't get fired, and to make a bigger bonus. When sales are good, Lijuan earns about $1,500 a month, a handsome amount in China. She is good at her job, having mastered the art of building relationships with doctors and paying them off.

"I have around a hundred doctors, but right now I'm only paying kickbacks to three of them," she explained.[17] She used to bribe them all, but because of the law enforcement crackdowns in the United States and China, her company has had to become more careful, so she now concentrates on just three. "Because these three are very, very important doctors, they can provide huge sales for me. They have critical positions and are able to prescribe a lot." One doctor in particular is a cash cow—a high influencer at a prominent hospital. "He has a lot of patients who come to see him," Lijuan explains. "He can prescribe like one hundred to two hundred boxes of drugs per month."

The bribes Lijuan pays are not large. "I give around [ninety dollars] to [one hundred dollars] to the higher- level doctors every month," she explained. For every five-dollar box of medicine a doctor prescribes, he or she receives a dollar in bribes, about 20 percent of the sale. "That's the higher level," she added.

Because kickbacks are based on how many prescriptions a doctor writes each month, how does Lijuan calculate her bribes? "Every month I go to the statistics department of my hospitals," she explained. "Usually the boss of the IT department or his colleagues can provide a list of the statistics, showing the sales of drugs." To get access to those figures, Lijuan pays another bribe, which ranges from $33 to $50 for every $150 worth of her drugs that the hospital sells. (Other drug reps and doctors confirmed that bribing hospital IT departments is an industrywide practice.) Lijuan's descriptions highlighted not only how organized the bribery system is but how expensive it is for her company. Roughly 20 percent of all her sales go to bribing her doctors, and 25 percent to IT departments.

Lijuan uses the statistics to carefully track the progress of her bribes every month to determine how they are affecting sales. "It's like you have an internet company, and every month you look at the statistics [of web traffic]." Sometimes she pays bribes to a doctor who then doesn't necessarily prescribe more. She might need to bribe him a little more to get sales up, or simply stop wasting the money on him altogether. "It's like big data," Lijuan said, smiling, apparently amused by the fact that any of this might be puzzling to an outsider at all. For Lijuan, bribery simply makes sense. "The doctors are helping me, so I should take care of them," she explained, adding that her managers are fully aware of what she does and in fact provide the money for the bribes.

Lijuan's story is just one among thousands. Institutionalized bribery on an industrial scale has been rampant in China for more than ten years. The effort required to actually generate the cash for these countless kickbacks, and the subterfuge required to cover them up, would be exposed only by far-ranging investigations in the United States and China. As those investigations continue, they have revealed that Western pharmaceutical companies have become models of exuberant irrationality.

*  *  *

On September 19, 2014, Mark Reilly, the China head of GlaxoSmithKline, a British company worth roughly $125 billion, stood before a judge in a small courtroom in Changsha, the capital of Hunan province. State television cameras rolled in the background. Reilly, wearing a dark suit, his face slightly pinched, appeared tense.

GSK's history dates back to the 1850s. A pioneer in treatments for asthma and HIV, it is one the largest companies traded on the London Stock Exchange. Reilly, then fifty-two, had worked at GSK for twenty-five years. In 2009, he was given the plum assignment of running GSK's China operations. Under his stewardship, sales of its products, including hepatitis B medicine and antibiotics, rose from $573 million to $1.2 billion by 2012 nearly doubling in just three years.[18]

According to the Chinese government, however, GSK's extraordinary success masked an extraordinary crime. A year earlier, state police had accused the company of a massive bribery scheme and arrested dozens of GSK employees across China. They also arrested Reilly, raising alarms throughout the global pharmaceutical industry. Following months of investigation and a secret one-day trial, GSK and Reilly now awaited the verdict.

The charges were extensive. GSK was accused of paying

more than $489 million in bribes to countless doctors throughout China between 2010 and 2013. According to the police report, it generated these funds by inventing several thousand so-called educational conference trips for doctors. Sometimes the physicians were actually sent on all expenses paid junkets—perhaps to Hong Kong or Hawaii—by the company. But the "educational" part of the conference typically lasted just a day or two, after which the doctors were treated to several more days of lavish sightseeing, entertainment, and cash bribes as a way of encouraging them to prescribe GSK products.

Very often, however, there were no actual conferences or trips at all. Instead, GSK's sales department devised a ruse with the assistance of Chinese travel agencies. An agency would issue a doctored receipt—either inflating the costs of a trip that did take place, or fabricating a receipt for a trip that never occurred. Sales and marketing would then submit the receipt to finance, claiming the expenses as marketing costs, and get reimbursed. This effectively provided the sales team with a slush fund with which to pay cash bribes. GSK worked with seven hundred travel agencies throughout China to run this operation, which meant that several thousand people within and outside the company were involved. It was a bribery operation unparalleled in Chinese corporate history.

The Chinese word for receipt is *fapiao*. At the heart of pharmaceutical sales in China, generating billions and billions of dollars for top drug companies, has been a system in which thousands of employees in major cities across the nation fabricated fake *fapiao* every month. To amass the cash to pay off her doctors each month, Lijuan submits phony receipts to her managers, gets reimbursed, and then uses the cash for bribes. "You say it's restaurant spending. So I ask my friends, or I save up some receipts when I go out to eat, to cover that." Lijuan's managers know the receipts are fake, but as long as they look legitimate, they reimburse her.

Ping, the other drug rep, described how the same process goes on in his own company, even now. "I will create a fake meeting," Ping explained. "I will use my credit card, and the hotel will give the receipt back to me. I will reimburse this bill to the company. So that's it, you got the money," he explained.

The judge in Changsha, Wu Jixiang, found Reilly guilty and fined GSK $489 million—the amount it had paid in bribes, and the largest corporate fine ever imposed in China. Judge Wu also sentenced Reilly to three years in prison. (Reilly was, in fact, deported to the United Kingdom and never served his jail sentence.)

Wu was clearly sending a message, not only to Reilly and GSK, but to the wider market and to the Chinese people. The verdict came as public anger over the state of the country's health services, including skyrocketing costs and corruption, had reached a peak. According to Chinese state figures, there were 4,599 altercations between patients and hospital staff in 2014 alone.[19] In some cases, patients and their families have even murdered doctors in their workplaces. "If the government is viewed as unable to provide adequate health care to their people, that will be viewed as a violation of the implicit social contract," Yanzhong Huang, an expert on China's health-care system at the Council on Foreign Relations, explained.[20] Failure to address these problems had become a critical threat to the Communist Party's political legitimacy. With the GSK case, they were able to show their proactive resolve.

Many in China believe the case against GSK was politically motivated, and that the government acted as it did in an effort to boost the domestic Chinese pharmaceutical industry. That may well be true. But in September 2016, the Securities and Exchange

Commission conducted its own investigation of GSK and found a similarly vast scale of bribery. It charged that "improper practices were pervasive" at the company's China subsidiary, noting: "Among the ways employees were able to fund payments to [doctors] was the use of collusive third-party vendors, such as those used to perform planning and travel services for events involving [doctors]." The SEC did not allege, as the Chinese police had, that GSK paid half a billion dollars in bribes. Instead, U.S. regulators found that "between 2010 and June 2013, [GSK] spent nearly RMB 1.4 billion ($225 million) on planning and travel services. Test sampling showed that approximately 44 percent of the sampled invoices were inflated and approximately 12 percent were for events that did not occur."[21] Although it appears that a majority of the company's invoices were doctored, and that it spent hundreds of millions of dollars on bribes in just three years, the true amount of the kickbacks is unknown.

GSK is the seventh industry leader to resolve a bribery investigation with the SEC. Beginning in 2012, U.S. regulators brought FCPA charges against Pfizer, Eli Lilly and Bristol-Myers Squibb. In 2016, they charged SciClone, Novartis, AstraZeneca, and GSK. In general, the time frame of these alleged bribes was between 2003 and 2014. The companies collectively paid $131.5 million in fines to the U.S. Treasury to settle the charges.

The U.S. investigations have gathered from the world's premier pharmaceutical companies a rich array of documentary evidence—emails, strategy plans, and other company documents—detailing how, in the go-go days of the late 2000s, they organized elaborate, tightly structured bribery operations in the Chinese drug market. In one July 2013 email, a Bristol-Myers Squibb sales representative in China wrote to a regional manager, reporting that a certain high-level doctor must be bribed before he will agree to use the company's products: "The attitude of the director of the infectious diseases department was extremely clear when I took over: 'No money, no prescription.'"[22] In 2006, a Pfizer China marketing manager wrote to his regional manager, explaining how two Chinese doctors would be bribed with a trip to Australia. In return, the doctors promised "to use no less than 4,200 injections a year" of a certain Pfizer product, and to prescribe it to "more than 80 percent of their patients."[23] In a sales report, a SciClone sales manager referred to the use of bribes to doctors as "luring them with the promise of profit."[24]

Bribes were carefully logged by sales reps and their managers. Pfizer China, which pushed antihypertension medicine and antibiotics, even had a point system "under which government doctors could accumulate points based upon the number of Pfizer prescriptions they had written. The points could be redeemed for various gifts," as the SEC alleged.[25] Novartis and SciClone sales reps kept spreadsheets tracking the amounts of money that doctors were owed each month. Key prescribing physicians were known as "money worshippers" at Novartis and "VIP clients" at SciClone.[26] AstraZeneca reps and managers "maintained written charts and schedules that recorded the amount of forecasted or actual payments."[27]

As well as direct cash payments and travel, physicians were also bribed with gifts. Sometimes they consisted of minor items like cigarettes, fancy meals, eyeglasses, or gift cards; at other times they were sexual in nature. The Chinese government, for example, accused GSK of hiring prostitutes for doctors. In an incident documented by the SEC, employees of Novartis's Chinese subsidiary paid for doctors visiting Chicago to go to a strip club.[28]

Multinationals used bribes not only to drive prescriptions and sales but also to influence several stages of a drug's entry to the Chinese market, from licensing to inclusion on hospital formulary lists. A SciClone employee bribed two government officials to ensure that a pending renewal for one of its drugs was approved. Between 2008 and 2009, Eli Lilly reps gave kickbacks to government officials "to list Lilly products on government reimbursement lists"—in other words, to ensure that certain hospitals used them.[29]

\* \* \*

For twelve years, Edward Chen was the chief financial officer in Taiwan of a top-ten pharmaceutical company headquartered in Europe. Prior to that he spent many years working in China's pharmaceutical sector. Though he retired in 2012, Chen regularly travels to China, consulting for large pharmaceutical companies doing business there. Executives of his stature rarely speak openly about bribery, but Chen has been profoundly disappointed by its prevalence.

He now lives in Taipei, a bustling city of large shopping malls, eighteenth-century temples, and garish neon avenues. Over dinner at an elegant restaurant in the city's fashionable Western district, Chen, who is by nature affable and quietly gracious, reminisced, often with laughter, about his career in Asia. He was the opposite of a hard-charging executive: a fastidious accountant and stickler for the rules, he saw to it that the numbers always added up correctly, literally and figuratively. He had seen things that offended his sensibilities, such as a senior corporate manager passing ten thousand dollars to a government official through a car window in order get a drug approved.

"My argument is: this is not a right process. It's illegal. It's not ethical," Chen said.[30] He had once worked for an engineering company that routinely bribed Taiwanese government officials. The officials in turn authorized contracts that were inflated in price or unnecessary altogether. Sometimes Chen himself had to hand out bottles of liquor as backhanders. He had long ago concluded that by bribing the government to sign a wasteful contract, he was cheating himself, the taxpayer—the government was wasting *his* money.

Chen inevitably faced a struggle at his global pharmaceutical company, and his dilemma illustrates a central clash playing out within multinationals around the world: a conflict between the sales department and the compliance department, between those willing to use bribery and those who believe the pursuit of profit should—and can—comply with ethics, with internal corporate control standards, with accepted business practices. If corporations are people, legally speaking, then this is, metaphorically, the battle for their souls.

The problem, Chen said, starts with the fact the global drug companies are bound to international equities markets—and the markets demand growth. "For those corporates that are publicly listed in Wall Street, in Tokyo—they are facing shareholders' pressure, facing the pressure from investors, from the market. Growth is the issue. Growth is some kind of curse, or nightmare."

The prospects for growth are, of course, what drove global drug companies to China, a gamble that certainly seemed to pay off. Between 2007 and 2011, for example, Novartis's net sales there increased by more than 50 percent, from $329 million to more than $500 million. In its 2011 annual report, the company highlighted its business in China as a "major success story."[31] Between 2009 and 2014, Bristol-Myers Squibb's revenue in China more than doubled, from $200 million to $500 million. Between 2006 and 2011 alone, the combined revenues of the top ten multinational pharmaceutical companies in China rose from $4 billion to $10 billion, according to the consulting firm McKinsey.[32]

But it was not enough, as elsewhere throughout the developed world pharmaceutical companies continued to implode. In 2011, the *New York Times* reported that drug companies faced additional billions in lost revenue as patents continued to expire; that research costs had doubled to $45 billion for the industry, even as fewer and fewer drugs won government approval; and that collectively the industry had cut 114,00 jobs between 2009 and 2010. It was "panic time" in the market, and investors were fleeing from pharmaceutical stocks as if they were a "hurricane . . . making landfall," investment analysts told the *Times*. The share prices of Pfizer and Merck, industry giants, had fallen by 60 percent since 2000.[33]

Growth in China had become all the more critical for Big Pharma—as did bribery. In the case of GSK, arrested officials explicitly made this connection. Bribes were used to meet an annual sales growth goal of 25 percent, compared to an industry standard of 7 to 8 percent, Xinhua, China's official news agency reported.[34] "The sales target in China was raised every year to compensate for the reduction in U.S. and European markets," Zhang Guowei, GSK China's human resources director, was quoted as saying.

Why do pharmaceutical companies find it necessary to resort to such a ludicrously inefficient way of doing business when they have the best medicine in the world and a market of tens—if not hundreds—of millions of customers in China eager to buy their products? "I asked a similar question many times," Chen replied, "and the answer is always like this: 'Because the others all pay.

If we do not pay, we lose market.'" In a world where everyone competes via bribes, bribery is the most efficient way to ensure market share.

In 2015, Charney Research, a marketing firm based in New York, conducted a survey of nearly 2,300 companies operating in China. Roughly 35 percent reported paying bribes to Chinese government officials. "In general, companies say payments are made to keep up with the competition. The struggle for market share emerged as a key driver," their report concluded.[35]

"The threat [of growth] is not to the global CEO; it will gradually cascade down to the CEO in each country," Chen explained. Headquarters would not hesitate to dismiss senior management who fail to perform in China. "Those expatriates normally have just a two- or three-year contract," which means that they have a very short period in which to achieve extraordinary results. "And if continuously they cannot reach the target they will not get an extension."

Local CEOs turn to bribery not only because they are beholden to headquarters, Chen believes, but because they are also beholden to their own egos.

"Most of the CEOS are so-called highfliers or talents, stars in the organization. Normally their egos are high and they have high ambitions," Chen said. "They must deliver. And this 'must' kills people, kills organizations." A CEO who "must" deliver, Chen explained, is often willing to flout ethical business practices in order to succeed.

"For any significant or major breach, [sales] will definitely discuss and get approval from the local CEO. Without the verbal approval or encouragement from the local CEO, I do not believe that they will [pay bribes]."

One of the largest studies ever conducted of corporate bribery was undertaken by the OECD in 2014. It analyzed data from 427 large-scale corporate bribery cases, resolved in various legal jurisdictions and involving bribes paid in various countries, dating as far back as 1999. The report found that in 41 percent of those cases, evidence showed that corporate managers approved the actions of their employees. In 12 percent of the cases, the CEO knew about and endorsed the bribery. And these were the cases only in which direct evidence was found; many others go undetected. The findings, the OECD argued, debunk the " 'rogue employee' myth and demonstrate the need for a clear 'tone from the top' in implementing corporate antibribery policies."[36]

At his own company, Chen challenged the head of the sales department to eliminate cash bribes and suggested doing something innovative instead. "I asked . . . Can we invest more in education, in other services? I told the sales director in front of the regional management, I said, 'Let's provide a higher discount rate and that will impact to our top line.' " Chen's fundamental argument was: If we eliminate bribes now, we may lose some sales, but it is a one-time loss, and the company will eventually recoup the loss over time. "I said, let me fight this for you. [The sales director] rejected it. He said, once you take this out, business will collapse in this sector."

Chen ultimately came to see that any attempt to immediately end bribery in all its forms would not only be difficult in practical terms but would affect sales morale. So he concentrated on at least eliminating direct cash kickbacks, an effort that took him two years of fighting to achieve. Although he believes this practice has ended at the Taiwanese branch of his company, sales reps continue to send doctors on lavish trips, a practice that is difficult if not impossible to stop. It will take pharmaceutical companies in China a long time to end the practice of bribery, Chen said. "It's an evolution. It will take twenty years, at least."

Pharmaceutical companies' use of kickbacks was reinforced by an environment in which bribery was already endemic and loosely policed. It had long been common practice for local businesses to bribe Chinese doctors. International companies followed suit, perfecting their own systems to thrive. During the period in which international drug companies expanded in China, enforcement of the FCPA was virtually nonexistent, and most European countries barely applied whatever antibribery laws they had. Global drug companies faced virtually no pressure to avoid this practice.

China, of course, was all too happy that its doctors saw their incomes rise. But that was a decision that the nation, its patients, and its doctors have now come to regret.

*   *   *

"Our income is very, very low. So this has created a space for the drug manufacturers to come in and determine our prescriptions," Dr. Lee, a lung specialist, observed one evening over a pot of green tea.[37] He was describing how doctors are vulnerable to the allure of pharmaceutical bribes, and how it required a great amount of self-discipline to refuse them.

Thirty-six-year-old Lee is the deputy director at a public hospital in a prosperous eastern Chinese city. Despite having spent fourteen hours that day at work, he spoke passionately and at great length about the series of problems facing his profession: misguided government policies, venal officials, corrupt pharmaceutical companies, violently frustrated patients.

It took him a long time to acknowledge his own complicity, but finally, toward the end of the evening, he began to unburden himself. He doesn't like taking bribes, he insisted, but regularly accepts them, receiving a kickback for every prescription he writes. He has a wife and daughter to support. Half of his thirty-thousand-dollar salary comes from corporate bribes, and he could not afford even a basic middle-class lifestyle without them. "I've never told anyone about my black income. I feel terrible saying this," Dr. Lee admitted, a look of genuine defeat on his face.

At his level, Lee explained, bribes are easy to accept, because he doesn't have to experience receiving them directly: "Kickbacks from the pharmaceutical companies are given to the head of the department, and then given to me." He suspects that a small amount of these bribes come only from foreign companies now, with most of the black money supplied by Chinese companies. But he doesn't actually know that to be the case, because the head of the department handles this money.

He insisted, however, that bribery does not compromise his ethics. "Doctors would not prescribe medicines solely for incentives. The advice is based first of all on what kind of illness you have. And then maybe I overprescribe something else a little bit to make some money. It's not: because I get high kickbacks I give you this whether this is useful for you or not. Most Chinese doctors are kind. And if there's a poor person and we know he is poor then we won't take advantage."

Even if Lee is as principled as he claims, many doctors in China are not. The costs both to patients' wallets and to their well-being have been tremendous.

Between 2004 and 2015—the period when Western pharmaceutical bribery was at its height—spending on drugs in China grew from $9.5 billion to the $115 billion of today. "According to a conservative estimate, 20–30 percent of China's overall health care expenditures were spent on services and drugs that are unreasonable or unnecessary," a joint study by the Australian Centre for Economic Research on Health and the Fourth Military Medical University of Xi'an, has found. "The corruption in drug purchasing and prescribing within health facilities has contributed [to] the rapid rise in pharmaceutical expenditure."[38]

In Ningbo, a city about four hours from Shanghai, a surgeon named Dr. Ming described the public health fallout from bribery. Ming, who is in her early thirties, used to accept bribes for a GSK antibiotic called cefuroxime. Two GSK reps, both women, visited her office every month for about a year. They would shut the door, and then place money on her desk, about fifty dollars. "They say, 'Thank you for your support,'" Ming recalled, laughing at how polite the reps were in thanking her for her corruption.[39]

Dr. Ming believes that bribery is leading to overprescribing in China. "Because the kickbacks exist, some doctors will prescribe an antibiotic even if you don't really need it. This is creating harm to the patient by making them spend more money on unnecessary drugs and by overusing antibiotics."

China has, in fact, one of the highest rates of drug overprescription in the world, particularly of antibiotics. The Chinese government estimates that the average individual in China uses ten times as many antibiotics as the average American. Other research shows that 75 percent of Chinese patients suffering from a common cold are prescribed antibiotics—twice the international average. A growing collection of studies written by doctors in the United States, Europe, and China suggest that the bribes paid by companies like Pfizer and GSK are part of the problem. "These incentives mean that doctors not only have an incentive to prescribe, they have an incentive to prescribe more expensive drugs, which are often the newer and more powerful antibiotics that should be reserved for more dangerous infections," a 2011 joint study by Princeton University and Peking University states, adding, "This pattern is likely to exacerbate the problem of growing antibiotic resistance."[40]

Antibiotic resistance is a serious problem anywhere in the world, as it leads to the growth of bacterial strains that cannot be treated with antibiotics, but it has become particularly alarming in China. A variety of experts, including from the World Health Organization, believe that China's pronounced overuse of antibiotics is responsible for the appearance of antibiotic-resistant strains of various diseases, such as tuberculosis and syphilis, as well as various superbugs such as MRSA, mcr-1, and CRE.[41] Health officials have called the latter "nightmare bacteria" because they remain resistant to all known antibiotics and can therefore be lethal. Those strains are expected to spread globally. In fact, in March 2016, researchers at the Department of Defense disclosed that mcr-1 had been found in a human being in the United States for the first time. (The patient, a woman, had a strain of E. coli resistant to various drugs.)

Aside from resistance, overuse of antibiotics can also lead to adverse drug reactions. In 2010, Chinese scientists authored a study calculating that between 2001 and 2005 "there were 14,738,000 incidents of moderate to severe antibiotic adverse drug reactions in China yearly, and that 150,000 patients died."[42] Yanzhong Huang at the Council on Foreign Relations points out the Chinese government has set limits on the volume of antibiotics that doctors can prescribe. But he wonders whether these restrictions have come too little, too late. "It's no longer that you can buy [antibiotics] anywhere you want. But the damage, I believe, has already been done."

"We all became doctors because we have higher morals and ideals. And then we have to face this—we get slapped in the face," Dr. Lee observed. "There's no social status in being a doctor. Nobody wants to do this job. It's dishonest. And nobody wants to do something dishonest.

"Sometimes in China," he concluded, "if you think too much, you get depressed. You have to be a happy fool."

*  *  *

All the drug companies fined by U.S. regulators state that they have terminated the offering of bribes, and in many cases, fired the employees responsible for it. They are all under strict federal court orders to ensure that the practice does not continue. Many companies, including Novartis and GSK, have also reformed their compensation structures in China. Drug reps now receive fixed pay, not bonuses based on how many prescriptions they convince doctors to write. Still, drug reps in China said that although they are no longer using bribes as frequently and blatantly as before, they have not disappeared altogether.

The scale and duration of bribery within these companies, as well as the depth of its impact, invite important questions: Did executives at headquarters in the United States or Europe know it was taking place and approve it? The answer, as presented by U.S. regulators, is unclear. The SEC determined that Pfizer's officers were not aware of the improper payments in China themselves, but added that those officers took no steps to try to detect transgressions. The SEC did not explicitly rule out that Eli Lilly's management knew, and penalized the company for failing to be more proactive against bribery: "Despite an understanding that certain emerging markets were most vulnerable to FCPA violations, Lilly's audit department, based out of Indianapolis, had no procedures specifically designed to assess the FCPA or bribery risks of sales and purchases."[43] At Bristol-Myers Squibb, the SEC found that internal and external audit reports conducted between 2009 and 2011 repeatedly turned up fake invoices and *fapioa* used to generate cash for bribes. Both the external and internal reviews were passed up the chain, from management in China to corporate business managers, who reported back to senior management in Delaware. Although aware of the irregularities, headquarters consolidated the falsified accounts into its own books and records.

What is a just punishment for this crime, and who should ultimately be held responsible? After all, as Edward Chen pointed out, executives approve bribery from the top down, not employees from the bottom up. In 2009, Lanny Breuer, then the assistant attorney general of the Justice Department's Criminal Division, suggested an answer. Just as pharmaceutical bribery was beginning to peak and to be probed, he told a gathering of global pharmaceutical executives in Washington, D.C.: "We will be intensely focused on rooting out foreign bribery in your industry. That will mean investigation and, if warranted, prosecution of corporations, to be sure." Then he added: "But also it will involve investigation and prosecution of senior executives."[44] In the thirty years since the passing of the FCPA, corporate executives had rarely been held responsible for bribery committed on foreign shores, but Breuer seemed to be heralding a new, more muscular policy. But even given the extent of bribery in the pharmaceutical industry, which has been well established by far-ranging investigations and extensive documentation, neither a single executive or even an employee of any of these businesses has ever been identified as bearing responsibility, let alone been charged and sent to jail.

In China, the bribes were primarily small and widely dispersed to low-level officials involved in direct customer sales. But when a company wants to land a $100 million contract, it has to pay kickbacks much higher up the chain—to presidents and sheikhs. Bribing a doctor and hiding it with *fapioa* is one thing. Paying off a Middle Eastern potentate and hiding it is another. This requires someone who has access to high-level officials in the first place, and who has the expertise to make the payments look legitimate, enabling companies to claim, "Oh, we didn't know they were going to pay a bribe," as one former prosecutor described the process. This is where middlemen come in.

The story of middlemen provides a deeper look inside the corporate bribery system: namely how corporations, since at least the Second World War, have accessed the highest levels of political power, and paid off heads of state, by hiring shadowy figures who bridge the worlds of legitimate business and organized crime.

# Chapter 5

# **The Black Curtains**

Victor Phillip Michael Dahdaleh was born in Palestine in 1943, raised in Canada, and built a sprawling empire with the precious ore bauxite, the principal ingredient of aluminum. He is often referred to as an "aluminum king," resides in a $5 million townhouse in Belgravia, the most exclusive section of London, and counts Bill Clinton and Tony Blair among his personal friends. He is not very tall, and is rather portly, with a deeply receding hairline.

Dahdaleh's assets, which include an aluminum refinery in Stade, Germany, and exclusive bauxite contracts in the Republic of Guinea, are said to be worth several billion dollars. He made a fortune not only by sourcing and refining aluminum, but has by brokering, on behalf of others, some of the largest aluminum deals in history. In the $100 billion aluminum trade, Dahdaleh occupies a niche that is practically his own: a billionaire who also operates as a superagent, a middleman with the rarest of connections, both to powerful corporations and to reclusive Middle Eastern heads of state. "He was a wheeler dealer. He'd either flown in from Kuwait where he'd seen the emir, or he'd just come from Abu Dhabi where he'd just seen the ruler," Jeremy Nottingham, who worked with Dahdaleh in the 1990s, recalled. "He was the consummate middle-man."[1] Dahdaleh is also someone whom corporations and foreign officials have trusted to manage an enormous volume of bribes, according to law enforcement in the United States, the United Kingdom, Switzerland, and Norway.

When a Fortune 500 company wants to bribe a president or a Persian Gulf sheikh, they first have to gain access through an agent, and these agents are an elite group themselves. "The top level of corrupt agents, you're talking about a small number of people in the world—in the hundreds," Sasi-Kanth Mallela, a former investigator for Britain's Serious Fraud Office who investigated Dahdaleh, said. In the Middle East, he explained, there are probably only two or three agents whom sheikhs and emirs will trust with business—and with handling bribes. The agents also represent several companies at the same time. "Anyone who wants to do business has to go through one of these people. You're talking about billionaires.

"The reason many companies use agents to pay a bribe is so they have plausible deniability," Mallela continued.[2] Orchestrating such bribery schemes, which involve secretly breaking many international laws, sometimes for more than a decade, requires skill and discretion. It helps immeasurably if the agent involved has a great deal of respectability.

No agent in the world was more respectable than Victor Phillip Dahdaleh, with his governorship at the London School of Economics and a scholarship named for him at the Clinton Foundation.[3] But even as he donated to global charities and lavishly endowed university centers, Dahdaleh was secretively a corrupt middleman for Alcoa, one of America's blue-chip companies and the largest aluminum manufacturer in the world. Through Dahdaleh, Alcoa carried out one of the most illicit deals in the history of the modern Middle East—a deal that involved the supply of aluminum to one of the world's largest smelters, located in the tiny Arab monarchy of Bahrain. Alcoa used Dahdaleh to bribe Bahrain's corrupt sheikhs with more than $130 million, and the sheikhs agreed to look the other way as Alcoa inflated the price of the aluminum by $400 million over twenty years. In other words, Dahdaleh, a darling of the Western liberal elite, is personally responsible for the kind of corruption that compelled hundreds of thousands of angry citizens, including many in Bahrain, to protest during the Arab Spring.

That desert sheikhs are occasionally corrupt and that greedy Western corporations pay them off is by now almost a cliché. But what makes this case unique is that it illustrates an integral but often hidden dimension of bribery: the role of the agent. Corrupt middlemen—and middlewomen—have operated for decades, if not centuries, as shadow figures in global commerce. It is a testament to their skill that so little is actually known about them. Since the inception of the Foreign Corrupt Practices Act, law enforcement investigations have provided only fleeting glimpses of a handful of these individuals. And if little is known about agents in general, until recently much less has been known about agents at Dahdaleh's level. Dahdaleh himself would probably never have been exposed had it not been for a feud within the Bahraini royal family between traditionalists, whose power is sustained through corruption, and reformers, who view corruption as unsustainable within a system of stable power.

This story illuminates how deeply enmeshed modern international commerce has become with organized criminal behavior. It exposes the institution through which even highly regarded Western companies have outsourced bribery, and how doing so has often been the source of their success. Through men like Dahdaleh, foreign corruption affects our world, undermining the rule of law and compromising our supposedly free and democratic institutions.

* * *

In March 1987, Victor Dahdaleh formed a company called Rawmet Limited in the tax haven of Jersey, off the coast of Normandy. (Jersey is technically a dependency of the British Crown, but has its own parliament and judicial system, including laws that ensure a high level of secrecy for businesses.) Dahdaleh, then in his mid-forties, was already comfortable in the upper echelons of society, having been born into a global business. In 1915, his grandfather founded a private investment company called Dadco, which Dahdaleh inherited and now runs from its headquarters in Guernsey. During World War II, the family business built air force bases for the British government, according to an aluminum executive who has worked with Dahdaleh. His father, Phillip Michael, owned a bus company, as well as oil and soap factories in Ramleh, Palestine. The family fled to Jordan in 1948, following the creation of Israel, and used the family bus company, Ramleh Suda Buses, to evacuate many Arab Palestinians from the occupied territories.[4] Wealth afforded the family a life of privilege. After a period of childhood in Jordan, Victor Phillip grew up in Toronto and then attended the London School of Economics. He graduated in 1967, and soon afterward became the managing director of another family concern, Phillip M. Dahdaleh & Sons, purveyor of a variety of goods in the Middle East. (In the 1970s, Dahdaleh was lobbying the American embassy in Amman, Jordan, for help in selling medical equipment, according to diplomatic cables leaked by Wikileaks.)[5] By the time he formed Rawmet, Dahdaleh was already cultivating a global net-work of contacts, including royalty in the Persian Gulf.

Rawmet's incorporation documents list three shareholders: Dahdaleh, Sheikh Khalifa Abdullah Hamad Al Khalifa, and Sheikh Bader Abdullah Al Khalifa. The latter two are members of the royal Al Khalifa dynasty in Bahrain.[6] From 1987 until the mid-1990s, when it was dissolved, Dahdaleh owned six shares of the company, and the sheikhs three each. The shares themselves were never worth more than a few dollars, and Rawmet appears to have been nothing more than a shell.[7]

There are many mysteries surrounding Dahdaleh, a man who has meticulously guarded his public image. He has never given an interview to the press, and the personal details he has made public—on his websites and in public relations statements—are meager, carefully curated to burnish his credentials as a philan-thropist and benefactor of educational causes. One of the most enduring questions about him is how he became so closely linked with the ruling family of Bahrain. A hint comes from an interview that Gudvin Tofte, a Norwegian who was the CEO of Aluminum Bahrain, or Alba, in the early 2000s, gave to Bloomberg News sev-eral years ago. Tofte said that in the 1980s, Dahdaleh contacted the French embassy in Bahrain, through which he established a connection to the House of Khalifa.[8] A business executive who has known Dahdaleh for years provided a different take: Alcoa, the American company, had earlier enlisted Dahdaleh's services in Dubai, and then recommended him to the royals. It is a testament to his skill that he not only made it past the marble threshold of the Al-Qudaibiya Palace in Manama but into its inner sanctum, where, with his crisp manners, his Middle Eastern pedigree, and his business acumen, he no doubt presented himself as a valuable asset to the royal family. According to people who have known Dahdaleh, he is an infectious charmer who easily makes friends. "He had a way of making you feel that you were privileged," Jeremy Notthingham, who was deputy chief executive at Alba until 2004, recalled. "I think he was a guy who made you feel important. I think he was also very discreet. He was never up front in anything, he was always in the background." However Dahdaleh may have charmed his way into the House of Khalifa, the incorporation of Rawmet revealed that, by the mid-1980s, he had already become their trusted man and conduit for their bribes. The relationship would prove extremely valuable to Dahdaleh, the royals, and Western corporations.

Alcoa was founded in 1888 in Pittsburgh, Pennsylvania, and by the year 2000, it employed roughly 120,000 people around the world, generating annual revenues of $20.5 billion. The company sources and extracts bauxite, primarily in Australia and Guinea, and refines it into the compound alumina, which it then processes, using a smelter, into aluminum. Aluminum is such a lucrative commodity because of its widespread use in products ranging from soda cans to cars and airplane parts. Alcoa also sells about half of its alumina production to other companies, including Alba, the focus of Dahdaleh's illegal deal. Alba's smelter, one of the largest in the world, is technically owned and managed by the royal family of Bahrain. Alcoa's relationship with Alba began in 1969, and by the early 1980s, it was directly supplying Alba with large quantities of alumina.

But in 1988, the chairman of Alba, Sheikh Isa Bin Ali Al Khalifa, informed Alcoa officials that if the company wanted to continue doing business with Alba, it would have to sell its alumina to an intermediary, Victor Dahdaleh, who would in turn would sell it to Alba. In addition to overseeing the tender process for Alba, Sheikh Isa was then the country's oil minister, which gave him immense power. He is also the brother-in-law of Prince Khalifa bin Salman Al Khalifa, who has clung to power since 1970, the longest-serving prime minister in the world.[9] Prince Khalifa is heir to the House of Al Khalifa, the Sunni royal family that conquered the Shia majority of Bahrain in the late 1700s and has ruled ever since. (The Al Khalifas' institutionalized discrimination against Shias is well documented, and ethnic tensions are a constant.) Sheikh Isa was considered to be the prime minister's right-hand man, so it was difficult for Alcoa to refuse his demand if they wanted to continue to do billions of dollars in business with an oil-rich state.

Alcoa officials initially raised questions about Dahdaleh, who had no experience in the aluminum business, but ultimately complied with Sheikh Isa's demand and brought Dahdaleh on as their agent.

The decision to hire an agent is not always an unethical one. Agents have expert knowledge of markets, regulatory barriers, foreign customs, and export and trade laws, as well as networks of contacts. Another of the chief reasons for employing an agent is that it cuts costs: Rather than maintaining an expensive office in a foreign country, along with local staff, consultants can be hired on a project-by-project basis and paid on commission rather than a fixed salary. On paper, Alcoa hired Victor Dahdaleh because of his contacts and his expertise in Middle Eastern customs. A commercial manager at Alcoa wrote that Alumet, one of Dahdaleh's companies, was "a company well versed in the normal ways of Middle Eastern business" and could "keep the various stakeholders in the Alba smelter happy."[10]

There was nothing inherently untoward about Dahdaleh's forming a company with Bahraini royalty, but the arrangement became corrupt when Alcoa in Australia, an Alcoa subsidiary, paid Rawmet a commission of $1.28 million for selling alumina to Alba in 1989. That commission was demanded as a bribe by the royal family of Bahrain. By agreeing to it, Alcoa showed that it was willing to engage in a corrupt relationship with the royals, and they, in turn, showed their gratitude to the company: Alcoa became the "preferred supplier" to Alba, as an Alcoa of Australia sales manager would later explain in a company memo.[11]

Dahdaleh, meanwhile, had proven himself to both the royals and Alcoa by successfully passing on the bribes. "The middleman does have to prove that they can be trusted. Coming through on the bribe payments creates trust," a former U.S. law enforcement official with knowledge of the Alcoa case described.[12] Gaining this trust became the entry point to Dahdaleh's high-flying success and rise to the global elite, and ultimately to his fall from grace.

In 1990, Dahdaleh opened an office on avenue d'Ouchy, a fashionable street lush with trees that runs through Lausanne, Switzerland. Number 61 avenue d'Ouchy had once been the Hotel Meurice Lausanne. With its neoclassical balconies and cream-colored facade, the elegant four-story building is located just a short walk from the northern shore of Lake Geneva. In the 1960s, Alcoa purchased the property and turned it into the offices of its European subsidiary, Alcoa Europe S.A. It was here that Alcoa invited Dahdaleh to set up a new company, AA Alumina and Chemicals, with a small staff on the fourth floor. He even printed stationery with the Alcoa logo on it, indicating his deep and growing ties with the company. That year, Dahdaleh signed a contract that made him Alcoa's official business agent.

In return for what was described as local support and marketing services, Dahdaleh would receive 1 percent of all the transactions he conducted between Alcoa and Alba.[13] Between 1990 and 2009, Alcoa maintained a contract with Alba that was worth $3 billion—one of the most lucrative aluminum deals in history.[14]

It has never been clear precisely what service Dahdaleh performed for Alcoa or why he was paid such extravagant sums to perform it. Alcoa already had a long-standing relationship with Alba, supplying it with thousands of tons of alumina. Although Dahdaleh was technically now the middleman, his company never actually took possession of the alumina it sold to Alba, according to U.S. regulators. Neither did Dahdaleh himself manage the arrangements for shipping the material from Australia to Bahrain.[15]

By accepting Dahdaleh as an intermediary, Alcoa was consciously accepting the terms of a dubious financial structure—a structure that corporations that have resorted to bribery have been using since at least the 1950s, and probably since before the Second World War. How this structure came into being is a key part of the postwar era's history of foreign corporate bribery—and much of what it reveals about agents and political power remains true today.

\*  \*  \*

Lockheed Aircraft Company, founded in Burbank, California, was the nation's largest defense contractor after World War II, specializing in commercial and military aircraft. But by 1967, the company was on the brink of bankruptcy. It had just received a federal bailout of $250 million and still desperately needed a significant sale. All Nippon, Japan's leading commercial airline, was looking to purchase twenty-one aircraft, in a deal worth $430 million.

Lockheed's competitors—McDonnell Douglas and Boeing—had been given the early nod.

Carl Kotchian, who became Lockheed's president in 1967, was convinced his company would fail if it didn't manage to win the contract away from its competitors—by any means necessary. Kotchian was a plain-talking North Dakotan who had risen up Lockheed's corporate ladder since his arrival there in 1941. He flew to Japan more than a dozen times trying to close the All Nippon Airways deal, and when that effort failed, he took more extreme measures.

The method Kotchian eventually turned to involved hiring a power broker who could interface with Japan's top leadership. In postwar Japan—as in many countries today—the inner circle of political power was closed to *gaijin* (foreigners). Language, etiquette, and social custom required that foreigners approach government officials only through the proper connections. As Kotchian would later explain to Congress: "I think you should recognize that the Japanese establishment . . . is a fairly close-knit group of individuals, both in business and government, and somebody from the United States is not privy to enter into that group, and so you need some help."[16]

Lockheed did more than acquire "some help." The agent whom Lockheed eventually hired to gain access to Japan's power structure was the country's most infamous gangster and a former war crimes suspect during the American Occupation.

Yoshio Kodama was born in 1911 in Fukushima prefecture to a warrior clan "considered of the Samurai rank," as a recently declassified CIA dossier recounts.[17] The agency had been tracking Kodama's activity for more than 30 years, and its biographical record of him, contained in more than 100 once-secret documents, is a fascinating portrait of a man who is probably the modern world's first and most notorious superagent.

A college dropout, Kodama was a fanatical adherent to Japanese nationalism from a very young age. Throughout his twenties, he "was associated with terrorist incidents and rightist arrests that marked the upsurge of Japanese militarism in the early 1930's," one U.S. intelligence document states.[18] In 1932, he plotted unsuccessfully to assassinate Prime Minister Shishaku Saito Makoto, who did not share Kodama's vision of aggressive Japanese expansion. Kodama was convicted at trial, shooting himself during the proceedings in a failed attempt at suicide, and spent nearly five years in prison.

Upon his release, Kodama became an asset to the militarized Japanese government now in power, which set him up as a covert foreign agent, pressing Japanese military causes in China. As his cover, Kodama established a vast trade empire in Shanghai, the Kodama Agency, staffed, as U.S. intelligence officers wrote, by nationalist "ruffians," "drifters," and Japanese "soldiers of fortune."[19] Heroin trafficking, intelligence gathering, paramilitary operations, and black-market procurement were among its many activities. According to the CIA, Kodama amassed a private fortune in China, including large holdings of "platinum, diamonds, and radium."[20] Intelligence documents quote sources as saying that Kodama returned to Japan in 1942 with a thousand gold bars and several billion dollars.[21]

With this war chest, Kodama become Japan's greatest postwar *kuromaku*—a "black curtain." The word, derived from ancient Kabuki theater, literally means the screen that conceals actors offstage and refers to the individuals who truly control power from behind the scenes. By the 1950s, the U.S. intelligence community was describing Kodama as the "undisputed leader of the Japanese right." He had personally financed the creation of the dominant Liberal Party, and bankrolled numerous rightist causes. As a *New York Times* report noted: "One of his sources of power has been his skillful manipulation of a distinctively Japanese sense of personal obligation. He has done favors, great and small, for those in high places and later has collected."[22] Kodama was also a "blood brother to a number of *yakuza* (leaders of the Japanese underworld)," according to intelligence documents.

Kotchian met Kodama in Tokyo in 1971 and was surprised to find a physically unprepossessing, very soft-spoken man. "It was hard to imagine where the energy and capability were hidden in him," Kotchian later wrote in a candid book about the affair, one of the few firsthand accounts ever published about Kodama. According to Kotchian, Kodama told him that Lockheed would never make a sale in Japan if it did not pay bribes, which were effectively the "admission to a ball game." "[I]f you didn't pay the admission, you were not even qualified to participate in the game—your product would not even be considered."[23]

Lockheed complied with Kodama's advice, taking great pains to devise a structure to pay him surreptitiously. The arrangement, which corporations engaging in bribery have been employing ever since, involved using a Swiss subsidiary to conduct all the payments, because Switzerland's corporate secrecy laws provided a greater measure of protection against being caught. Because Kodama insisted that the bribe money be delivered in cash, Lockheed personnel in Switzerland would purchase millions of yen from a foreign exchange broker in Hong Kong, load the cash into specially designed packing cases, and deliver them directly to Kodama. They later switched to bearer checks, which Lockheed's vice president of international finance personally took to Tokyo.

Of the $12.5 million that Lockheed funneled in bribes and questionable payments to Japan between 1969 and 1975, Kodama received $7 million ($5 million was his consulting fee, and roughly $2 million was allegedly for kickbacks). The other $5.5 million was funneled to more than a dozen government officials through different agents.[24] Kotchian would later testify before Congress that he never asked his *kuromaku* for an accounting of what happened to the money, although in his book he acknowledges that he knew that at least $1.6 million of the bribes was going to Japan's prime minister, Kakuei Tanaka. Although the way Kodama passed the bribes to Tanaka remains a mystery, after they were paid, All Nippon reneged on its deal with Boeing and McDonnell Douglas and purchased Lockheed's aircraft instead.

In 1976, Senator Frank Church, chairman of the congressional committee that eventually investigated Lockheed's overseas bribery, asked William G. Findley, Lockheed's chief auditor at Arthur Young & Co.: "When you learned of these payments, did you inquire about the identity of [Kodama]? . . . Did you discover that he had been convicted as a war criminal?"* Lockheed's board of directors was aware of his history, Findley answered, but implied that they basically did not care. It was also revealed in great detail during the 1976 hearings that Kodama had, in fact, been Lockheed's secret agent since as early as 1958.[25]

Carl Kotchian's admission before Congress of having paid bribes

---

* In fact, Kodama had never been convicted. During the American occupation, the U.S. military arrested him as a Class A war crimes suspect. He was detained for three years at Sugamo Prison in Tokyo, but never went to trial. The U.S. military released him in 1948; according to some sources, the U.S. intelligence community intervened on Kodama's behalf, and cultivated him as an anti-Communist asset. Even without a conviction, Kodama was obviously a man of "very questionable character," as Senator Church said.

to the Japanese became Japan's greatest scandal since the end of the Second World War—their version of Watergate. In all, sixteen high-ranking Japanese politicians and businessmen were indicted on corruption and other charges. Prime Minister Tanaka resigned in 1974 and was indicted two years later on bribery charges. In 1983, he was found guilty and sentenced to four years in prison. He appealed but died in 1993, before Japan's Supreme Court returned its verdict.[26] Kodama was the only one never to be convicted. He died of heart failure in 1984 at the age of seventy-three.

*Rokkiedo Jiken*—the Lockheed Incident, as it was known in Japan—dramatized an essential truth: that the highest-level contracts in Japan—representing billions of dollars and the very future of the country's national development—were not awarded on the basis of merit alone, on the quality of a product or the competitiveness of its price. This is not to say that Lockheed's planes were inferior in quality; quite the contrary. But the scandal revealed for the first time not only that there was a system in place through which Japan's highest leadership, including its prime minister, could be influenced through bribery, but also that the secret key to accessing this system was a figure like Kodama.

We can never know for certain what impact Lockheed's paying an underworld king the equivalent today of at least $40 million may have had on Japan's political development and on its relations with the United States. Senator Charles Percy captured the disturbing ramifications of the Lockheed-Kodama connection when he described the "very sad state of affairs" that "the largest United States defense contractor" had paid millions to a ideologue who, through his leadership of Japan's militaristic right wing, had helped bring "a war on the world really, an attack on the United States. . . . From what I have learned, that kind of an association,

I am literally shocked that Lockheed would have that affiliation or feel it necessary in order to get business out there. Where is the responsibility?"[27]

*  *  *

By the early 1990s, Dahdaleh had created a number of shell companies to which Alcoa paid millions in "commissions," and which Dahdaleh then handed over to the royal family as bribes, U.S. and UK authorities allege. Dahdaleh managed much of the fraud from the comfort of his Edwardian townhouse on Eaton Place, using his fax machine to instruct various banks to wire the funds, according to British prosecutors.[28] In 1993, he created a new company, Kwinalum, registered in Singapore. Ostensibly it would handle additional shipments of alumina out of Australia, via Singapore. In reality, Alcoa of Australia was still managing those shipments. But through Kwinalum, Dahdaleh raised the stakes of his schemes and began marking up the price of alumina he sold to Alba. Between 1993 and 1996 alone, he overcharged Alba by almost $19 million.

Why did Alba agree to buy alumina at what must have been an obviously inflated price? Because the markup created a float, a large fund that could be skimmed off or kicked back by the sheikhs controlling Alba's board, according to U.S law enforcement. The plan worked as follows: Alcoa would sell Dahdaleh a ton of alumina at discounted prices, and Dahdaleh would in turn invoice Alba at a price marked up by as much as 14 percent. Alba would pay that sum into Kwinalum's bank account, and the 14 percent would create a float. Dahdaleh did not keep that money for himself, but had an arrangement to kick it back to the sheikhs who controlled Alba. Though the sheikhs could not blatantly steal millions of dollars from the company's finances, which would have posed too great a risk, this scheme enabled them to do so clandestinely. (In essence, they were stealing from the national treasury, given that Alba is a national company.)

According to Jeremy Nottingham, members of the royal family were aware that this corruption was taking place. In fact, Sheikh Isa, Alba's chairman, personally controlled a system whereby all of Alba's tenders, and not just those involving Alcoa, were awarded based on bribes. As Nottingham explained, "The rule was that any contract over 100,000 dinars, or $260,000, before being awarded, even though we had our own tender board and our own internal procedures, it had to go what we called 'downtown.' That was a euphemism. And downtown meant it went to the office of the minister [Sheikh Isa] and the minister told us to whom to award the contract." Nottingham, who later testified at Dahdaleh's corruption trial, added: "There was only one way that you got business, you were awarded any contract during that era. There was a bribe price that had to be paid. It was standard practice."

With Sheikh Isa's blessing, Dahdaleh marked up the price of alumina he sold to Alba by a total of $108 million between 1997 and 2001, according to the Justice Department. From 2002 to 2004, he marked up the price by $79 million; between 2005 and 2009, by $188 million. Over the course of two decades, then, the citizens of Bahrain overpaid $394 million for alumina, money that the royals skimmed off the public purse.

Throughout this period, Alcoa executives knowingly turned a blind eye to, or even facilitated, Dahdaleh's enterprise. When Alcoa's in-house attorneys become concerned about the agent's shell companies, citing possible violations of the FCPA, a senior Alcoa executive vouched for Dahdaleh, the Justice Department alleges (the executive in question was not named). When Bruce Allan Hall, who became Alba's CEO in 2000, started asking similar questions, William Rice, then vice president of marketing at an Alcoa subsidiary, faxed him a letter from Pittsburgh assuring him that Dahdaleh's company was Alcoa's trusted distributor, documents submitted as part of Alba's civil suit against Alcoa and Dahdaleh show. Hall, still unsatisfied, almost walked away from an aluminum deal, and in response Rice faxed him threatening to sell Alcoa's alumina to other buyers if Alba refused to work with Dahdaleh's company, according to a company letter. Rice says that he was merely the point person during the correspondence, and not responsible for the arrangement. "In my role, there was clearly management above me who were making the decisions," he said.[29] Eventually, Dahdaleh found his own way to convince Hall—by bribing him. Hall eventually took $10 million in kickbacks and was arrested in October 2011. (Alba eventually settled its civil lawsuit with Alcoa and William Rice. U.S. law enforcement has never charged any Alcoa executives for any wrongdoing.)

In 2013, Great Britain's Serious Fraud Office specifically named Sheikh Isa as one of the recipients of the Alcoa bribes. According to Dahdaleh's official charge sheet in the United Kingdom, he wired Sheikh Isa at least $6 million through offshore accounts. The U.S. Justice Department traced at least $131.2 million in bribes that Dahdaleh wired from various shell companies to the royals between 1993 and 2006; one official alone received a total of $83 million. He is not publicly named, but fits the description of Sheikh Isa. (In keeping with Justice Department policy, foreign officials are never publicly named because they cannot, under U.S. law, be charged with corruption for receiving bribes.) According to a businessman who worked closely with Sheikh Isa and did not want to be named, the sheikh almost certainly did not keep this money himself. "Sheikh Isa didn't live lavishly. He was a very simple guy," the businessman said. "He was the bag carrier for the guy who really made the money." Legal proceedings in the United States and the United Kingdom suggest that it was the prime minister, Prince Khalifa bin Salman al Khalifa, who was the recipient of most of the bribes. In Justice Department documents, the prince, like Sheikh Isa, is never overtly named, but is simply referred to as "Official D . . . a senior member of Bahrain's Royal Family and a senior government official of Bahrain for many decades."[30] According to the Justice Department's allegations, to which Alcoa ultimately pleaded guilty, Official D received at least $37 million in direct wire transfers from Dahdaleh's companies.

Alcoa was not the only company for which Dahdaleh acted as a middleman in the Alba deal. In 2014, Torvald Klaveness, the Norwegian shipping firm that transported Alcoa's alumina from Australia to Bahrain, paid a $5 million fine to Norwegian authorities following a four-year-long investigation. According to Økokrim, Norway's economic crimes agency, Dahdaleh had arranged freight contracts for one of Klaveness's subsidiaries, which in turn paid roughly $2.7 million in commissions to Alumet, Dahdaleh's shell, between 2003 and 2004.[31] Dahdaleh used other shell companies and bank accounts in Switzerland and Guernsey to secretly wire "a significant portion" of these commissions to Sheikh Isa.[32] Tom Erik Klaveness, whose father founded the company in 1946, told a Norwegian newspaper that some of the bribes were destined for the king of Bahrain, though he could not confirm this.[33] Both Økokrim and Tom Erik Klaveness declined to comment further.

None of these details would ever have come to light had Alba not sued Alcoa in U.S. federal court in 2008, seeking $1 billion in damages. That it did so signified a rift in the royal family, between the so-called "good Al Khalifas and the bad Al Khalifas," as one observer characterized them. The "good Al Khalifas" refers to Crown Prince Salman bin Hamad bin Isa Al Khalifa, a younger reformer who reportedly views the corruption of his uncle, the prime minister, as jeopardizing the stability of the Al Khalifa dynasty. The crown prince is believed to have authorized Alba's new management to investigate allegations of corruption within the company's tendering system, and then to have brought the lawsuit against Alcoa, allegedly to shame his uncle and the uncle's cronies.[34] Once the lawsuit became public, the Justice Department intervened and began its own criminal inquiry against Alcoa, as did the Serious Fraud Office in the United Kingdom.

Dahdaleh was arrested in London on October 24, 2011, against the backdrop of the Arab Spring, and just months after tens of thousands of Bahrainis, mostly Shias, took to the streets in an uprising against the corruption of the prime minister, an uprising that the Al Khalifas crushed to protect their corrupt interests. "The point was the defense of the privilege that they have, which enriches them immensely," a Bahraini human rights activist, Ala'a Shehabi, observed.[35] Although the prime minister and Sheikh Isa denied any accusations of corruption, Dahdaleh's trial, which began in 2013, exposed the truth about their involvement for the first time.

Dahdaleh never denied making the bribes. Instead, his defense team argued that the bribes were legitimate, and legal, because Bahrain's government knew about them and approved them. In court, Dahdaleh's barrister, Nicholas Purnell, contended that Sheikh Isa was acting only on the orders of Prime Minister Khalifa bin Salman Al Khalifa, who ultimately controlled Alba: "All the payments that had been made by Mr. Dahdaleh had been made

with the knowledge of the board in the form of the Bahraini majority and its relationship with the Prime Minister."[36]

But the Serious Fraud Office's case fell apart when the key witness for the prosecution—Bruce Allan Hall, the former CEO of
Alba—changed his testimony. The Serious Fraud Office had sought
to assign responsibility for the entire Alba scheme to Dahdaleh,
but Hall argued, as did many others, that Dahdaleh alone was not
responsible for devising the plan. He merely excelled at manipulating it. "This was government-sponsored corruption. And Victor
was a key player in the government-sponsored corruption, but he
wasn't the originator of it," Nottingham observed. Two American
lawyers who had represented Alba in its civil suit against Dahdaleh
also refused to testify in London, on the grounds of attorney-client
privilege, which proved the coup de grâce. The judge ruled that
without the right to cross-examine these witnesses Dahdaleh could
not have a fair trial, and the charges against him were dropped. In
2014, Alcoa paid $161 million in penalties to settle an SEC inves-
tigation of its FCPA violations, and its subsidiary, Alcoa World
Alumina pled guilty to charges brought by the Justice Department,
paying an additional $223 million in fines.[37]

\* \* \*

Not every agent is a dangerous ideologue like Kodama, or as
wealthy and well-connected as Dahdaleh. Not all overseas business is conducted through agents, and certainly not all agents are
corrupt. But ever since Lockheed first employed them, agents have
played a critical role in the multibillion-dollar international corporate bribery system.

Siemens Corporation kept 2,700 hundred "consultants" on its

payroll, a veritable army of bribe payers. A Justice Department investigation found that, in many cases, their only function was "passing along corrupt payments for Siemens to foreign government officials responsible for awarding business."[38] Its large staff of said consultants enabled Siemens to conduct bribery on a breathtaking scale: At least 4,283 corrupt payments, involving nearly $1.4 billion, were paid in more than a dozen countries around the world. Some of its intermediaries were low-level businessmen who did little more than courier cash to high-level officials. Others were men like Carlos Sergi, a prominent entrepreneur in Argentina with long-standing ties to the Argentine Air Force, who had allegedly brokered questionable arms sales during Argentina's Malvinas War, and been a shadowy figure in large radar procurements during the administration of Nestor Kirchner. Sergi also allegedly helped orchestrate the flow of $100 million in bribes to Argentinian government officials, including President Carlos Menem in the 1990s and President Fernando De la Rúa in the 2000s.[39] As the Justice Department noted, Sergi's "value to the conspiracy was his access to influential members of the Argentine government and role as a facilitator." Evidence discovered in the investigation revealed that Sergi passed $16 million to Menem, though the former president has never been charged and has denied any wrongdoing.

After the Siemens deal, Sergi fell back into the shadows, where he remains today, still under investigation by the Justice Department. His name has since resurfaced in another scandal. In 2011, Spanish authorities at Barcelona Airport detained a private jet. Inside two couches on the plane they found hidden more than a ton of cocaine, worth roughly $42 million. The jet, which had flown from Argentina to Cape Verde in Africa, had been piloted by Gustavo Julia and his brother Eduardo, who planned to smuggle the drugs into Argentina. The Julia brothers are the sons of Jose Julia, the deceased former head of the Argentine Air Force under Carlos Menem. (In 2013, a Spanish court sentenced the Julia brothers to thirteen years in prison.) Argentine newspapers have quoted unnamed Spanish magistrates as indicating that five hundred thousand dollars had been paid to charter the jet, and that Carlos Sergi paid the fee.[40]

For a time, Siemen's brazen use of intermediaries seemed an extreme and isolated case. Since then, however, many of the most recognizable companies in the world—including Daimler, Hewlett-Packard, and Johnson & Johnson—have been investigated and fined by international law enforcement for using corrupt agents. Although none employed as many agents as Siemens, in more than a dozen cases intermediaries played a crucial role in aiding leading multinationals to penetrate and thrive in the emerging markets of the world.

For more than fifty years, Rolls-Royce has manufactured the most cutting-edge commercial and military jet engines in the world. The dominant narrative in the United Kingdom and globally has been that Rolls became one of the world's premiere blue-chip companies as a result of its superior engineering, coupled with its brilliant corporate leadership. Indeed, Rolls-Royce's revenue skyrocketed from £2.8 billion in 1987 to £76 billion in 2016, as the *Financial Times* reported.[41] According to British and American law enforcement, however, from 1989 until 2013—the very period of its explosive growth—Rolls-Royce maintained a widespread system of bribery, involving at least eight international middlemen who paid off government officials in Nigeria, China, Russia, Indonesia, Kazakhstan, and Angola, among other countries. The bribes generated at least £250 million in profits for the company.

In the 1990s, Rolls paid more than $10 million to its agents in Thailand, who in turn bribed senior government officials to buy Rolls's T800 engine, thereby beating out competition like Pratt & Whitney. In 2012, Rolls's agent in Nigeria bribed government officials to obtain inside information about its competitors, including General Electric. Rolls used the information to ensure that its bids were more favorable, and won lucrative contracts. It pleaded guilty to the bribery in 2017 and paid a total of $800 million in fines to authorities in the United States and the United Kingdom, making it another of the largest bribery schemes on record.[42]

* * *

On June 20, 2016, Victor Dahdaleh rose from his chair on the stage of the Convocation Pavilion at York University, Toronto, wearing a crimson and blue graduate's gown. He was greeted by a round of applause. York is one of Canada's most respected universities, and in recent years has built a global reputation for excellence, particularly for its business and law schools. Since the early 2000s, Dahdaleh has become one of the school's single largest benefactors, with a building on campus named for him, and another soon to follow. In 2015, Dahdaleh donated $20 million to found its Dahdaleh Institute for Global Health Research. Mamdouh Shoukri, York's president and vice-chancellor, called it a "transformational gift" and "the largest ever received in the university's history from an alum."[43] In May 2016, Dahdaleh donated $3.5 million to Montreal's McGill University, where he received a graduate diploma in management in 1975, to fund a new chair in neuroscience research. McGill hailed him as its single largest donor from the United Kingdom.[44] In November 2016, Dahdaleh donated more than $6 million to the British Lung Foundation—again, the largest donation the organization has ever received.[45]

In recognition of his philanthropy, York awarded Dahdaleh with an honorary degree in law, the highest of its kind. As he took center stage at the Convocation Pavilion, he exhorted his audience, "Try your best to be a good citizen. And most importantly," he continued, "when you succeed, give something back."[46] As he stood at the lectern, extolling the virtues of altruism, his assets in Switzerland lay frozen. Since 2009, the Attorney General's Office in Bern has been leading a criminal proceeding against Dahdaleh on suspicions of money laundering, and has blocked more than $60 million—an extraordinary sum, but likely just a fraction of Dahdaleh's overall wealth.[47]

That Dahdaleh made millions through bribery was just the first act in his extraordinary career. In successive acts he laundered his riches and purchased access to prestige and a position within the liberal global elite. That process began with Alcoa. Once he had moved into Alcoa's Switzerland office, Dahdaleh was brought closer into the company's orbit. In May 2000, Alcoa merged with another American aluminum giant, Reynolds, making it the largest aluminum company in the world. Before approving the merger, the European Commission required Alcoa to divest itself of certain of its European assets to prevent monopolies. Among the holdings it had to sell was 50 percent of its ownership in an aluminum refinery in Stade, Germany, acquired through Reynolds.[48] The buyer was Dahdaleh, who was now no longer just a corrupt middleman but a significant player in the global aluminum business.[49]

In June 2004, the remaining 50 percent of the Stade refinery went up for sale. The seller was Norsk Hydro, a Norwegian energy firm. Dahdaleh paid $110 million and now owned all of the Stade refinery.[50] With this purchase he also acquired a 10 percent interest in a company called Halco, a consortium of companies (including Rio Tinto Alcan and Alcoa) that owns 51 percent of La Compagnie des Bauxites de Guinée (CBG), a bauxite mining company in the Republic of Guinea. (The government of Guinea owns the remaining 49 percent of the business.)[51] CBG has exclusive rights to one of the largest proven reserves of bauxite in the world, of which Dahdaleh now owned a piece. Now, from his mansion in Belgravia, he began sourcing his own bauxite directly from Africa and refining the ore at his refinery in Germany. He had become a vertically integrated aluminum magnate.

By the mid-2000s, Dahdaleh began his third act: as global benefactor. He formed a foundation in his name and began giving away millions of dollars to universities, medical research, and liberal causes. Thousands of dollars went to the International Crisis Group, the Brussels-based human rights organization; to cancer research at Imperial College, London; and more than twenty thousand dollars to the Institute for Public Policy Research, a center-left think tank in London. In 2007, the National Ethnic Coalition of Organizations presented Dahdaleh with the International Ellis Island Medal of Honor, which honors individuals "whose professional, personal or philanthropic contributions benefit our global community."[52]

Ascending through ever higher circles, Dahdaleh donated to the Labour Party in England and became a friend of Tony Blair's, and then of Bill Clinton's. By 2004, the year he took complete control of Stade, Dahdaleh had already begun donating to the Clinton Foundation and is reported to have given between $1 million to $5 million. (The foundation has not disclosed the exact amount.)[53] Together the Clinton and Dahdaleh foundations have endowed a scholarship that enables promising students from poor countries, particularly in the Middle East, to attend McGill University.[54]

Fittingly, it was McGill that was the scene of the crowning moment in Dahdaleh's philanthropy: In 2009, he persuaded the school to present Bill Clinton with an honorary degree. Even more impressively, he persuaded Bill Clinton to travel to Montreal to accept the honor at a time when the Justice Department's criminal inquiry into Alcoa, and Dahdaleh, was widely publicized.[55] As Clinton stood before an audience of some seven hundred on the morning of October 16, it was Dahdaleh himself, beaming proudly, who placed the hood conferring the degree over his shoulders. Dahdaleh, captured in video of the event, then gave Clinton a lingering hug.

In his acceptance speech, Clinton referred to Dahdaleh as "my great friend" and spoke for nearly an hour, returning time and again to the imperative of "moral responsibility." He marshaled many statistics in his fine oratory, precise and damning figures about global inequality, about the structures rigged against the poor. The Dahdaleh story, had he recounted it, could have spoken volumes about how corporate bribery, particularly on Alcoa's scale, deepens inequality and dampens the prospects for democracy by empowering authoritarian regimes.

Today, Dahdaleh continues his philanthropy, dividing his time between London and a sprawling home he and his wife own in the Paudex region of Switzerland. The house, located on a secluded cul-de-sac, is just a fifteen-minute drive to the headquarters of Dadco in Lausanne, where it all began. There, from the old Hotel Meurice building, Dahdaleh continues to reap the benefits of his long relationship with Alcoa. Halco, their joint venture in Guinea, reported $117 million in net income between 2015 and 2017—of which Dahdaleh derives 5 percent.[56]

The role of agents illuminates one of the most destructive consequences of high-level commercial graft: a disturbing cycle in which public prestige paves the way to corruption, and corruption, in turn, to even greater public prestige. "Truth walks toward you along the path of the questions that you ask," Charles Gibbons, a lawyer who represented Alba, said one afternoon during the Alcoa civil trial in Pittsburgh. Dahdaleh's career illustrates that lies accumulate in the place of questions that no one dares to ask.

The same can be said of the foreign government officials who receive bribes. As the following chapter will show, corrupt foreign officials are able to receive and launder this money only because powerful institutions and professions in the West—corporations, banks, lawyers—choose to overlook black money. And as is the case with middlemen, the impact of this corruption, far from remaining overseas, comes back to haunt us at home.

## Chapter 6

# A Houseboat in the Swamps

In late 2007, as the British and Nigerian police were closing in on him, James Ibori, the former governor of Nigeria's Delta State, had his lawyer in London make an unusual purchase: a 7,000-square-foot mansion in Houston, Texas. Ibori paid for the $1.8 million property in cash.[1] He had no particular reason to own a mansion in Houston and, in fact, had no ties to Texas at all. Between 1999 and 2007, he made an annual salary of only eighteen thousand dollars as governor.

Nigeria is Africa's largest economy, one powered almost exclusively by oil production. Most of that oil—37 billion barrels—lies buried in the Delta's swampy creeks, making it one of the world's most coveted properties. Ibori ruled the Delta during a pivotal period in its history, a period of both unprecedented oil development and violence. As leading oil companies signed multi-billion-dollar contracts, the Delta's ethnic clans, from whose land the crude was taken, slaughtered one another for control of the resource, and then terrorized foreign oil companies. All the while, James Ibori secretly amassed an illicit fortune through corporate bribes, embezzlement, and fraud.

With the help of professional financiers and lawyers in London, Ibori secreted millions of dollars in real estate and in bank accounts across the world. His lawyers arranged everything so that his assets were owned by a dense web of shell companies, none bearing a trace of Ibori's name. The Houston mansion was deeded in the name of MER Engineering—a shell company that British and Nigerian law enforcement were just then identifying as the central spoke in a mysterious bribery case.

The British police had been investigating Ibori's shadow empire since 2005, because much of his money flowed through London, and had traced and frozen $35 million of his assets. Detectives from Scotland Yard had been jetting back and forth to Abuja, the Nigerian capital, gathering evidence—including a suspicious-looking business contract that linked Ibori to two of the largest oil companies in the world: Chevron and Shell Oil.

Chevron and Shell, they learned, rented two houseboats in the Niger Delta, essentially floating hostels for oil workers and security personnel in the swamps to sleep. Between 2004 and 2007—Ibori's second term—the two oil companies deposited $3.4 million into a bank account at Barclays in London, purportedly for the rental of the houseboats. It seemed a routine transaction, except for the fact that Chevron and Shell paid for the rentals to MER Engineering. The bank account at Barclays, also held in MER's name, was controlled by Ibori.[2] Chevron and Shell have argued that it is not suspicious that they paid MER millions while Ibori was governor, and Ibori has claimed that the deposits were legitimate business income, because, in fact, he had resigned from the company. Court proceedings in the United States, the United Kingdom, and Nigeria have told a different story. At the heart of what became the most consequential corruption trial in British history is the question of whether or not Chevron and Shell Oil bribed Ibori, Nigeria's most ruthless political figure. "He's in the class of the Pablo Escobars," said Nuhu Ribadu, a former Nigerian police official who investigated Ibori.[3]

After MER's houseboat revenue was deposited into Ibori's account, his lawyers laundered it through secret bank accounts and ultimately dispersed it into other assets, including a luxury car, real estate in the United Kingdom, a down payment on a private jet, and the Texas mansion. If the money from Chevron and Shell was legitimate business revenue, why did Ibori go to such lengths to hide and launder it—for his own personal use? "I believe the contracts with Chevron were corrupt," a Scotland Yard detective would tell a packed courtroom in London in 2013.

Though Chevron and Shell have never been charged with any wrongdoing, an account of Ibori's dealings with the companies and what he did with their money illustrates how corrupt officials go about receiving, moving, and hiding their bribes. In high-level bribery, the kind involving millions of dollars, the recipients typically do not want hard cash, and certainly not delivered to their home country. "People like James Ibori want access to the international financial system to be bribed, to cream off the top, and to launder that money. They want a safety net, a financial safety deposit box," Robert Palmer, a money-laundering expert at the London-based anticorruption organization Tax Justice UK explained.[4]

To fully enjoy the proceeds of bribery, foreign officials need shell companies through which they can mask their true ownership; bank accounts held in the name of those shell companies at respectable banks like Barclays; real estate titled in the name of the shell companies in first-tier cities like New York or Washington; and a team of lawyers and financial consultants to incorporate and manage the shell companies and execute the necessary transactions. Taken together, these elements constitute a kind of encryption technology, masking both the bribe and its recipient. Nearly every corporate bribery scheme investigated by international law enforcement in the last ten years—and even dating back to Lockheed's bribes in 1976—has used these methods.

Ibori's particular story illuminates how the extraordinary corruption of one man was possible only because of a chain of institutional failures—a chain linking together two of the world's largest oil companies, many of the world's largest banks, the system of offshore shell companies, the legal and financial services professions, and the luxury real estate market in the United States and the United Kingdom.

*    *    *

Escravos is an ancient settlement on the Gulf of Guinea, in the western part of the Delta. As early as the sixteenth century it was a major source of slaves for Portuguese traders. Portuguese sources refer to the region as *rios dos escravos,* or slave rivers. The name endured. In 1998, Chevron commissioned a billion-dollar facility amid this swampy desolation, to be manned by a workforce of seven hundred Nigerians. By early 1999, when Ibori took office, Chevron was producing 420,000 barrels of Delta crude a day, making it one of the most lucrative oil facilities in the world.

But then the violence struck.

The Ijaw, the Itsekiri, and the Urhobo, the ethnic clans that comprise the Delta community, have long vied for power and territory. Oil, first discovered in 1956, further deepened the ethnic fault lines.[5] The clans watched as $300 billion in crude was pumped from their land, swelling the coffers of the oil majors and the power elite in Abuja, while their own villages remained in poverty, most with no electricity or running water. Each clan wanted a share of the oil wealth, to build roads and schools. Each blamed the others when this failed to happen. By 1999, ethnic differences set Ijaw against Itsekiri, and Itsekiri against Urhobo, in a full-scale war.

By 2000, Chevron's Escravos terminal became a focal point of the bloodshed. For years, ethnic militias battled one another in the creeks, until they began attacking Chevron's facility itself, kidnapping workers and killing American consultants. "We have informed Chevron and Shell, we have informed everybody—withdraw your workers from all installations," an Ijaw militant leader warned.[6] By March 2003, Chevron and Shell had essentially complied, abandoning dozens of oil wells. Escravos would stand idle for the following year, costing Chevron $1 billion in lost revenue. The impact reverberated far beyond the Delta. Nigeria was then the sixth-largest producer of oil in the world, exporting two million barrels a day. Global oil supplies were already tight because of unrest in Venezuela and Iraq at the time. When the Delta's oil production plummeted by more than 30 percent, the price of oil spiked internationally, causing panic in markets around the world.

It was Ibori who finally brokered a fragile peace among the clans, exhorting the militants, chastising the ethnic chiefs, and sympathizing with the ravaged communities, all while traveling in a luxury yacht, his security detail armed with RPGs and assault rifles. When he visited one of Chevron's damaged facilities at Abiteye, he choked back tears as reporters looked on. "These flow stations were built to advance the socio-economic development of the nation," Ibori said. "So, the action of these undesirable elements is a monumental waste."[7]

It has never been clear precisely what Ibori promised to whom behind closed doors, but his diplomacy worked. During the tense negotiations, he had proven adept at telling all sides what they wanted to hear. He met privately with Chevron executives and publicly lamented that their property had been vandalized. But he also agreed with locals that they were not being treated fairly by the oil companies. "I deeply sympathize with them. I am from this community, so I feel what they feel," Ibori told reporters.[8] "Unless we take this oil money to build schools so that our children can go to school, put it in industries, you cannot really go very far. . . . God forbids that we put it in anybody's pocket," he told his constituents.[9] What he did not tell them was that he had secretly gone into business with Chevron and Shell, making a handsome profit from the companies just when they needed him the most.

The clans agreed to maintain the peace, and Chevron and Shell returned to the Delta. In February 2004, it was Ibori himself, not officials from Chevron, who led a delegation of community leaders and reporters to the Abiteye oil field, signaling Chevron's return. Thanks to Ibori, the Escravos plant is today the crown jewel in Chevron's Nigerian ventures.

On January 28, 2008, the U.S. ambassador to Nigeria, John Campbell, took a tour of Chevron's Escravos plant, accompanied by Donna Blair, his consul general. They were hosted by Fred Nelson, then Chevron's managing director in Nigeria.[10] The embassy delegation noticed dozens of houseboats sitting along the edge of the Escravos river, as Donna Blair recounted in a State Department cable leaked by Wikileaks. Houseboats are a common feature throughout the Niger delta, but these quarters were unusual.

Chevron's executives volunteered that the company was leasing several of its houseboats from a concern owned by Ibori. Blair noted in her cable that Ibori was then under indictment for one hundred counts of corruption by Nigerian authorities, adding, "The executives said that Chevron had been unaware that the leasing company belonged to Ibori at the time the boats were leased. The executives were concerned about this connection and said Chevron was investigating its options with regard to these leases."

A few weeks later, Fred Nelson attended a luncheon hosted by Nigerian newspaper editors in Abuja. Questions were then circulating about whether Chevron had, in fact, had contracts with MER, and whether those documents were legal—the implication being that the houseboat contracts were merely a pretext through which Chevron and Shell had bribed Ibori. "We had a contract with MER on houseboats," Nelson explained, according to newspaper accounts at the time. But then he added, "I've heard that the company belongs to the former governor. However, there is nothing in the contract that is abnormal. We see nothing untoward."[11]

At the same time that Chevron's and Shell's wells started flowing again in 2004, the companies began depositing more than $3 million into MER's bank account at Barclays in London. Chevron's payments came directly from the company's bankers in San Ramon, California, where the company is headquartered, according to a former Scotland Yard detective, speaking on condition of anonymity. It was then that a lawyer in London began moving the funds around the world, so that they would end up in the pocket of James Ibori.

* * *

Arlingtons Sharmas Solicitors, a two-person law firm in London, specializes in commercial law and property transactions. Its offices are housed in a four-story brick building on Arlington Street in the St. James area of Central London. One of the firm's partners, Vijay Kumar Sharma, is considered a pillar of the legal community. He has sat on the boards of various international nonprofit organizations, including the Salzburg Global Seminar, an Austrian-based think tank. In 2004, Sharma was one of several distinguished speakers at a Salzburg symposium on the new European constitution; the other participants included U.S. Supreme Court Justice Anthony Kennedy and Václav Klaus, then president of the Czech Republic. Sharma's wife, Baroness Usha Prashar, has been a member of the House of Lords since 1999.

Arlingtons Sharmas's other partner was Bhadresh Gohil, who headed the firm's commercial department and was also its anti-money laundering officer. Gohil, who joined the firm in the early 1990s, is now in his fifties, tall and broad-shouldered, with the posh accent and self-possession one would expect of a former Mayfair solicitor. He was convicted at trial in 2011 for being the central money launderer in one of the largest corruption scandals in UK history, and served three years in prison for the crime, but he continues to deny all the allegations. "I know in my conscience that I've done nothing," he said.[12] He asserted that he never laundered any of Ibori's money, and never tried to hide Ibori's ownership of any assets, but merely used special-purpose vehicles to organize those assets.

According to the UK police, Gohil lived a double life. Although he was the firm's anti-money laundering officer, he began to specialize in hiding illegal funds. Staying out of the limelight himself, he took on high-profile clients whose spectacular political power, wealth, and corruption would prove to be his undoing. He had a secret compartment behind the fireplace in his office, where he hid two hard drives containing evidence of his crimes. "[He was] holding out as a man of integrity," a judge in Southwark Crown Court would later describe him.[13]

Since as early as 1996, when he was in his early thirties, Gohil had begun incorporating an extraordinary number of offshore shell companies in countries like Mauritius, Lebanon, Switzerland, and the Seychelles. Such concerns can have legitimate business functions—they are often used as holding companies when two companies merge—but their primary purpose is providing anonymity to their owners. "The veils of secrecy created by shell corporations are used as successfully by organized crime figures as they are by politically corrupt kleptocrats," an FBI agent who works on anti-money laundering cases observed.[14]

If an individual wants to buy property, for example, but doesn't want the property titled in his name—an option often used by celebrities—he can incorporate a shell company (or hire a lawyer to do it), and then title the property in the name of the shell. In the United Kingdom, as in the United States, it is surprisingly easy to incorporate such a business. The whole process takes only a few minutes, and can be done entirely online for just a few hundred dollars, and little supporting documentation is required other than a driver's license or government-issued ID.

Although a single shell company has limited functionality, it can become part of a constellation of shells, arranged in such a way that Shell A owns Shell B, and Shell B owns Shell C, which in turn owns 50 percent of Shell A, and so on—until the true ownership of an entity is hidden in a cascade of paperwork scattered around the globe. It requires forensic mastery to uncover what anti-money laundering experts call layering—the process of distancing an owner, through layers upon layers of fictitious entities, from what he actually owns. Layering places obstacles in the way of law enforcement, allowing criminals time to hide their crimes and escape. "For every one dollar or minute a person spends on layering, they know the government is going to have to spend ten times that amount of time and money to try to trace it," Ryan Rohlfsen, a former Justice Department prosecutor explained.[15] A group of layered shells becomes more powerful still when each shell is connected to a series of bank accounts. The bank accounts do not have to be in the same country in which the business is incorporated. In fact, it is often advantageous if they are not, as it adds another level of layering.

By the spring of 2005, Gohil was at the height of his career. "I was very successful. I was high profile. I believe I was a very good lawyer," Gohil recalled. His name was eventually passed on to a prospective new client: James Ibori.[16] Gohil did not know it at the time, but Scotland Yard's Proceeds of Corruption unit had just opened an investigation into Ibori.[17] Gohil flew down to Abuja to perform his KYC—"Know your customer," a financial industry term that refers to due diligence—to certify that his potential client was legitimate and not involved in anything untoward. Ibori wined and dined Gohil for several hours at his palatial home. "It was quite exciting to have a state governor as a client. There was wealth and opulence. This was a man you could see was powerful," Gohil recalled.

Gohil asserts that he detected no "warning shots" that indicated he should be wary of Ibori. "[Ibori] never asked me to launder money," he insists. "He was very transparent. His first thing was, 'I live in Nigeria, but my children go to school in the United Kingdom. Can you handle my payments for me?' The funds came from British banks, from Barclays. It wasn't, 'Bhadresh, here's cash and go hide it for me.'"

According to British police, however, that is precisely what Gohil did. Around April 2005, Gohil began moving millions of dollars from MER's bank account in London into a Swiss account controlled by Stanhope Investments, a company registered in the Seychelles. He recorded the details of the transaction on his external hard drive and then returned it to its secret compartment. (Gohil explained that he hid the hard drive because his office had twice been broken into, and he worried that privileged client information would be lost if his computer were stolen.) In London's West End, Ibori soon visited a Mercedes-Benz dealership. With money wired from Stanhope's Swiss account, he purchased for $422,000 an armor-plated Maybach 62, a limousine-style, custom-built, mostly handmade vehicle favored by celebrities. He shipped the Maybach to Johannesburg, South Africa, where he owned a house worth more than $5 million.[18]

*  *  *

In the world of international corporate bribery, sometimes a document like a houseboat contract is not what it seems. "You have to look at something which, on its face, perhaps in isolation, is innocuous. But in the context of what's going on, it's problematic and it raises a red flag," explains Andrew Warren, who retired from the Justice Department's FCPA Unit in 2015, regarding the challenge of investigating bribery deals.[19] He added that in bribery cases, investigators have to keep scrutinizing, peeling back layer after layer of a deal to arrive at the truth: "Was this coincidence or was this intentional? Or was this structured just to conceal the payment of bribes?"

Chevron's and Shell's contracts with MER Engineering raise precisely those questions: Why did the two companies hire Ibori's houseboats, out of all those available in the Delta, and begin paying MER millions of dollars at the very moment a gas crisis was threatening the Delta, global oil supplies, and the oil companies' revenue? Was this part of a bribe that Ibori extorted by refusing to negotiate a peace settlement among the local clans unless the companies paid him off? In Nigeria's oil and gas sector, such bribes are a common practice, according to people who have pleaded guilty to them. They are often paid to ensure that a project continues to run smoothly, as a former executive of Kellogg Brown & Root, the American engineering company, told a judge in Texas when he was sentenced to prison: "It's considered necessary . . . in Nigeria, not so much to win the project, as to make sure that the project goes ahead. Without certain arrangements in place, various personalities in Nigeria would just impede the project, as they have done it before."[20]

Or did Chevron and Shell take the initiative and offer Ibori millions to buy his continued support and ensure he promoted their best interests in an unstable environment? "In the oil and gas industry, you're not paying bribes—you're paying thank yous," Paul Novak, an American businessman who spent a year in U.S. federal prison after pleading guilty to paying bribes in Nigeria, said. He explained that foreign companies generating millions in revenue are expected, by the Nigerian officials in power, to display their gratitude through graft. "There's a feeling that God blessed you. You're going to make money. You should be grateful. You should spread the wealth."[21]

Since 1977, the Foreign Corrupt Practices Act has mandated that companies like Chevron maintain a system of internal controls that mitigates the risk of paying bribes to a government official. The cornerstone of this process is performing due diligence on third parties—such as a houseboat company—before entering into a contract with them, to ensure that they have no questionable links to a government official. Such ties are common in bribery schemes, and have been unearthed in several FCPA cases adjudicated by the Justice Department. Between 2004 and 2008, Weatherford International, a large oil services company, went into business with a local contractor in Angola. What appeared to be a legitimate business arrangement was in fact secretly controlled by an Angolan government official and his relatives. The sole purpose of the contract was to enable a Weatherford subsidiary to pass hundreds of thousands of dollars in bribes to the official.[22]

According to the U.S. State Department cable leaked by Wikileaks, Chevron executives stated they were unaware the company from which they rented houseboats had been owned by Ibori. Either the company failed to perform even rudimentary due diligence on MER, or it chose to ignore the very obvious signs linking the houseboats back to the Nigerian leader. Bracon Limited, the company that built MER's houseboats for Chevron and Shell, features photos on its website that indicate that the boats in question were called the *Lady Teresa*, the name of Ibori's wife, and the *Lady Comfort*, the name of Ibori's mother.[23]

Even if this connection was not obvious enough, a simple check of MER's ownership structure would have revealed Ibori's long-standing link to the company. Nigeria's Corporate Affairs Commission maintains the corporate filing of companies registered in Nigeria, and though their archives are not open to the public, lawyers can access information from the files. MER's records reveal that Ibori incorporated MER on April 6, 1992, and held 9,999 of 10,000 shares. (The one remaining share was held by his lawyer, Chiedu Ebie, who conducted the purchase of the Houston mansion.) The MER documents state that Ibori resigned as director of the company and relinquished his shares on May 21,

1999, shortly before he became governor. But they also indicate that Ibori continued to have a connection to the company. In 2002, MER's shares were reallocated: Ebie was given 9,999, and a woman named Adebimpe Pogoson was given one.[24] It was well known in Nigeria that Pogoson was Ibori's personal assistant. According to a Nigerian newspaper report, Ibori hired her in 1997 when, prior to his career in politics, he was the editor of the Nigerian newspaper the *Diet*. According to British and U.S. law enforcement, Pogoson was the sole signatory to MER's bank account at Barclays. Given the millions of dollars that Chevron and Shell were wiring to her in London, it stands to reason that they should have performed some due diligence to learn who she was.

"Paying third parties is the number-one area where companies get in trouble," James Koukios, who until 2014 was the assistant chief of the Justice Department's FCPA Unit, observed. He added that it might not have been a sufficient defense for a company to claim that it was unaware of a foreign concern's actual ownership. "There are scenarios where it might be. The FCPA says if you're aware of a high probability that the money's going to go to a foreign official, that's enough. So you can't just close your eyes to it. But at the same time, if you were really duped, if really you were lied to, it could potentially be a defense."[25]

Ibori himself has never denied that he owned MER Engineering and has repeatedly confirmed that MER received payments from Chevron and Shell. But he claims that the payments from the oil companies were entirely legitimate, because he had resigned from the company when he became governor in 1999. That claim, however, has turned out to be false. In 2012, the U.S. Justice Department, acting on an official request from the UK's Crown Prosecution Service, filed a restraining order against all of Ibori's assets in the United States, including his mansion in Houston and two apartments worth $4 million at the Ritz-Carlton in Washington, D.C. The U.S. documents reveal that Ibori "continued to manage actively MER's operations while serving as Delta's governor." As evidence, they stated that "Governor Ibori admitted (i) in 2002 to RBC Trustees (Guernsey), Ltd. to have business interests in various companies, including MER; (ii) in 2004 to Privatbank that he was a major shareholder in MER." Most important, Ibori also certified "in February 2004 to Barclays Bank that he owned several companies, including MER."[26]

Gary Walters, a former Scotland Yard detective who headed the UK's investigation into Ibori, also came to believe that the contracts with Chevron and Shell were corrupt. "The explanation was that these boats were supposed to be housing for workers and/or security personnel to provide a secure place because kidnappings were going on—that Chevron and Shell would use them, but they hadn't," Walters, who is now retired in London, said. "All the companies like Chevron and Shell have their own security," he added, explaining that the companies would have no need for a houseboat when they already had elaborate security measures in place. Walters said that an investigation was never opened into Chevron and Shell because the police were too focused on Ibori and not sufficiently on the alleged bribes of the oil companies, because at that point in time corporate bribery was not as much of a priority for the British police as it is now.[27]

Both Walters's team and Nigerian investigators tried to learn more about the MER contracts but, they allege, were thwarted on several occasions. A Nigerian investigator in Abuja claimed that Ibori used his influence to have several investigators with the Economic and Financial Crimes Commission (EFCC), a police agency, including himself, sacked and harassed. Other EFCC investigators working on the MER bribes were arrested, he said, and evidence related to MER's contracts with Chevron went missing.[28] (In emails at the time, Ibori, Gohil, and other associates discussed that although the Ibori investigation "cannot be neutralised in the UK", it could be neutralized from Nigeria.)[29] When a team of Scotland Yard detectives was scheduled to visit Escravos along with the EFCC to examine the houseboats, Nigeria's attorney general at the time served an injunction against the EFCC, preventing them from making inquiries in the Delta, a former Scotland Yard detective said on condition of anonymity, adding: "A few weeks later there was a fire within Delta State Government House in which a large amount of documents requested by the EFCC were destroyed."[30]

*   *   *

Court 9 at Southwark Crown Court in London was tightly packed on the morning of April 16, 2012, when James Ibori, then fifty-three years old, stood in the dock at the back, behind a glass partition. He wore a gray suit and blue tie, and waved to his supporters, who had been congregating outside the courthouse since 7:00 A.M. Many had flown from Nigeria to cheer him on. By 11:00 the crowds had become so large that police formed a cordon around the courthouse and called in a helicopter to provide surveillance from the air.

"From the moment Ibori was elected he set about enriching himself at the expense of some of the poorest people in the world," Sasha Wass, the lead prosecutor in the UK's corruption case against Ibori, told the courtroom after the trial began. "His

greed increased exponentially during the course of his governorship, as did his arrogance."[31]

Bringing Ibori to justice had not been easy. Twice the former
governor had slipped through the fingers of the Nigerian police
before fleeing to Dubai. In April 2010, just days after settling into a
five-star hotel, he was arrested by local police acting on an official
request from the British government. Scotland Yard had decided to
take matters into its own hands, claiming jurisdiction because Ibori
had laundered his kickbacks and embezzled money through UK
banks and UK-registered shell companies, using a London-based
solicitor. Ibori spent a year in jail in Dubai and was finally flown to
London in April 2011.

The Crown's investigation produced sixty-five thousand pages
of evidence. Wass and her team brought twenty-three charges
against Ibori, claiming he defrauded the Delta State out of as much
as $250 million. He was charged with keeping $79 million for himself and helping various business associates and accomplices pilfer
the rest. In one deal alone, the Crown alleged that Ibori rigged a
contract and kept $37 million when the Delta State sold its shares
of Vmobile, a Nigerian company. Though he had been prepared to
fight the charges at trial, Ibori changed his mind on the opening day
and instead entered ten guilty pleas to conspiracy to defraud and
money laundering, but only for his personal share of $79 million.
He pled not guilty to the remaining charges.

After his plea, it remained for the Crown Prosecution Service
to confiscate Ibori's stolen assets, but hearings would first have
to determine how much he had actually stolen. Throughout the
proceedings, Sasha Wass had placed MER Engineering, along
with its controversial relationship with Chevron and Shell, firmly
at the center of Ibori's global web of corruption. As Wass's sen-

tencing statement read: "It was Ibori who was able to influence the contracts with Chevron and Shell and the [Nigerian National Petroleum Corporation], the state-owned oil company. . . . The contracts between MER and various oil companies operating in the Delta State were corrupt."[32]

Corporate bribery was certainly not the only way that Ibori became wealthy, but it was a vital stream in his enriching himself. If Chevron and Shell did bribe him, those funds played an integral role in the rise of one of Africa's power brokers and his reign of violence and misrule. "That's the message we're trying to convey," a Justice Department official said, explaining the hypothetical concern of cases like this, "a big oil company goes to a small African nation and pays the president of the country and meets in cloak-and-dagger fashion, paying bribes to the president through the president's henchmen—who are also on the side leading efforts to murder the president's detractors."[33]

The question that was never fully addressed during legal proceedings against Ibori was whether Chevron and Shell's payments to MER were legitimate, and if so, why the money paid into MER's bank account was laundered and used for Ibori's personal benefit. Because neither the British Crown nor American authorities ever charged Chevron or Shell with any wrongdoing for their purported dealings with MER, they were under no legal obligation to cooperate with the British police. In fact, when approached by British authorities, both companies refused to provide witness statements or any other documents certifying that their contracts with MER were legitimate. As Gary Walters observed, "If you've got a witness that's reluctant—in other words Chevron and Shell—you can't make them tell you things."

The continuation of Ibori's confiscation hearings might have brought more details about MER's contracts with Shell and Chevron to light, but because of an unexpected new twist of bribery, this one ironically implicating the British police, the hearings would never resume.

\* \* \*

The Iboris of the world do not, and cannot, act alone. Though Gohil knew how to set up the necessary money-laundering structures, even he did not act on his own. For high-level officials there is usually an army of professionals in the first world—solicitors, bankers, financiers—that facilitates the crime and gains extraordinary wealth of its own from it. They are essential not only for their skills, but because their professional status opens doors at financial institutions.

Elias Preko, for example, certainly had the proper credentials. A Harvard graduate who once made $12 million a year as a Goldman Sachs banker, he then went into private practice, where he advised Ibori's wife and mistress how to set up anonymous trusts and how to bypass due diligence requirements in Guernsey, so that Ibori would not be identified as their actual owner. Preko used his reputation to allay concerns raised by officials at the Royal Bank of Canada about the trusts.[34] Ibori laundered $5 million from inflated state contracts through these trusts, the Crown alleged. In December 2013, Preko was convicted by a jury at Southwark Court and sentenced to four and a half years in prison.[35]

The secrecy afforded by complex legal structures such as Ibori's—particularly the use of shell companies—is perhaps the single greatest legal loophole that allows corporate bribery to thrive, and the single greatest impediment to international law enforcement's effort to detect and prosecute this crime. The regulation of these structures, therefore, is one of the greatest challenges in controlling bribery, as it involves balancing transparency with an individual's right to privacy, and discerning between legally sanctioned anonymity and organized crime.

Both the United States and the United Kingdom are struggling to impose stricter regulation on the incorporation of shell companies. It is a multibillion-dollar business globally but increasingly common domestically in states like Delaware, Nevada, Oregon, Wyoming, and South Dakota. In the United States, anonymous business incorporation is perfectly legal, and there is no federal legislation that regulates such companies. States like Delaware and Oregon have therefore provided in their own laws for extremely limited public disclosure of company ownership. "There's not just some computer database where we can punch in and just go boom, James Ibori owns this company," one Justice Department official explained.[36]

The businesses are never required to file public records or keep any records at all. To ensure greater secrecy, the actual directors of the company can even nominate proxies to serve as a director or shareholder in their place, such as a relative or associate. The nominee's name, and not the true owner's, will then appear on any documents that might ever be found. To add even greater secrecy, a global law firm such as Mossack Fonseca can be hired to do the work of appointing nominees. Mossack Fonseca, which was founded in Panama and has offices in thirty-five countries, specializes in creating complex legal structures: It might create shell company A, and then either appoints itself as the nominee director of company A, or appoints another shell, company B, as the nominee director—or both.

Stanhope Investments was one such shell company used by Ibori. It was Stanhope's bank account in Geneva that, after receiving funds from MER, become a conduit through which he bought his Maybach, and through which he made a down payment on his private jet. Scotland Yard was aware of Stanhope from Gohil, but there was no publicly available documentation proving Ibori's link to the shell—at least not until the nonprofit news organization International Consortium of Investigative Journalists (ICIJ) published the Panama Papers in March 2016, the largest leak of offshore company records in history. A hacker stole the 11.5 million internal records—emails, photos of passports, correspondence—from Mossack Fonseca's computer servers and leaked them to ICIJ, which then published them as a public searchable database online. This material provides documentation and information about the true ownership of 214,000 shell companies around the world.

Through the leaked documents, ICIJ was able to establish a link between Stanhope and a foundation called Julex, which was incorporated in Panama in 2003. On paper, Mossack Fonseca is the agent of Julex, essentially its only owner. But internal Mossack Fonseca records reveal that Ibori and his family members are the foundation's true beneficiaries. Julex, in turn, is the only shareholder of Stanhope Investments, meaning Ibori, through Julex, controls Stanhope. The paper trail tying Ibori to Stanhope is a rare instance of such a clear connection.[37]

Almost every high-level bribery scheme investigated by U.S. authorities in the last decade has involved the use of shell companies. In one particularly elaborate case, consultants hired by the Russian subsidiary of Hewlett-Packard used a vast network of shell companies—registered in the United States, the United Kingdom, and the British Virgin Islands—to route millions in bribes to high-level Russian officials. Many of these shell companies were in turn owned by other shell companies, making their true owners nearly impossible to identify. The recipients of the bribes then laundered the money through yet another cascade of shell companies in places like Latvia, Bosnia, and Lithuania, creating in effect a "a global labyrinth," as the Justice Department described it. Hewlett-Packard's Russian subsidiary pleaded guilty to the charges and paid a fine of $108 million in 2014.[38]

"There's definitely a point where you do hit a brick wall oftentimes in these matters," according to Ryan Rohlfsen, who spent years investigating such cases, including the Hewlett-Packard case. "The spiraling black hole of shell companies would go so deep that you have to call the ball and just quit. You're throwing good money and resources after it, and at some point it's a diminishing return."

In the wake of the Panama Papers a global effort is now under way to challenge the protection provided by this legal and financial architecture. In the United States, several pieces of proposed legislation have taken aim at shell companies. In 2016, Representatives Peter King and Carolyn Maloney of New York, along with Senator Sheldon Whitehouse of Rhode Island, introduced a bill calling for all shell companies registered in the United States to disclose their "beneficial owners," meaning those who ultimately benefit from that ownership. In his 2015 budget, President Barack Obama likewise proposed that all companies, not just shells, be required to report their beneficial owners to the IRS as part of their tax filings.

These reforms face stiff resistance from both the business incorporation industry and the states and jurisdictions that permit ownership secrecy. An extraordinary amount of money is on the line. The British Virgin Islands, which offers ironclad secrecy for the six hundred thousand companies registered there,[39] generates

almost $200 million a year in revenue from company incorpo-
ration. Nevada, where state authorities have pushed to expand
secrecy for corporations, generated $138 million from incorpora-
tion fees, according to *USA Today*.[40]

The United Kingdom, which has similarly easy and extremely
private company registration, has also become a haven for secrecy.
As Ibori's case and others have shown, abuse of its system has been
rampant. In 2015, during a speech in Singapore, David Cameron,
then the British prime minister, singled out the Ibori affair as an
example of why the United Kingdom needed to do more to address
the problem: "I'm determined that the UK must not become a safe
haven for corrupt money from around the world. We need to stop
corrupt officials or organized criminals using anonymous shell
companies to invest their ill-gotten gains in London property, without being tracked down. People like convicted Nigerian fraudster
James Ibori, who owned property in St John's Wood, Hampstead,
Regent's Park, Dorset all paid for with money stolen from some of
the world's poorest people."[41] In July 2016, a new law went into
effect whereby companies registered in the United Kingdom are
now required to publicly identify in their filings the "persons with
significant control"—essentially the beneficial owner.

But despite the efforts of lawmakers, other loopholes remain.
"If you are going to, say, launder money and you want to do so
in the shadows, and you want to do it without someone watch-
ing, maybe real estate would be something that you might want to
consider," a Justice Department official explained. "You can buy a
nice house in Beverly Hills, and there's no agency or department
necessarily whose sole job is to sit there and watch for suspicious
real estate transactions."

After the terrorist attacks of September 11, the USA Patriot

Act was adopted, and one of its provisions required real estate and escrow agents to implement anti-money laundering programs. But six months later, after lobbying from the real estate industry, the Treasury Department exempted them from the requirement. Today, real estate and escrow agents are not required to know the identity of their customers or the source of the funds those customers use to make purchases. Shell companies, meanwhile, are increasingly used to buy property in the United States. According to a study by the *Washington Post*, anonymous companies acquired $61.2 billion in U.S. real estate in the last quarter of 2015—which amounted to 58 percent of all transactions of $3 million or more.[42] An associate of Ibori's, Victor Uduaghan, incorporated the shell company Flatwillow LLC, to hide Ibori's ownership of the two apartmentsin the Ritz-Carlton.

"I'm always amazed at how many foreign corrupt politicians own property in either California or the DC metropolitan area," an FBI money-laundering expert observed, but this situation is only beginning to change. In 2016, the Financial Crimes Enforcement Network (FinCEN), part of the Treasury Department, issued a new order targeting real estate purchases in Manhattan and Miami-Dade. The order, which is temporary for now, requires title companies to identify the beneficial owner of shell companies used to make all-cash purchases of more than $1 million in Miami and more than $3 million in Manhattan.

Regulations in the United Kingdom require that estate agents perform due diligence on only the seller of a property, not the purchaser.[43] The law assumes that the purchaser's solicitor will have done this checking, but in cases like Ibori's, the solicitor is actually involved in the crimes. Just as in the United States, it is a simple matter for anonymous shell companies, even ones registered halfway around the world, to acquire property in the United Kingdom. A study by the *Guardian* recently revealed that offshore shell companies own ninety thousand properties there. (Twenty-two thousand of those companies are registered in the British Virgin Islands alone.)[44]

\* \* \*

Shell companies and a lax real estate market were critical to the opulence that Ibori enjoyed at the expense of the poor people he fleeced. But nothing was as essential to Ibori's corruption, or as alarming, as the breaches in the banking system.

As the Justice Department detailed in its seizure of his U.S. assets, Ibori had certified to Barclays that he was in the fact the owner of MER's bank account. That disclosure itself was a tacit admission of illegal activity, as Nigeria's constitution prohibits governors from controlling foreign bank accounts, possessing undeclared assets outside of Nigeria, and maintaining ownership of a private company. When Ibori identified himself as the owner of the MER account, the bank's compliance officials should have raised a red flag. Ibori was officially a "politically exposed person" (PEP)—a designation used in financial regulation for a foreign government official, or for a person in a prominent political office. Banks in the United Kingdom are required by law to use a high level of caution and ongoing screening when potentially doing business with politically exposed persons, because accepting their money carries a high risk of money laundering.

Following years of media coverage, Ibori was by then already internationally known as the governor of a region engulfed in violence—violence deeply intertwined with the oil extraction industry.

An internet search would have revealed his political status and the controversy surrounding him, in a country well known for high levels of corruption. Barclays appears not to have put the accounts under enhanced scrutiny, as required by law, and MER's Barclays account continued to receive deposits for three more years.

The revelations at Southwark Crown Court that Ibori used the City of London as a laundering operation were all the more embarrassing—for the banks, for the regulators, and for the city in general—because corrupt Nigerian officials had done so before. Sani Abacha, the former president of Nigeria, is said to have stolen $4 billion while in office between 1993 and 1998. Nigerian investigators believe that more than one quarter of that sum was derived from corporate bribes, including $166 million in payments from Siemens, from the German arms company Ferrostaal, and from the French construction company Dumez.[45] In the early 2000s, British regulators learned that Abacha had laundered a total of $1.3 billion, including portions of his bribes, through forty-two bank accounts in London between 1996 and 2000, with $170 million going through Barclays.[46] Like Ibori, Abacha used a network of shell companies and professional financiers. Following the revelations, Barclays and other banks vowed to tighten their money-laundering controls.

Yet, as a 2010 report by Global Witness highlighted, Barclays, along with HSBC, NatWest, UBS, and RBS, continued to take millions in suspect deposits, from among others Diepreye Alamieyeseigha, the governor of Nigeria's Bayelsa State, and Joshua Dariye of Plateau State. Between 1999 and 2004, Dariye deposited nearly seven hundred thousand dollars in cash into his Barclays account, and the bank appears not to have monitored it. (Alamieyeseigha was later convicted of thirty-three counts of money laundering by a Nigerian court, while Dariye was arrested by British police on embezzlement charges but fled back to Nigeria after skipping bail.)[47] Neither Barclays nor any other UK bank has ever been censured, fined, or otherwise held to account for what appear to be breaches of UK banking regulations in the money-laundering operations of Abacha, Alamieyeseigh, Dariye, or Ibori.

The laxity that enabled this corruption to thrive still continues at British banks, critics and regulators allege. In 2015, British banking regulators probed how Barclays was willing to bypass due diligence requirements for high-level clients in a $2.8 billion deal, the largest transaction the bank had ever undertaken for individuals. While bank regulators said they found no evidence of financial crimes, they reported that Barclays went "to unacceptable lengths" to avoid asking the PEPs further questions as required by law: "Barclays thereby threatened confidence in the UK financial system and failed to mitigate the risk to society of financial crime."[48] When asked what has changed to prevent another foreign official like Ibori from laundering money through London again, Gary Walters replied, "Nothing."

Like their British counterparts, American banks are supposed to "know their customers." But American banks have a similarly long history of lax oversight, with an untold number of foreign officials laundering their bribes through them. Recent U.S. bribery investigations, however, suggest that domestic banks have become more proactive in monitoring accounts owned by foreign government officials when those accounts appear to be used for suspicious transactions. In 2010, two U.S. banks (which the Justice Department did not publicly name) took notice of accounts owned by Mahmoud Thiam, then the minister of mines in Guinea, after they began receiving million-dollar transfers from other accounts Thiam owned in Hong Kong. The banks both proactively shut down Thiam's accounts long before the Justice Department opened an investigation alleging the money was, in fact, a bribe that Thiam was trying to launder.[49]

In this case, however, the accounts were held in Thiam's own name. He could have exploited a major loophole in the U.S. banking system by using a shell company, and the banks would probably never have flagged the transactions. To this day, American banks are not required to have information about the owners of accounts registered in the name of a shell company—a significant deficiency in "know your customer" compliance regulations. It was only in 2016 that FinCEN put forward new financial regulations to attempt to close this loophole by requiring banks to proactively identity the beneficial owner of any company with which they do business. According to FinCEN's guidelines, a beneficial owner would be anyone with a 25 percent or higher ownership stake in a company. Even this new rule, however, would still be easy to circumvent. By keeping their ownership stake below 25 percent, at least on paper, a determined kleptocrat or his associates would escape a bank's notice. Moreover, under the new FinCEN rule, banks have to rely on the shell companies themselves to identify the beneficial owner.

\* \* \*

As he sat in his jail cell at Wandsworth prison, Bhadresh Gohil devised a plan to appeal his conviction. He began anonymously sending documents to the Metropolitan Police, public officials, and journalists. The documents, which Gohil said he had received anonymously while incarcerated, purported to expose a troubling twist in Ibori's case: Scotland Yard officers who had been investigating the matter had, in turn, taken bribes from a private detective agency in London—a firm, in fact, hired by Ibori. That agency, RISC Management, paid the bribes to get inside information that might help Ibori's defense.

The Crown Prosecution Service vehemently denied these allegations, and Scotland Yard, which spent months investigating the claims, also found no support for them. British prosecutors in turn charged Gohil with forging the documents and with trying to pervert the course of justice. He was scheduled to go on trial again in January 2016.

But then the case took another turn. At a court hearing prior to his new trial, the Crown Prosecution Service turned over documents supporting his bribery claims—documents the Crown had insisted did not exist. According to the *Daily Mail,* the material in question consists of receipts and notes indicating that Clifford Knuckey, the director of RISC Management, had a personal meeting in 2007 with Detective Sergeant John McDonald, who was leading Scotland Yard's Ibori investigation. RISC had been employed by Speechly Bircham, a leading London law firm that Ibori had hired to prepare his defense. Internal RISC documents reveal that two days after his meeting with McDonald, Knuckey paid a "confidential source" five thousand pounds for "information provided." Another document shows that in the midst of the Ibori investigation in 2007, McDonald made a total of nineteen cash deposits to his bank account, the *Daily Mail* reported.[50] McDonald admitted meeting with Knuckey but denied any wrongdoing, and RISC and Knuckey denied the allegations. Speechly Bircham stated that it had no knowledge that RISC was making any improper payments.

In May 2016, more than a year after Ibori's confiscation hearing was postponed, the Crown Prosecution Service admitted in court that it had been aware of "intelligence" suggesting that Knuckey had met with McDonald and allegedly paid him off. The intelligence, the Crown argued, was unfounded given that it came from RISC documents, and a subsequent investigation could not substantiate it as evidence, hence it was never disclosed.[51] McDonald was never charged. Sasha Wass, meanwhile, voluntarily removed herself from the case, and returned her briefs to the Crown Prosecution Service, according to the *Times*. [52] In April 2018, a Crown Court rejected Gohil's appeal, arguing that his lawyers failed to advance the evidence that McDonald was bribed.

As a result of these developments, it appears that the United Kingdom's most high-profile prosecution of a foreign official—an investigation that was supposed to set a new standard for justice and transparency, that has lasted more than a decade, has involved some of Scotland Yard's most experienced detectives, and has cost more than £5 million in taxpayer money—could come undone, because of the taint of corruption still hanging over the officer who led the investigation.[53] Like Gohil, Ibori too has petitioned to appeal his conviction on the grounds of police misconduct.

In February 2017, Ibori was quietly released from prison after serving half of his thirteen-year sentence. He boarded a plane and flew back to Nigeria. His release received almost no coverage from major British newspapers at the time but made major headlines in Nigeria. Its news media featured the former governor waving his fists triumphantly in the air, thronged by ecstatic crowds on his return to his hometown, Oghara, in the Niger Delta.

Now lost in the swirl of these developments are the allegations of Ibori's own corruption, particularly his relationship with Chevron and Shell. Can the oil companies be taken at their word that there was nothing untoward in their relationship with MER? Ibori's confiscation hearings might have shed more light on the matter. Wass had been scheduled to present evidence that had been prepared for Ibori's trial before he pleaded guilty, but these details may now never be revealed. Ibori has effectively managed to deflect attention from himself, and as a former Nigerian official who worked with Ibori observed, "The more dirt they throw at him, the more clean he becomes."[54]

Whatever Ibori's legacy, it has reinforced how the West's abetting of corrupt political figures feeds a cycle of impunity, of crooked patronage and power that has stymied regions like the Nigerian Delta for decades. "A few people take advantage of their positions, take everything for themselves, and leave the rest dry," Nuhu Ribadu said. "And if that happens, certainly there will be no growth, no development, no change in the lives of people."

Ordinary Deltans like Victor, a twenty-five-year-old man from Port Harcourt, in Rivers State, are among the victims of this cycle. Victor has a degree in mechanical engineering, but has been unable to find a job since he graduated several years ago. While people like him suffer, he said, an elite clique continues to enjoy all the spoils. "We are very, very angry. From the day we are born we have been hearing the same names. Ibori's daughter is in the House of Assembly. Her father was once the governor," Victor said. "It's just one thing roving around the family, you understand me? They are still ruling us. And they're telling us we are the future of tomorrow. What makes me feel I will be the future of tomorrow, when the people, since I was born, are still in power? What is the hope?"[55]

Part of that hope rests in holding to account the corporations that pay the bribes and the officials who receive them—in setting an example by challenging the forces that allow corruption to thrive.

But as Part III of this book explores in greater detail, corporate bribery's impact is often so deep and lasting and insidious—destabilizing economies and even helping to foment terrorism—that truly addressing is an elusive struggle for nations around the world.

# Part III

# Impact

# Chapter 7

## *Miza*

Dionysiou Areopagitou Street runs along the south slope of the Acropolis, in an ancient, teeming section of Athens. Whereas many of the nearby streets are winding and narrow, densely packed and crowded with tourists, Dionysiou Areopagitou itself is pleasantly wide, straight, and long. Cars are not permitted, creating the feeling of a grand pedestrian thoroughfare. It is virtually silent, paved with a mixture of small cobblestone and large marble slabs, and is shaded on both sides by olive trees. Splendid two- and three-story mansions, varying in style from Art Nouveau to neoclassical, adorn the southern side of the street, adding to its beauty and charm. The mansions have unobstructed views of the Parthenon, which, when lit up at night, is a particularly majestic sight and makes Dionysiou Areopagitou the most exclusive address in all of Athens.

Number 33 on the street is a pale-yellow building, with a delicate marble balcony perched on a neoclassical facade. On the morning of April 11, 2012, it became—and remains—one of the most infamous addresses in a country plunged into economic ruin. That morning, a contingent of police arrested the home's owner, Akis Tsochatzopoulos, then seventy-three. Photographs of the event show an elegantly dressed man being escorted from his door, chin jutting out in an expression of indignation. Tsochatzopoulos believed he had the kind of pedigree that was supposed to protect him from the law: a founder of the leading PASOK party and a former defense minister, he was one of the most recognizable politicians in Greece.

He may have been corrupt, but he'd done nothing that others in his circle had not been doing for decades, which is to say, steal. And he'd done so the proper way, smartly hiding deceit behind layers of intricately planned obfuscation. Number 33 was the crown jewel of a long career of corporate bribery and money laundering, the kind of systemic abuse that brought Greece to the brink of collapse.

As the police took Tsochatzopoulos away, thousands of Greeks gathered on streets nearby, protesting the cataclysm that had become their lives: sinking salaries and gutted pensions, soaring unemployment, bread lines and tear gas—the symptoms of austerity measures meant to avert a financial crisis, spawned in part by men like Tsochatzopoulos. For the protestors, the injustice had reached a climax a week earlier, when a seventy-seven-year-old retired pharmacist, Dimitris Christoulas, shot himself just steps from the Greek Parliament. His pension slashed, he preferred death to picking through "rubbish to feed myself," his suicide note read.[1]

Accompanying the police that morning was a thirty-six-year-old public prosecutor named Papi Papandreou. While most of the Greek public had never seen her face, she had been making news, along with her boss, the equally enigmatic Eleni Raikou, the first woman ever to be elected the top prosecutor in Athens. When Papandreou appeared at Tsochatzopoulos's door, he is said to have exploded in rage that she showed up unannounced. "Should I have informed you that I was coming to arrest you?" Papandreou snapped back before leading him away.

The single known photograph of Papandreou was taken the morning of the arrest. She appears slightly out of focus, visible from only the shoulder up, in profile. She has long blond hair and a look of focused attention, eyes trained on a target. In the insular male world of backroom deals and bribery that constituted Greek politics, Papandreou and Raikou dared to do what generations of prosecutors before them had not: They probed behind its facade, starting with a suspicious mansion at 33 Dionysiou Areopagitou Street.

* * *

The Greeks, a young journalist named Thanassis explained, have two different terms for bribery. One is *fakelaki*, which literally means "little envelopes." These are the small bribes that locals pay to civil servants to get simple things done—jumping a long queue at the social service office, for example, or obtaining a permit for home repairs.

The other word for bribery is *miza*, which is the term for the starter that gets a car engine running. *Miza* refers to the kickbacks that foreign companies pay to government officials like Tsochatzopoulos in return for huge state contracts.[2]

*Miza* has become deeply intertwined with the economic situation in Greece. Since the start of the euro crisis in 2010, as Greeks have learned that their leaders borrowed too much and saved too little, overspent and lied about it, they have also become aware of the role that *miza* has played in this abuse of power.

In 2008, before the crisis began, Greek unemployment stood at about 7.7 percent. By 2015, it had risen to 25 percent, with 1.7 million working-age people having lost their jobs.[3] Suicide rates, meanwhile, have doubled. Many feel their lives have been upended, and that there is no going back. A taxi driver's pension had been cut to six hundred euros, down from fifteen hundred. Her daughter, who speaks five languages, had gone to Dubai to work in a hotel for fifteen euros an hour. A fashion photographer in her fifties, who only years earlier had traveled around the world shooting spreads for *Vogue* and *Marie Claire*, was now lucky if she could rent out a section of her house to tourists. "I thought I would retire with a long career behind me," she said through tears, "but now I'm like a butler, cleaning bathrooms and folding towels for my guests."

Hubris has become the standard explanation for the Greek economic calamity. That part of the story is well known. When Greece joined the European Union in 2001, it immediately gained access to boundless funds in the form of cheap credit. European banks were more willing to buy Greek government bonds, because the country's economy was now backed by the euro, and no longer the drachma. Under reckless leadership, the nation started drawing more debt than it collected in taxes and certainly more than it saved. The government covered up just how much it was spending, and by 2009 its budget deficit was 15.4 percent of its GDP, the worst in the EU. (Germany's, by contrast, was 3 percent, consistent with EU rules.) Its public debt had reached $442 billion[4]—the highest in the country's history. (Germany, by contrast, had a $150 billion surplus.)

But financial imprudence was only one aspect of the financial crisis. Greeks have come to learn, through scandals unfolding in their courts, as well as in the United States and across Europe, that American medical device producers, German and French arms manufacturers, and many others companies paid huge amounts of *miza* to Greek officials and lied about their role for years. In return for *miza,* the bribed officials signed contracts for products the country couldn't afford and often didn't need. With access to cheap credit, Greece had embarked on a massive weapons expansion program and borrowed heavily to support a bloated, corrupt public health system, spending more in these two areas, relative to GDP, than any other country in Europe. To purchase billions of dollars worth of German arms and American medical devices, it borrowed from European banks, which lent the funds with few questions asked, aware that Greece hadn't the means to pay it back. (In May 2010, Greece's initial bailout of €110 billion [$146 billion] was used primarily to repay German banks, which owned €32 billion of Greek debt, and French banks, which owned €52 billion of Greek debt. The remaining €50 billion was held by other European banks.)[5]

These transactions made the companies, the banks, and Greek officials very rich, but bankrupted the ordinary Greek taxpayer. The businesses involved were some of the most prestigious brands in the world, including Johnson & Johnson, Smith & Nephew, Ericsson, Daimler, Siemens, and Ferrostaal. Although corporate bribery did not cause the worst sovereign debt crisis in modern history, *miza* was an inextricable element of how it began.

\* \* \*

Eleni Raikou and Papi Papandreou started working out of the Court of Appeal building in Athens in 2010, when the country was just beginning its decline. They were given one room in the basement, a dusty warehouse with barely enough chairs. Raikou filled the room with dozens of boxes of investigative files, usually using one of them as her chair. The staff consisted of three other prosecutors and two part-time consultants. Whenever someone wanted to leave the office, a desk had to be moved to get it out of the way. Because there were no windows, "It felt strange because we didn't know if it was night or day, or what the weather was outside," one prosecutor recalled.[6] This was the origin of the Economic Crime Squad of the Athens Public Prosecutor's Office—the brainchild of Raikou and the first of its kind.

Eleni Raikou is known to the Greek public only through her work. By reputation she is hard, unsparing, and relentless. In person, she is tall and striking at fifty-four years of age, intensely focused yet surprisingly warm. Raikou makes a point of never giving interviews to the press. She is from a poor family and an impoverished neighborhood of Athens. Her background, her colleagues suggest, accounts for why she was willing to take on the elites, who meant little to her.

Raikou had already made a name for herself by breaking barriers as a wife and mother who rose to the heights of her male-dominated profession. In 2010, she was elected the chief prosecutor in Athens—the first woman in history in that position. Her coworkers say Raikou didn't make an issue of her gender. "It could be said that everybody dealt with her as if she were a man, both her colleagues and policemen," one judicial official observed. "They usually curse before her as if she were a man."

It was then that the idea of creating a specialized corruption unit came to Raikou. Prosecutors in Athens, like everywhere, are stretched thin, simultaneously working on drug cases, terrorism investigations, and bribery. When they actually had the time to focus on large-scale corruption cases, they usually uncovered a massive drain on state resources. "We realized that through public contracts there was a large waste of money, that the amounts paid by the state were much more than they needed to be," one prosecutor recalled.

Coincidentally, a month after the Economics Crimes Squad was established, Greece signed its first memorandum of understanding for a bailout package with the European Commission, the European Central Bank, and the International Monetary Fund. The MOU, which publicly revealed for the first time the extent of Greece's debt, was a revelation to Raikou's team. "It was then that we saw the real situation in Greece with corruption. Up until that point it was not known the financial situation of Greece was in such dire straits," a prosecutor explained.

Raikou found a natural ally in Papi Papandreou, a young public prosecutor recently out of law school. Like Raikou, Papandreou is also from a poor family. She, too, decided to be a prosecutor at a young age, driven by an almost romantic notion: As one of her colleagues explained, she liked the idea that, through her work, good could prevail. Raikou became her mentor and teacher.

One morning in May 2010, Papandreou read an article in the leading *Kathimerini* newspaper that featured Tsochatzopoulos and his mansion.[7] The piece described how the mansion was valued at seven thousand euros per square meter and was located on one of the most expensive streets "in all of Europe." It also noted that Tsochatzopoulos had purchased the property through an offshore bank account.

The offshore reference caught Papandreou's eye, though at the time her team knew little about offshore banking. But Papandreou did know that Tsochatzopoulos, who served as minister of defense between 1996 and 2001, had long been trailed by allegations of corruption, which had never been proven. In 2004, Tsochatzopoulos married his second wife, Vassiliki Stamati, at a lavish wedding in Paris. They arrived at the ceremony in a brand-new Jaguar and stayed in a 2,600-square-foot suite at the Four Seasons, as press accounts reported. This led the public and the media to wonder how Tsochatzopoulos, a former government minister with a modest salary, could have afforded such luxury.

The suspicions about him eventually led to a parliamentary inquiry. A special committee began looking into several arms deals that Tsochatzopoulos had overseen while defense minister—"one for American radar systems critics consider useless and unsuitable for the military's needs, and the other for Russian surface-to-air missile systems deemed too expensive and marginally functional," according to one account.[8] The committee's findings were inconclusive, and Tsochatzopoulos avoided any censure. But questions about the former defense minister's judgment and his lifestyle, and the elaborate structure of the arms deals he oversaw, remained. "Everyone knew that something wrong was going on with the minister, that he was corrupt," one judicial source recalled. "But you could not see the fire."

Raikou and Papandreou were determined to find that fire. They worked at night and on weekends. The more they learned, the more they realized how little they knew, so each decided to study specific areas. Papandreou chose finance, and Raikou, international banking laws. They reached out to colleagues, family members, friends, and anyone else who might have expertise in a particular area of finance or law. Then they began culling documents from around the world. They sent out requests for mutual legal assistance.

As they pieced the evidence from abroad with what they had assembled, they discovered that the mansion at 33 Dionysiou Areopagitou Street had originally been owned by a legal entity called Torcaso. A shell company incorporated in Cyprus, Torcaso had no function other than to provide its owners a legal means to hold and transfer assets. In 2001, Torcaso sold the property to another offshore shell company, Nobilis International, which had been incorporated in March 1999 in Cheyenne, Wyoming. Following the trail of the ownership record further, Papandreou learned something interesting: In 2010, Nobilis sold the mansion to Vassiliki Stamati—Tsochatzopoulos's wife.

When Raikou's team probed the incorporation records for Torcaso and Nobilis, they found that the companies were actually owned by Tsochatzopoulos, with his cousin serving as director. That meant that the former defense minister had owned the mansion all along but wanted it kept secret; he merely transferred his ownership to different offshore companies, before finally "selling" the property to his wife. It looked to be classic money laundering.

The investigators kept digging. Papandreou and Raikou had sent official requests to Swiss authorities seeking the bank records of Nobilis and Torcaso. Those documents suggested more telltale signs of black money: More than $17 million had been deposited to a Nobilis bank account in Switzerland throughout the 1990s. And that was just one of several accounts Nobilis controlled across Europe.

It was not just the deposits that were interesting, but who had made them: some of the largest defense and arms companies in the world. Bank records showed transfers to Tsochatzopoulos's offshore companies from the Russian company Almaz-Antey, which supplied the surface-to-air missiles that had come under parliamentary review; and the German conglomerate Ferrostaal, which had won a controversial $4 billion Greek submarine deal in the 1990s.

The timing of the deposits to Nobilis was also suspicious: They began in 1997 and peaked between 1999 and 2002—the period when Tsochatzopoulos was minister of defense. The flow of money from large arms companies to offshore accounts controlled by the minister bore all the signs of high-level corporate bribery.

When they assembled all their evidence, Raikou and her team marveled at what they had. Because the statute of limitation had passed, they couldn't go after Tsochatzopoulos for the bribery itself (in all, they identified at least $75 million in bribes paid to him). But they did have enough compelling evidence, corroborated by international affidavits and bank statements, to bring a money-laundering charge against him. "Big joy" is what they felt, in the words of one prosecutor.

"Finally, we had the proof. Nobody believed that Greek justice could come after someone like him. They thought that nothing would happen," another prosecutor who worked on the case said.

In October 2013, Tsochatzopoulos was convicted of money laundering and sentenced to twenty years in prison. Ten other people, including his cousin, his wife, and one of his lawyers, were convicted along with him.

The mansion at 33 Dionysiou Areopagitou Street had been a facade masking Tsochatzopoulos's criminal life. But it also had proven to be a doorway into another hidden world, for in following the money trail further, from Tsochatzopoulos outward, Raikou and her team soon uncovered a much larger scheme: International defense and arms companies had been bribing the Greek armed forces for a decade, resulting in billions of dollars in waste that had helped pushed Greece to the brink of collapse.

\* \* \*

In the first decade of the twenty-first century, Greece went on a massive militarization spree. In 1996, the year Tsochatzopoulos took office, the country had nearly gone to war with Turkey, following a dispute over an uninhabited islet known as Imia. The Defense Ministry justified the ensuing arms purchases by continuously evoking that threat. In capitals across Europe, Tsochatzopoulos signed contracts and brokered military alliances, all the while emphasizing the "destabilizing impact"[9] of Turkey, which, in his words, was an "international troublemaker."[10] In 1996, state spending on arms reached $7 billion; by 2000 it had risen to nearly $9 billion, a disproportionately large amount for such a small country.[11] Among its purchases were missiles from Russia, F-16s from the United States, artillery from Czechoslovakia, and submarines from Germany.

The submarines had always stood out as an especially questionable acquisition. For one thing, they were a new, experimental class of nuclear sub, the first of their kind. Few doubted that Ferrostaal, the German conglomerate, was capable of building them. The question was why Greece's navy would even need them. What was even more notable was the price tag. When the agreement was first negotiated in 1998, Ferrostaal negotiated a price of roughly €1.8 billion ($4 billion dollars) to build three new craft. But by the early 2000s, the contract had been expanded to include an upgrade on three submarines the navy already owned, at a new cost of nearly €3 billion. Today, over a decade later, this curious deal has resurfaced as one of the most controversial scandals in Greece.

The affair has exposed how the country's exorbitant arms expenditure was driven by human greed. Purchasing committees within the military were essentially bribery syndicates, according to a prosecutor who is investigating the massive bribery scandal in Greece's defense industry: "The opinion I have is that when the minister makes a committee to supervise the purchase, and he says, 'In the committee will be Officer A and Officer B,' he makes a present to them. I put you in that committee and I make sure that you will sign every contract, and for every contract you will receive bribes."[12]

He recounted that in the submarine deal, Ferrostaal executives allegedly bribed the former chief of the Hellenic navy, Georgios Theodoroulakis, with nine hundred fifty thousand euros.. (Theodoroulakis served between 2001 and 2002, and died in 2008). Several of his subordinate officers received five hundred thousand euros each. Although these were large sums, about €60 million was earmarked for Tsochatzopoulos alone. Sotiris Emmanouil, the former managing director of Hellenic Shipyards, where the submarines were being built, allegedly received €23 million in bribes. (In 2011, Ferrostaal admitted to paying bribes in Greece and paid a fine of $190 million to settle a criminal investigation by the German police. Prosecutors in Munich have been investigating the company and its contracts since 2010, including a number of bribes allegedly paid in South Africa.)

The prosecutor said that more recently his investigation had widened to include thirty-two additional suspects, including ten who worked for the shipyard administration, and five who worked for trade unions. He also cited the case of Panagiotis Efstathiou, an eighty-three-year-old Greek arms dealer currently on trial for corruption. Several international arms companies had allegedly used Efstatiou to funnel bribes. (According to Reuters, Efstathiou named the German company Atlas as complicit;[13] another German company, Rheinmetall, also admitted to the bribes.)[14] Efstathiou's payments were dispersed throughout the military, for contracts involving antiaircraft missiles and tanks, among other things. "He bribed about twenty officers. The whole army system was corrupt," said the prosecutor. The companies so far alleged to have paid bribes are German, French, Swedish, and Russian. Antonis Kantas, the former deputy director of procurement for the Defense Ministry, who is also on trial, reportedly told one magistrate: "I took so many bribes that I've lost count."[15] Investigators did the tabulation for him: He received $16 million in bribes in connection with ten separate arms deals.

What especially concerned the prosecutor and many anticorruption officials in Greece was how the rampant bribery had led to grossly inflated costs—costs that contributed to the state's catastrophic debt. "They sell expensive weapons at double the price," he explained. Greek defense officials didn't balk at such overvaluations because they knew they were going to get their cut as a percentage of the overall contract.

In the case of Ferrostaal, the prosecutor said, evidence suggested that as early as 1996, before the submarine contract was even signed, the company began scheming to inflate its prices by almost 100 percent. "The real price for the submarines was one billion euros plus. The other eight hundred million to one billion euros was not for the submarine, it was for the German company." From that inflated profit, "one hundred twenty million euros went to use for the bribes," or about 7 percent of the original price tag of the submarines.

Greek investigators who have been reviewing every major arms sale transacted by the Greek state over the last two decades estimate that the loss to the Greek taxpayer in bribes alone has been in the billions. "In ten years, thirty-six billion euros was spent on arms, and four percent was possibly paid in bribes," one investigator said. The bribes alone were equivalent to at least €1.5 billion. The €1.5 billion, however, does not include the overall loss to the state due to inflated prices.

What made the situation even worse was the fact that the submarines were faulty. "There was a problem with the balance," Constantinos P. Fraggos, a retired brigadier general and military expert, explained.[16] In the end, the submarines were never even delivered. Today, nearly a decade later, they still sit unfinished at the Skaramangas Shipyard, outside of Athens.

Fraggos, who served as a military advisor to the Defense Ministry for three and a half years, has written a book that details at least twenty cases in which defense contracts resulted not only in inflated prices, but in wasteful or useless purchases. "They bought 60 F-16s without radar defense," he recalled. "They bought 150 tanks, the first [of their kind] in the world," he said, referring to German Leopard 2 tanks Greece purchased in 2009. "But they bought them without ammunition. They bought the ammunition after ten years." (In 2014, police in Munich raided the offices of Krauss-Maffei Wegmann, the manufacturer of the tank. The company is currently under investigation for allegedly paying bribes in Greece).[17]

Fraggos, one of the country's most outspoken critics of the military, believes that the conviction of Tsochatzopoulos only begins to address the problem. "They are just two or three brought before justice. They don't have the documents to send the guilty to jail. They have to find the black money. Because there is a big resistance of the banks, of the system." He stressed that the state's losses in the defense industry were relatively easy to calculate because the sums involved were so large, and the bribes so concentrated—€60 million alone went to the former defense minister.

"It's very easy to speak about the armaments—armament, armaments, armaments. But there are other sectors in which the percentage of corruption was bigger. What to say about health?" Fraggos asked.

* * *

On April 14, 2010, John Dougall, a Scotsman then forty-four years old, stood before Justice David Bean in the dock at Southwark Crown Court in London. A man of acerbic humor whom colleagues have described as "whip smart," Dougall was about to make history. For more than a decade, he had been a rising star at DePuy, one of the world's premiere manufacturers of orthopedic devices, known particularly for its artificial knees and hips. The company, which has twenty-three thousand employees worldwide, is headquartered in Leeds, England, but is owned by Johnson & Johnson, the American health-care giant. Dougall had been vice president of marketing until 2007 and had lived a relatively luxurious life, making two hundred thousand dollars a year and often flying business class and driving expensive cars. But that morning it had all come to an inglorious end: Justice Bean sentenced Dougall to a year in prison—not a harsh sentence but an unprecedented one nonetheless. Dougall was the first executive ever to be jailed in the United Kingdom for corrupting foreign officials in order to win business—and also the first witness to cooperate with British authorities in an international corruption case.

His case would soon become groundbreaking for Greece as well. DePuy had an annual turnover of roughly $100 million there, making it one of the top five players in the orthopedic market in the country. Dougall testified that the company's sales were driven by *miza*. Between 2002 and 2005, he acknowledged helping funnel more than $10 million in bribes to surgeons at Greek public hospitals. In return, the surgeons helped DePuy generate at least $40 million in sales. Dougall's cooperation with British and American authorities, who had jointly investigated DePuy since 2007, helped crack open the case—and eventually exposed the role of *miza* in Greece's state-run health-care sector.

In 2011, Johnson & Johnson paid a $70 million fine to the Department of Justice to settle the criminal investigation of its actions in Greece, and also admitted to paying bribes in Poland, Romania, and Iraq. Dougall was—and remains—the only individual jailed for the offense. But internal company emails and documents that he submitted to the police made it clear that DePuy ran a large bribery operation in Greece, often with the consent of senior management, between 1999 and 2007—the very time frame in which health-care costs in Greece were exploding. "I accept the corruption was in effect a company policy, predating your involvement and approved by your superiors," Justice Bean stated at Dougall's sentencing.[18]

DePuy executives, Dougall told investigators, had developed institutional code words for the bribes, calling them "cash incentives" and payments for "professional education"—or "ProfEd." To channel the ProfEd to surgeons, he explained, DePuy hired an experienced middleman in Greece, Nikolaos Karagiannis. In one of his emails to DePuy, Karagiannis wrote that "the existence of cash incentives to surgeons is common knowledge in Greece."[19] Dougall warned his superiors that if they stopped paying them "we'd lose 95 percent of our business by the end of the year."[20]

In 2012, using evidence from the U.S. and UK investigations, particularly Dougall's testimony, the Greeks opened an inquiry of their own. At around the time Tsochatzopoulos was arrested, a team of investigators arrived at a public hospital in Athens, hoping to make a breakthrough. The team had come to inquire about the hospital's director, a prominent orthopedic surgeon whose finances had raised suspicions. "We discovered certain bizarre movements in his account but also in the accounts of his father-in-law, who was actually a priest," Panagiotis Nikoloudis, the former head of Greece's Financial Intelligence Unit, recalled.[21]

In Greece's universal health-care system, nearly 70 percent of the country's hospitals are state run, and nearly all the country's seventy thousand doctors are employed by the government. (As in China, public doctors in Greece are considered foreign officials under U.S. and UK law.) Since the 1970s, Greek hospitals have purchased supplies and medicine not through transparent, competitive tenders, but based on the decisions of hospital directors and prominent surgeons. This virtually unchallenged discretion allows bribery to flourish.

At the Athens hospital Nikoloudis's team analyzed dozens of the hospital director's purchases, dating back to the early 2000s. Johnson & Johnson orders appeared repeatedly. When they compared the dates and the prices with the director's bank account records, a striking pattern emerged: Every time the director ordered supplies from Johnson & Johnson, a week later he received a deposit into his bank account, which was always equivalent to 23 percent of the Johnson & Johnson order. "We could see the money," Nikoloudis recalled.

Nikoloudis was appointed to the Cabinet of Prime Minister Alexis Tsipras as State Minister for Combating Corruption in January 2015. He has been a district attorney for twenty-eight years, specializing in corruption, but even for him, the discovery of those hospital bribes was a revelation: The margin of corruption was larger in health care than in any other sector. "The bribe represented an inflation of price by twenty-three percent, sometimes twenty or twenty-one percent. In arms contracts it was only four percent. In other fields it was no more than two or two and a half percent."

When Johnson & Johnson paid a fine to the Department of Justice in 2011, neither the company nor U.S. authorities took into consideration what impact the corruption might have had. But for Nikoloudis its ramifications were clear. "In the decade between 2000 and 2010, an enormous amount of money, amounting to billions of euros—some say fifteen billion euros—was wasted in these kinds of orders for medical supply companies for public hospitals." The DePuy case was emblematic of the recklessness that had precipitated Greece's financial meltdown.

According to public filings by U.S., British, and Greek law enforcement, the DePuy bribery worked as follows: The company deposited millions into Karagiannis's offshore account on the Isle of Man, and he, in turn, bribed the surgeons for every knee or hip replacement they performed, and for using expensive supplies related to the surgeries, such as orthopedic screws. Each time a surgeon used an expensive screw, he or she received a bribe worth at least 20 percent of the product's value, sometimes more. "In case it is not clear to you, please understand that I am paying cash incentives right after each surgery," Karagiannis once explained in an email to a client.[22]

Karagiannis and his employees often wrote emails explicitly referencing bribery. Some within DePuy's management structure wanted to terminate their relationship with him, concerned that his bribes, the so-called ProfEd, exposed them to legal risk. But DePuy's president at the time, Michael J. Dormer, also a senior executive at Johnson & Johnson, overruled them. "The only problem with the proposal was that we would lose half our business even by year 3," he wrote in an email. He continued, "To lose approximately $4m in sales in end user terms to the competition is totally unacceptable."[23] Dormer eventually arranged for DePuy to acquire Karagiannis's company, Medec, to ensure that the ProfEd kept flowing.

The ProfEd came in different forms. "The bribery was not only in cash. It was in expenses, it was in luxurious travel, in equipment," another investigator said. "We heard some stories, in Cuba for instance, concerning doctors who had female company in luxurious hotels. We have heard too many stories." Either in cash or in kind, many of Greece's best orthopedic surgeons made hundreds of thousands of dollars in black money, investigators allege.

To recoup the costs of the bribes, plus the cost of taxes and Karagiannis's cut, DePuy inflated the price of its products by 35 percent.[24] This meant the state overpaid by that amount every time a surgeon performed a knee surgery. By the mid-2000s, the price of a knee replacement in Greece had risen to more than eight thousand dollars—double the cost in the rest of Europe. "There is no doubt one of the reasons why the prices were so high in Greece is that the market was corrupt," John Kelsey-Fry, a British Crown prosecutor had argued at John Dougall's sentencing.[25] There were dozens, possibly hundreds, of doctors on DePuy's black money list. According to Greek prosecutors, Depuy's bribes compromised the majority of public hospitals in Greece—114 out of a total of 143.

The loss to the Greek state, at least as it has been calculated so far by American, British, and Greek investigators, is upwards of $16 million (the amount DePuy paid in bribes between 1998 and 2006). Though that amount is certainly small relative to the billions Greece owes, it does not represent the full extent of the problem, according to Spyros Georgouleas, the head of the Public Prosecutor's Office in Athens. "We have seen the tip of the iceberg here," he said. "Just think that we're talking about only one company, and only in orthopedics."[26]

Georgouleas, who is overseeing the DePuy investigation, pointed out that since 2012, Smith & Nephew and Stryker, two other leading American orthopedic manufacturers, are now under investigation in Greece; both also paid large fines to the U.S. government to settle charges that they systematically paid bribes there. Public filings from the U.S. investigation indicate that between 1998 to 2008, Smith & Nephew paid more than $9 million in bribes to surgeons and inflated its costs by 40 percent. It, too, used Karagiannis as its middleman, paying bribes so that it could outcompete DePuy. In an email to a Smith & Nephew vice president in 2002, Karagiannis warned that he needed more money for bribes to keep up with major competitors, who were paying 30 percent to 40 percent more than Smith & Nephew.[27] "It was the accepted universal practice in Greece that twenty percent was set aside in order to pay surgeons," John Dougall had testified to the British police. "All companies that wanted to participate in the market had to set aside this twenty percent."[28] (John Dougall declined to comment about the DePuy affair).

"Think about other categories of doctors," Georgouleas continued. "We're not talking about the eyes, about cancer. We're not investigating, for instance, drugs or medicine." To his point, Greek prosecutors have recently opened an investigation into the German pharmaceutical giant Bayer, alleging that it bribed eight hundred doctors in Greece, as well as Novartis, based in Switzerland. "So you can understand that we're talking about billions, billions, if you add all these sums of money," Georgouleas said.

An examination of skyrocketing health-care costs in Greece today supports Greek investigators' claims of the deleterious effects of kickbacks. The cost of a heart stent was five times higher in Greece than in Germany, according to former prime minister George Papandreou.[29] Because Greek doctors have been induced to overprescribe expensive medicines, the state paid three to four times more than any other European country for prescription drugs, a former health minister told the press. Some doctors wrote prescriptions for nonexistent patients in order to get a kickback in return. With more and more physicians on the take, spending on pharmaceuticals rose from $1.4 billion in 2000 to $7.6 billion in 2009.[30] Between 2000 and 2009, the country's overall health budget deficit reached €50 billion because of overspending.[31] Part of this was due to inflated prices caused by bribery. By 2010, state hospitals owed pharmaceutical companies and medical suppliers nearly $7 billion, Reuters reported.[32]

"I cannot say corruption is *the* reason for the crisis," Nikoloudis said. "But it's one of the main reasons Greece is having a crisis." Whereas Greek doctors are guilty of willingly accepting bribes, Georgouleas charges foreign companies with a callous disregard for the greater impact of their bribery. "I have heard, as a general defense, companies say: We could not do our job here in Greece in another way," Georgouleas said. "Let me say that they could. This is an insult for us, as people. It's too easy to say that all Greeks are scum, and present yourself as an angel who has to work this way in order to make profit."

*   *   *

When the International Monetary Fund and the European Commission agreed to a $273 billion bailout for Greece, two of their central conditions were that the country overhaul its anticorruption strategy and slash $3 billion from its health bill, which was running at $17 billion—about 5 percent of GDP, among the highest in the European Union. Since the bailout began in 2010, the government has committed to greater transparency in procurement, mandating that hospitals install computers to track purchases and spending, and has centralized a once fragmented system for buying drugs. It has also reduced hospital expenditures by 25 percent since 2009, in part by lowering the price of pharmaceuticals, but primarily by cutting wages and the number of health-care workers, according to a study by the European Commission.[33] In the government's efforts to address waste and corruption in the health-care industry, health-care itself has become the greatest victim.

"Since 2009, forty percent of our income has been horizontally cut," the vice president of a doctor's union at a prominent hospital in Athens said. "The primary health-care system has been destroyed," he added, referring to the thousands of jobs lost. "People can't find doctors in primary care, which means most people come to the hospitals. The needs of the hospital have doubled while costs have been cut," he said. "I have an ultrasound machine that is fifteen years old. I should change it, but I put it off for now."

"People are facing something completely new and strange," observed a volunteer at the Metropolitan Social Clinic, located in Elliniko, forty minutes by subway from central Athens. "I never imaged that I would come to the point where I am unemployed," she said. After she had been laid off from another job when the crisis hit, she was angry for months and began showing up at the street protests in Athens. Because she no longer has health insurance, she can't pay for visits to a doctor. "For the first time, the public system is turning away people without insurance. I've stopped going for blood tests," she explained.

Under existing legislation, Greece's National Health Services Organization provides the unemployed insurance coverage for only two years, even though many Greek citizens have been jobless for longer. According to one study citing estimates from the Ministry of Labor, two million Greeks lack insurance.[34] "Those people don't have money," a doctor explained. "If you don't have money, you don't go to a doctor—because people who don't have money have dignity. But it means that when they do come to the doctor, they come too late; it's more complicated by then, it's more expensive."

Greece is now not only dealing with a fiscal crisis and the emerging problems caused by the flood of refugees from the Syrian war, but a mounting public health crisis as well. Because of cuts to mosquito prevention programs, malaria has reappeared in the country for the first time in forty years. Reductions in street work programs have led to the distribution of fewer clean syringes and condoms to drug users, according to a 2014 study published in the *Lancet*. As result, new cases of HIV infection increased from 15 in 2009 to 484 in 2012, "while preliminary data for 2013 suggest that the incidence of tuberculosis among this population has more than doubled compared with 2012." The same study reported other troubling signs, including that stillborn deaths had risen 21 percent between 2008 and 2011 because of lack of access to prenatal health services. Infant mortality, meanwhile, increased by 43 percent between 2008 and 2010 because of worsening economic conditions.[35]

"You have a system that has collapsed," a doctor said. "You have to build it again, but carefully. We have to give new motivation to the doctors, and we have to clean the market of the malpractices—we have to give clear rules."

* * *

When the Greek government created a new, national-level post of Prosecutor for Corruption in 2013, Eleni Raikou was appointed its first-ever head and given a new suite of offices at the Supreme Court complex in Athens. Papi Papandreou joined her team. They had scarcely more resources than before—their team still consisted of only five prosecutors, with Raikou often still paying for supplies out of pocket—but in the eyes of many, they have become powerful symbols of Greece's resurgent justice system.

As the ancient legend goes, the goddess Athena is the protector of Athens, the custodian of civilization, a warrior maiden prepared to fight for just causes. The Greek public and media often draw an analogy between Raikou, Papandreou, and Athena; one article, published in a Greek online newspaper features a cartoon of Papandreou dressed in ancient Greek robes, holding a sword and the scales of justice. In truth, however, justice has been more elusive.

Since Tsochatzopoulos's arrest, Raikou and her colleagues have been conducting bribery investigations involving several of the largest companies in the world—including Siemens, Bayer, and, recently, Ericsson, the Finnish telecommunications company. They have seized and repatriated $45 million in funds stolen through corruption. "And four hundred million euros have been charged from several cases and are going to court," one of Raikou's colleagues said. "We cannot say we have eliminated corruption, but through the efforts of public prosecutors in Greece, there is a resistance. This resistance is very important. We will continue even if they don't give us any means."

There is no doubt that Raikou will, buttressed by new political support and institutional backing, play a critical role in the changes that appear to be taking place in Greece. But by her team's own admission, they have not yet succeeded in bringing charges against an official of Tsochatzopoulos's stature, even though evidence suggests that that are many such individuals.

In 2012, Nikoloudis and his team believed they had made a breakthrough. Karagiannis's company, Madison, had taken great pains to hide the flow of bribes into it, transferring different tranches of funds through a complex web of offshore accounts in Liberia, Monrovia, Cyprus, and Malta. But Karagiannis made a critical error: From those separate locations, Madison transferred all the bribes into a single bank account at a specific bank branch in Syntagma Square, in the center of Athens. When police discovered the account, they closed in.

"We thought we had cracked the case," Nikoloudis said, and the investigators assumed their task would be simple. "We believed we would just go the bank, find out that those funds had been transferred to certain specific accounts, and then we would obviously locate these people," referring to the doctors who had received the bribes.

But when investigators arrived at the bank, the staff had troubling news. "The bank said, well, 'The money was not transferred. Some people came with suitcases and just took the money,'" Nikoloudis recounted. Though the bribes had entered Greece through sophisticated means, once there, the payments were delivered to the doctors by hand, in cash, so there was no way to trace it.

During their investigation, prosecutors had searched the home of Despina Filippou, the managing director of Karagiannis's company. In her garage they found a list of 250 doctors who they believed were on DePuy's bribe list. But because prosecutors simply didn't have the resources to investigate them all, they narrowed their pursuit to twelve surgeons, each of whom had been found to have more than two hundred thousand euros in his bank account, an amount that seemed suspicious. One of them, Panagiotis Soukakos, is among the most famous surgeons in Greece, a leading professor of orthopedics, politically well connected and a close friend of the Greek king. Because the bribes had allegedly been given to the surgeons by hand, though, prosecutors had no direct evidence proving that money had gone from Karagiannis directly to them. All twelve of the suspects, including Soukokos, were acquitted after trial in 2012.

"What I realized through investigating those pharmaceutical and medical supply companies was that the people involved in all these deals were actually experts in money laundering," Nikoloudis observed. The criminals are "several steps ahead of justice," a member of Raikou's team said. "Through the internet, [they] can move money quickly. It takes years for justice to keep up."

Six years after the DePuy investigation began in Greece, the case has yet to result in a single conviction, either of DePuy employees or of the doctors implicated. Prosecutors still hope that situation can change. In 2013, they brought new charges against twenty-five suspects, including several former DePuy executives, like Michael Dormer. Documents from the UK and U.S. investigations allege that Dormer, a British citizen, "knowingly continued" DePuy's bribery scheme, but he was never charged in either country; he had resigned from Johnson & Johnson in 2007 (when the bribery allegations first surfaced in the United States) after accepting "ulti-mate responsibility by virtue of my position."[36] It remains to be seen whether Greece can mount a successful prosecution against a corporate executive like Dormer, a foreign citizen. The outcome of the DePuy case will prove a critical test of the country's ability to prosecute high-level financial crimes.

Greece today is a different country than the one afflicted by the Ferrostaal and DePuy scandals. Procurement rules in both defense contracting and health care have dramatically changed, creating more transparency and limiting the opportunities for bribery to take place. More important, as the Greek economy continues to contract—as it has for seven out of the last eight years—the state is spending far less on weapons and health care, so there is simply no market for bribery.

What remains unchanged is that the individuals responsible for one of the greatest financial collapses in modern history, includ-ing the corporate executives whose bribery helped precipitate it, have not been held to account. Most of them remain virtually unknown, let alone prosecuted, as investigators continue to exca-vate the extent of the ruins. The capacity of the Greek government to hold the powerful to account is uncertain. The outcome will not be determined by a contest of wills, Eleni Raikou's resolve pitted against that of organized financial criminals. The contest is one of resources—a confrontation between countless multinationals, who spent enormous money and effort over decades to pump black money into Greece, and the paltry means of a bankrupt state trying to uncover the evidence and make it stick in court.

That effort has already suffered a setback. In March 2017, Eleni Raikou resigned under controversy. Among her many cases, she had been investigating a sprawling kickback scheme allegedly orchestrated by Novartis. Raikou had apparently turned up important evidence, including $30 million in payments from the company's bank account to four thousand doctors throughout Greece, as well as high-level politicians, including two former prime ministers. An article then appeared about her in the newspaper *Documento* that, quoting anonymous sources, claimed that Raikou had improperly withheld evidence in a separate investigation of a state procurement deal involving helicopters and frigates.[37] In a letter of resignation she delivered to Greece's Supreme Court in late March, Raikou claimed the article was only the latest attempt by "corrupt government officials and major interests in the pharmaceutical field" to "plan my moral annihilation so as to allow the degradation of our research." According to documents Novartis filed with the SEC in January 2017, the Justice Department and the SEC have now opened an investigation into the Greek bribes.[38] In all likelihood, Novartis will reach a corporate settlement yet again, and simply pay another fine.

# Chapter 8

# Fueling the Fire

His son's murder lives on in Mohsin Ali's memory, an inescapable pain, instantly accessible. Ali lives in Natore, a village in Rajshahi, a large district six hours to the northwest of Bangladesh's capital, Dhaka. Rajshahi has become a dangerously conservative stronghold, an incubator for intolerant religious views. Islamist extremists recently killed a professor of sociology at Rajshahi University who was known for encouraging his students to question traditional Islamic values. His attackers hacked him to death with machetes. Bangladesh's intelligence agencies continue to uncover such Islamist militant cells throughout the country, including several more in Rajshahi. Many have connections to international terrorist groups like Al Qaeda, and their recruits claim to have received training in Afghanistan and Pakistan. Police have even begun arresting cells linked to the Islamic State, an alarming new development in Bangladesh's growing problem with extremism. It was at Mohsin Ali's small farm in Natore, a pastoral setting of shimmering mustard fields and narrow dirt roads, that this militant violence was first born—a fire fueled by the bribes of one of the largest corporations in the world.

On the morning of April 1, 2004, Mohsin Ali and his wife, Tahura, rose early as usual to tend to their chores. Their farm, on roughly an acre of land, has a two-storied house of packed mud and a large covered dwelling for the chickens and the cows. Ali tended to the animals that morning while Tahura prepared breakfast, and they then waited to eat with their son, Monwar. A handsome young man then twenty years old, Monwar was a student at Tahirpur College, a local university. In a photo from that time, he is tall and lanky, like his father, in slim-fitting jeans and a stylish shirt. He sits at a fountain, wearing large sunglasses, and holds up a lotus flower, the symbol of his university. He has a look of solemn intensity—a boy trying hard to be a man.

Between studying, helping with the farm, and running the local student chapter of the Awami League, one of Bangladesh's two main political parties, Monwar led a busy life. He was the pride of his family, not only because he was hard working, but because of his principles. "He had a habit to protest when he saw an unfairness or injustice anywhere," his father recalled.[1] "If anyone was in trouble, he used to rush to help that person. And if he came to know that you are bothering someone, he would come to you and say, 'Don't do that. Don't bother him.'"

In Monwar, his parents had seen the possibility of a better future. Life was difficult, but Ali remembers how his son used to reassure him. "He used to say to me: Father, now we have a lot of hardship, a lot of struggle. But just hold on a few more years, then I will graduate, and I will take a job—and our hardship will be over. Just wait a little while longer, and our good days will come."

Monwar was a passionate supporter of the Awami League, which traces its origins back to 1971, when the eastern part of Pakistan violently broke away to form Bangladesh. The Awami League advocated for that break, because its members felt that Bangladesh should be its own secular democracy, comprised of both Hindus and Muslims, bound together in tolerance by a common Bengali culture, history, and language. Not everyone shared that belief.

Many thought that Bengalis should remain part of Pakistan, and that Pakistan should be restricted to Muslims. Eventually the two sides fought a civil war, thousands died, and Bangladesh was born. But the feud did not end, and those who supported the religious point of view formed a new political party, the Bangladesh Nationalist Party (BNP). Decades after those bloody days, these opposing factions continued to struggle, and the conflict had now found its way to Mohsin Ali's doorstep. At ten o'clock that morning a crowd of men brandishing weapons appeared there and began calling for Monwar to come outside.

What happened next was more than just an incident of violence in an isolated region. It was also a tragic example of how corporate bribes, paid by Western corporations in the pursuit of business, can ultimately affect the lives of ordinary people in countries like Bangladesh. Monwar's story puts a face on the otherwise hidden victims of these crimes, as it was connected, through a secret chain of people and events, to millions of dollars in payments that Siemens, one of the largest industrial companies in the world, had been making to a man named Aminul Haque. Haque was one of the most powerful officials in the Bangladesh Nationalist Party, which then ruled the country. At the same time that Haque was receiving kickbacks from Siemens, he and his allies were also secretly building a private army, a terrorist group determined to destroy secular-minded people who opposed the BNP—people like Monwar. The bribes that Siemens paid would help push Bangladesh to the brink of collapse, and open rifts from which Bangladesh has never recovered.

Thirteen years have passed since Monwar was taken away to a paddy field, shot, and then beheaded—the first victim of Jamaat-ul-Mujahideen Bangladesh (JMB), or the Holy Warriors of

Bangladesh, an extremist group that has opened the floodgates to Islamist militancy in Bangladesh. Even now, as JMB menaces the entire country, it continues to threaten Mohsin Ali personally.

How Monwar's murder is linked to Siemens is a larger narrative about political power and corruption in Bangladesh and one of the most infamous and consequential of all bribery cases. It reveals that, long after that matter has been adjudicated in the West, the victims in Bangladesh have never even been recognized, let alone granted justice.

*  *  *

On December 15, 2008, the U.S. Justice Department announced the resolution of a bribery investigation that was one of the largest in FCPA history, spanning several years and involving multiple branches of U.S. and German law enforcement. Siemens Corporation, the department disclosed, had pleaded guilty to paying more than $800 million in bribes in dozens of countries around the world, including Nigeria, Argentina, China, and Saddam Hussein's regime during the Oil-for-Food Program. Matthew H. Friedrich, then the acting assistant attorney general, cited billions of dollars in projects that Siemens had corruptly acquired across the globe. In Venezuela, for example, it had used kickbacks to win a $340 million railway system contract. In Bangladesh, Siemens's local subsidiary used bribes to be awarded a $40 million contract for a national telecommunications project.

In 2001, the Bangladesh Telephone and Telegraph Board (BTTB), the state-owned telephone company, announced that it planned to build a national mobile phone network called Teletalk, which would compete with the many private cellular networks emerging at the time. The project had a price tag of $75 million and would be contracted out to foreign companies.

From its headquarters in Italy, Siemens's telecom group began strategizing how to win the contract. In an email sent that year, one of the company's employees listed its formidable competition—Motorola, Ericcson, Nortel, and several Chinese firms, including ZTE and Huawei.[2] But Siemens could prevail, the employee continued, not because the company had a better proposal, but because it would use bribes. The bribes would "neutralize the offer of the competitors . . . who had high contacts in the [Bangladeshi government]" and "probably had a more advantageous financial proposal."[3]

Starting that year, Siemens spent enormous time and effort engineering a sophisticated global bribery structure to win Teletalk. It set up a special subsidiary in Switzerland, Intercom, to generate bribe payments, and a series of shell companies with bank accounts in Cyprus and Austria to secretly funnel them. It also hired two Bangladeshi middlemen to handle the delivery of the bribes. The two men had already had "significant success in several projects" over the past fifteen years for Siemens, the email noted.

Peter Albrich, who was then the CEO of Siemens Bangladesh, referred to the bribes as "fuel on the fire." Winning Teletalk was a long and arduous process, given both the competitors for the project and the bureaucratic hurdles of the Bangladeshi government. Whenever Siemens hit a rough patch in negotiations, Albrich would request more money from Intercom for bribes. "We need some fuel to keep the fire going," he wrote in one email.[4] Intercom would then wire more money to its shell companies, from where it was routed to bank accounts that the middlemen had hidden away in Singapore.

Between 2001 and 2006, Siemens paid at least $5.3 million in bribes to government officials in Bangladesh, the Justice Department disclosed. It never revealed, however, the identity of these officials, other than to state one was the son of a prime minister in Bangladesh, and another was Bangladesh's minister of telecommunications. Justice Department policy prevents prosecutors from publicly identifying the foreign officials who receive corporate bribes, unless those individuals are subsequently charged with a related offense, such as money laundering.

In the end, Siemens agreed to pay $1 billion in penalties and fines to the U.S. government, and roughly $500 million in fines to the German government—still the largest such settlement in history. To avoid criminal charges, it also agreed to dramatically reform itself as a company. It fired its management board, instituted a companywide system of antibribery compliance, including intense antibribery training for its staff, and hired an independent, court-appointed corporate monitor to evaluate the company's progress in implementing these reforms.

Today Siemens is lauded for having transformed itself into a more transparent and disciplined company. That certainly may be true, but its record fines, the DOJ's remarks, the ensuing news coverage, and even Siemens's own commitment to internal reform have all failed to address the damage that the corporation's bribes inflicted in Bangladesh, or even to acknowledge that any individual communities in Bangladesh might have been affected. The larger account of who received the bribes and what they did with the money has still never been told. Instead, it remains the story of a company that pleaded guilty to little more than failing to keep accurate books and records—in other words, for lying to the so-called free market, which constitutes little more than a white-collar crime.

Months before Siemens settled the case, however, an FBI agent and a legendary Justice Department prosecutor began working tirelessly behind the scenes to trace the consequences of Siemens's bribes, and in a rare example of such a collaboration, helped Bangladesh bring to judgment the people who were paid off.

\* \* \*

In January 2008, Debra LaPrevotte made her first trip to Bangladesh.[5] Like most new visitors, she was shocked. Dhaka, a city of 18 million people, is unsparing in its assault on the senses: the gnarled traffic, the skyline dominated by water-stained high rises, the sheer volume of bodies. But what struck her most deeply was the poverty—the cruelty and pervasiveness of it. Beggars flood the streets of Dhaka, some badly scarred, some missing limbs, some covered in boils. The helpless and poor tend to swarm around cars at stoplights, pleading with those inside for a handout. It made LaPrevotte think of the powerful politicians ruling the country, siphoning off money through corruption. "How do you look your people in the eye and reconcile that?" she recalls thinking.[6] Her own firsthand experience of that remained with LaPrevotte.

LaPrevotte became an anti-money laundering expert at the FBI almost by accident. As a young bureau recruit, she spent eight hours a day sitting in surveillance cars, waiting to catch sight of suspects. She was energetic and driven, but restless. To while away the time, she started learning foreign languages on tape, studying nine in two years.

In 1999, a position opened at the Asset Forfeiture and Money Laundering squad at the bureau's Washington field office. The unit specialized in seizing the proceeds of criminal activity—cars purchased with drug money or luxury estates acquired through banking fraud. LaPrevotte welcomed the chance to do something different and eventually discovered she was drawn to "going after the heads of [state] who are corrupt and destabilizing their countries," as a colleague close to her describes it.

Her experience in Dhaka convinced LaPrevotte that she had to get people at the FBI to turn their attention to the corruption in Bangladesh. That would become something of a personal crusade, for both her and her friend Linda Samuel, a prosecutor with Justice's Asset Forfeiture Program. "The fact that the Justice Department pursued it as they did was the result of the fact that two people were involved. They were extraordinary, Debra and Linda," Salahuddin Ahmad, Bangladesh's former attorney general, observed.[7]

Bangladesh's Anti-Corruption Commission (ACC) lies in the dense heart of the city. Since its creation in 2004, the ACC has been empowered by the executive branch to independently investigate corporate crimes, money laundering, and political corruption in the nation. It is also the FBI and DOJ's principal liaison in tracking down international money-laundering cases and violations of the FCPA. LaPrevotte went to the ACC to discuss where Siemens's money had gone, and to enlist the ACC's help in retrieving it.

Under the best of circumstances, Bangladesh is an unwieldy political proposition. It has half the population of the entire United States crowded into a landmass the size of Pennsylvania, most of it desperately poor. The entire country is bitterly divided between the right-wing BNP and the secular-leaning Awami League. BNP is led by a woman named Khaleda Zia, who has twice been the prime minister, including between 2001 and 2006. Her husband, who founded the party, was assassinated in 1981; Zia blames the Awami League. The Awami League is led by a woman named Sheikh Hasina, who currently serves as prime minister. Her father, who was considered the founder of Bangladesh, was assassinated in 1975; Hasina blames the BNP. Perhaps the only thing stopping all-out civil war is a moderate indigenous culture, but that too is increasingly beset by extremist Islam.

LaPrevotte had arrived in Bangladesh in the middle of two of the most calamitous years in the country's history. A year earlier, in January 2007, the army had seized control of civilian rule, believing the country was on the brink of chaos. The terrorist group JMB, after murdering Monwar, had been unleashing a violent campaign to impose Shariah law, killing dozens. At the same time, Bangladesh had become the most corrupt country in the world, according to Transparency International. Pitched battles between the Awami League and the BNP, meanwhile, had been raging for days in the run-up to a national election, with many casualties. A report at the time by the International Crisis Group warned: "Bangladesh faces twin threats to its democracy and stability: the risk that its political system will founder in a deadlock over elections and the growing challenge of militant Islamism, which has brought a spate of violence. The issues are linked; Islamic militancy has flourished in a time of dysfunctional politics, popular discontent and violence."[8]

When the army finally emerged from its barracks on January 11, 2007 (a date the country still refers to as 1/11), it bestowed upon itself the benign-sounding title of "caretaker government" and launched a sweeping crackdown against corruption, arresting tens of thousands of people, as well as Islamist militants. The jails of Dhaka soon swelled with the country's wealthiest, most privileged, and most powerful citizens, including Sheikh Hasina and Khaleda Zia.

Locked away in the prison cells were also the two men many believed truly responsible for Bangladesh's unraveling: Tarique and Arafat "Koko" Rahman, the sons of former prime minister Khaleda Zia. Although neither brother was officially a member of the government, both were known to operate a "shadow government" from an office building in Dhaka, an address every Bangladeshi knew and feared. They were the secret godfathers of the BNP, close allies of Aminul Haque's, but given their family connection, even more powerful. From their office, the Rahman brothers issued threats and extorted loyalty payments, and regularly took bribes from foreign companies in return for awarding public contracts worth millions. What they did with the money was more alarming. For years, political insiders and retired military officials had been warning the U.S. embassy that Tarique, along with Aminul Haque, was patronizing extremist groups, including JMB.

"Tarique had engulfed the entire political culture of this country. That is when it became impossible for the state to function. And that is when the army stepped in," Anisul Huq, Bangladesh's law minister, explained.[9]

The brothers were both arrested in early March 2007 in a series of large raids by the police. Rumors spread that they were severely beaten, and that the generals running the crackdown took particular pleasure in mistreating Tarique. "Tarique thought the army chiefs were his mother's servants," a member of the caretaker government said. "The generals became really angry with Tarique."[10] Whether or not the rumors were true, Tarique used them to his advantage. Though officially imprisoned, he managed to hold television interviews from a wheelchair, insisting he needed to seek medical treatment abroad.

Though 1/11 momentarily promised a chance to purge Bangladesh of the corruption of the Rahmans, it also offered a unique opportunity for Debra LaPrevotte and U.S. investigators in the form of a neutral government, aligned neither to BNP or the Awami League, and willing to cooperate on corruption, specifically by neutralizing Tarique Rahman. For the United States, as for Bangladesh, addressing the country's corruption required more than cleaning up bad business. It meant preventing Bangladesh from becoming a failed state, as James F. Moriarty, the U.S. ambassador to Bangladesh at the time, explained in a State Department cable leaked by Wikileaks:

"Embassy Dhaka has three key priorities for Bangladesh: democratization, development, and denial of space to terrorists. Tarique's audaciously corrupt activities jeopardize all three. His history of embezzlement, extortion, and interference in the judicial process undermines the rule of law and threatens to upend the U.S. goal of a stable, democratic Bangladesh. The climate of corrupt business practices and bribe solicitation that Tarique fostered derailed U.S. efforts to promote economic development by discouraging much needed foreign investment and complicating the international operations of U.S. companies. Finally, his flagrant disregard for the rule of law has provided potent ground for terrorists to gain a foothold in Bangladesh while also exacerbating poverty and weakening democratic institutions. In short, much of what is wrong in Bangladesh can be blamed on Tarique and his cronies."[11]

Since 2010, when the Justice Department launched the Anti-Kleptocracy Initiative, the United States has begun to exert extraordinary influence to prevent foreign officials from enjoying the fruits of corruption—including by dispatching agents like LaPrevotte to find and seize their illicit funds. If a foreign official uses the U.S. banking system to launder his money—for example if bribery payments were wired in American dollars—the United States has jurisdiction to seize their money and any assets derived from it. The United Nations Conventions against Corruption (UNCAC), a treaty ratified by more than 150 countries, provides the legal framework for the United States and Bangladesh to cooperate on the asset recovery.

In Bangladesh, LaPrevotte and Samuel found a small cadre of dedicated allies, which included Anisul Huq, then an ACC prosecutor; Salahuddin Ahmad, the Columbia-educated economist serving as the attorney general at the time; and Saleh, a hard-driving financial investigator who continues to fight corruption (Saleh is not his real name).

When LaPrevotte met with the the ACC chairman, Hasan Masood Chowdhury, a highly respected former four-star general, she handed him a copy of an intricate graph containing numerous intersecting lines. "The FBI has this computer program that allows them to trace money from bank accounts. You can get a printout that shows the money trail," Ahmad said. "[The] ACC chairman . . . was shocked. He didn't expect Debra to have so much detail, to go so much into the nitty-gritty."

LaPrevotte explained that since 2001 bribes had been flowing from Siemens shell companies in Austria and Cyprus to bank accounts in Singapore. Through forensic accounting, she discovered that the account belonged to a company called Zasz Trading, registered in Singapore. Zasz actually belonged to Arafat Rahman, Tarique Rahman's younger brother. (The name "Zasz" was derived from the initials of Arafat Rahman's two daughters and his wife: Zahia, Sharmila, and Zafia.) In August 2005, the Zasz account had received $180,000 in payments from a Siemens middleman. LaPrevotte insisted that Bangladesh, with the United States' help, could get the money back.

There was more. Roughly $1.7 million of Siemens's money had also flowed through shell companies in the United States to a bank account at HSBC in Hong Kong. That amount had been given as a bribe to Bangladesh's minister of telecommunications at the time, Aminul Haque, who had then been leading a dangerous double life.

\* \* \*

In the days before the armed crowd arrived at his farmhouse, Mohsin Ali learned that a feud had arisen between members of his son's student group and the local BNP faction controlled by Aminul Haque.

In 2003, unknown assailants had gunned down the BNP's municipality leader in Rajshahi City, the provincial capital. In February 2004, the nephew of a former BNP Parliamentarian from Rajshahi was shot and killed. Two more assassinations followed, targeting BNP leaders and their families—men who were close to Aminul Haque and his powerful allies. The police never apprehended the assailants, and their identities were never discovered. But local BNP activists immediately blamed members of the Awami League. According to a police report, one of Haque's close allies led a rampaging mob to Natore, an Awami League stronghold, and burned down nearly forty houses and shops.

It was only weeks later that Monwar became another of the victims of BNP. "As my son was one of the leading activists of the

Awami League student wing, he became one of the targets," Mohsin Ali said, adding that his son had never, to his knowledge, been involved in any attacks or any violence.

Clashes between the BNP and the Awami League were common, and had been for years. They could be violent, sometimes even deadly. But the attack on Monwar was of a different magnitude, for after killing Monwar, his attackers left his decapitated body as a warning, effectively announcing the birth of Jamaat-ul-Mujahideen Bangladesh.

Four days later, at around eleven in the morning of April 5, Ali heard the deafening roar of motorbike engines outside. Rushing to the door, he saw a large crowd descending on his farm, this time consisting of between 100 and 150 men. Some were armed with shotguns and pistols; others carried sticks and iron rods. As they shouted "Long live Aminul!" the mob began firing bullets into the air. Mohsin and Tahura hid in a small building on the farm, while their neighbors began to flee in panic. The mob proceeded to destroy Ali's house, reducing it to rubble. The job done, they chanted triumphantly, mounted their motorbikes, and disappeared behind a cloud of dust down the road.

Mohsin Ali was now convinced that Aminul Haque was implicated in his son's murder.

* * *

Aminul Haque was then sixty-one years old, with a crown of thick, wavy gray hair, a prominent nose, and eyes shaded behind large, darkened glasses. He was at the height of his career, the culmination of a long, illustrious rise to power in Bangladesh.

Haque was the scion of a prominent land-owning Bangladeshi

family. He had studied law in England and was called to the bar at Lincoln's Inn in 1974, at the age of thirty-one.[12] Returning to Bangladesh, he thrived and became a barrister, arguing cases before the nation's Supreme Court. In 1991, he ran as a BNP candidate in parliamentary elections, winning the seat for Rajshahi three times throughout the 1990s.

Rajshahi is a crucial vote bank in Bangladesh's fractured political landscape, as it is key to BNP's hold on power. Haque was instrumental in maintaining that hold. In 2001, he once again secured a seat there and the BNP won the national elections. In return, he was rewarded with the post of telecommunications minister, a coveted position overseeing projects worth billions of dollars. Haque became one of the most influential players in his party, a member of BNP's Central Executive Committee—and soon, a close ally of Tarique Rahman's. He was also the public face of Bangladesh's technological development and progress, often appearing at news conferences to extol the benefits of the new Teletalk initiative, and how it would reshape Bangladesh's future. In fact, that project was also reshaping his own future, making him extraordinarily rich.

Siemens had first arranged to bribe Haque in early 2002, when the company's management realized it would have to pay him to clinch the Teletalk deal. Mizanur Rahman, a close family friend of Haque's, approached Siemens about the arrangement. "He set up businesses specifically when Aminul Haque came to power, for the Siemens account. Mizanur was the one who was saying, 'Without me, there's no deal for Siemens,'" Saleh, the Bangladeshi investigator, explained.[13] By December 2002, Siemens Bangladesh entered into an agreement with Mizanur Rahman. As in many bribery cases, Rahman would serve as Aminul Haque's middleman, receiving a "consulting fee" that he would actually pass on to Haque as a bribe. Mizanur's contract stipulated that he would receive 5 percent of the overall BTTB contract if Siemens won—a total of roughly $3.75 million.

It is not clear how much money began flowing to Aminul Haque during that period, but he began working tirelessly behind the scenes to ensure that Siemens's bid got as far as the National Purchase Committee. He had been indispensable to Siemens's corrupt scheme—and their bribes appear to have been indispensable to his own designs.

In 2004, news of Monwar's murder made headlines across Bangladesh, shocking the country. Even more disturbing was the fact that JMB had continued its bloodshed, killing twenty-five people and maiming as many as five hundred in the span of four months, targeting many Awami League supporters. As the member of Parliament for Rajshahi, Haque was also in charge of its overall administration and public safety. When a police official pleaded with him for more resources to fight JMB, he alleged that Haque replied, "You don't have to worry because the prime minister and her sons know what is happening." Taken aback, the official replied, "I have to do something; it's my job." Haque then warned him, "You can't do anything, because that organization is sponsored by the highest level of government, the prime minister, her sons, the intelligence agencies."[14]

"Haque was supporting [JMB] and he asked me to support them," the police official recently recalled. Although nearly eleven years had passed since his encounter with Haque, he was still angry that he had been prevented from confronting JMB at a time when the group was still small and could possibly have been stopped. But he had soon found that he could no longer command his lower-ranking officers, who were taking orders from Haque. "If I asked them to arrest someone," the officer said, "they would send a message to the prime minister and they would stop me."

After Haque effectively neutralized the local police, JMB carved out Rajshahi as a base of operations. Around that time, Julfikar Ali Manik, a Bangladeshi journalist, traveled to the province and managed to interview the group's leader, Siddiqi Islam, who used the nickname Bangla Bhai, or Bangla Brother. Islam had received training in guerrilla warfare while fighting with the Taliban in Afghanistan. He boasted to the journalist that he now commanded ten thousand men,[15] a number there was no possible way to verify. But one afternoon the group held a large, raucous march through the center of Rajshahi City. Thousands of JMB supporters turned out, in a fleet of sixty buses and hundreds of motorbikes, and were escorted by police.[16] Word spread that Haque was openly patronizing the group.

Many people who knew Haque were shocked that a man of such standing was closely associated with terrorism in Bangladesh. "He was brilliant," one Western diplomat who knew Haque observed. "I thought he had outstanding analytical skills. And patience. That patience, and understanding of the larger picture and long-term goals, was what struck me."[17]

Haque and Tarique Rahman were not themselves religious fundamentalists. Their support of a terrorist group was almost purely strategic and political, according to a former criminal intelligence officer in Dhaka who has spent years tracking the rise of terrorism in Bangladesh. "Tarique Rahman probably does not pray five times a day—he doesn't want Shariah himself," the officer said.[18] "But he wanted to use the Islamists against his political rivals." He went on to describe the Faustian deal that Haque and Rahman forged with Bangla Bhai and JMB: "By giving shelter to these groups, they wanted to use them to get rid of Awami League. The Islamists, on the other hand, got shelter and political support and patronization, which helped them to press their campaign."

But the situation soon got out of control, the officer continued. He described JMB as a monster that eventually developed a will of its own, styling itself after the Taliban in Afghanistan. "JMB went against BNP," the officer explained. "It created a crisis for BNP. There was a clash between the militants and their patrons."

The rift between them exploded, literally, on August 17, 2005. That morning, JMB operatives simultaneously detonated nearly five hundred small bombs in sixty-three of the sixty-four districts in Bangladesh. No one was killed, but casualties were not the point: JMB was sending a signal that its ambitions had grown beyond the confines of merely killing Awami League supporters in provincial Rajshahi. It now wanted an Islamic state and was willing to go to war against anyone, including its former patrons, who stood in its way.

Immediately after the attacks, local newspapers reported that Bangladesh's intelligence agencies and police officials scrambled to answer a pressing question. An attack of this scale indicated that JMB had sophisticated training, a large national network, bomb experts, and access to lethal material. Where had the funding for the group come from?[19]

Coincidentally, on August 18, 2005, a day after the attacks, as banks records later showed, Siemens Corporation wired $150,000 into a Hong Kong bank account. The money was a bribe for Aminul Haque.

* * *

In 2009, Debra LaPrevotte and Linda Samuel sat in a secure location in Dhaka, a kind of safe house provided by Bangladesh's military police. Their surroundings looked like an ordinary conference room, with a large table and office chairs. LaPrevotte had made several trips to Bangladesh over the past year, most of them with Samuel. Together the women had developed a good working relationship with Bangladesh's generals and the ACC. In the United States and Germany, the Siemens bribery case had already been adjudicated and brought to a close, and the company, having done its penance, had essentially moved on. But the work of tracking the bribes, bringing to justice those who had taken them, and understanding what role they might have played in the cycle of violence and militancy in Bangladesh was still under way.

Neither Tarique Rahman nor his brother, Koko, would be questioned by the women that day. In September 2008, Tarique had won bail on medical grounds and immediately flew to London. "With deep political ties that reach the highest court in the land, Tarique managed to manipulate the judicial process and overcome a concerted effort by the Caretaker Government to block his bail," a State Department cable leaked by Wikileaks reported.[20] Koko also secured bail on medical grounds, flying first to a hospital in Bangkok, and then moving to Malaysia, where he was rumored to own a mansion.

In the brothers' absence, the military arranged for LaPrevotte and Samuel to interview suspects, informants, middlemen, and mules in the Siemens scandal. The men were picked up by Bangladesh's military police and brought to the undisclosed location. The atmosphere was tense; many of those brought in cried, knowing they might be threatened or harmed for speaking with the FBI.

The Americans took a soft approach, telling them, "Look, we are helping the government to fight corruption. We have an ongoing investigation regarding Siemens. We understand that you have information. We want you to know that this is voluntary; you're welcome to leave at any time."[21] Some did leave, but most stayed. Many had worked closely with the Rahman brothers and began to reveal their secrets. "You'd be surprised how many people want to talk because they want their country to be better than it is," a former FBI investigator noted.

Among those brought in were Fezle Selim and Zulfikar Ali, Siemens's principal middlemen in the bribery scheme. Selim acknowledged that the money he received from Siemens was used for bribes, and told the Americans that a Siemens executive directed the entire scheme, deciding which "government officials were to receive bribe payments and how much to pay them."[22] Ali alleged that Haque and other officials picked Siemens for the Tele-talk project not because it offered the best deal for the country, but because the bribes promised to enrich them personally.

Over hours and days of meetings with informants, a picture began to emerge of the Siemens black money flow. LaPrevotte and her colleagues not only confirmed the bribes going to Aminul Haque and Koko, but also learned of a previously unknown trail: Selim and Ali would take portions of the money they received from Siemens and pass it on to Tarique Rahman.

"The Siemens money went to [Tarique] in cash. It was removed from accounts in *taka* [the local Bangladeshi currency]. We interviewed people who said, 'We would wait. We would either be asked to courier it over to him.' Or he would come by their office and pick it up. Or he would send a representative," an FBI investigator said. By using agents upon agents to move cash, Tarique created an intricate system of layering, distancing himself from the source of the bribes and from culpability. "It was said that people would fly out of Bangladesh with suitcases full of Tarique's money to places like Dubai," Salahuddin Ahmad recalled. Koko, who had been less careful, had had Siemens's money wired directly to his Singapore account. "In Koko's case, it was foolishly transparent."

Siemens's internal investigation had traced a total of $5.3 million in wire transfers paid as bribes in Bangladesh. The company continued to pay Aminul Haque for a year after the August bomb attacks, in large tranches of $250,000 or $340,000. They added up to $1.7 million in total, all wired to the bank account of Mizanur Rahman. The agents Ali and Selim together received $3.2 million, of which they dispersed more than $2.2 million. It is unclear how much of their distribution ended up in Tarique's pockets. The FBI declined to comment, citing an ongoing investigation, as did Saleh.

There may be even more money unaccounted for. Witnesses interviewed by Samuel and LaPrevotte told them the total amount of bribes paid in the Teletalk deal was actually closer to $12 million.[23] It is possible that Tarique and Aminul received much more than has previously been reported.

A State Department cable, leaked by Wikileaks, suggests that the Teletalk payments were only part of the Siemens money allocated to Tarique Rahman: "According to a witness who funneled bribes from Siemens to Tarique and his brother Koko, Tarique received a bribe of approximately two percent on all Siemens deals in Bangladesh [paid in U.S. dollars]."[24] If the witness is correct, it means Siemens paid potentially tens of millions of dollars in bribes to Rahman while his mother was in power between 2001 and 2006.

Her time in Bangladesh left LaPrevotte wondering: "Bribery

has a domino effect. Millions of dollars for contracts are coming into the country. Where's it going?"

*  *  *

The investigator Saleh is an anti-money laundering expert, and an operator with influence at the highest levels of power in Bangladesh. He is not officially part of the government, and therefore not bound by its bureaucratic rules. Instead, he occupies a kind of gray zone, conducting his work in the shadows.

While over the past decade the U.S. government has demonstrated its commitment to fighting corporate bribery, its legal jurisdiction, policy mandate, and resources stretch only so far. As a result, its prosecutions almost never extend to the aftermath of bribery. Likewise, companies are never penalized based on how bribed foreign officials like Aminul Haque may actually use the money they receive.

Saleh, however, has spent years following the track of these funds. Having closely analyzed the Siemens bribes, he has grown increasingly concerned by the nexus between Bangladesh's crippling corruption; the millions in corporate bribes allegedly paid to Aminul Haque, Tarique Rahman, and Koko; and Bangladesh's rising Islamist terrorism.

A former military officer with combat experience, he conducts himself in a deeply focused, almost grave manner. His anticorruption efforts have made him many enemies in Bangladesh, and he keeps his identity hidden out of concern not so much for his own safety, but for that of his family, which he moved out of Bangladesh as a precaution.

In recent weeks, Saleh had picked up Haque's trail, tracing

him to a rented house near a park about ninety minutes outside of Dhaka. Since his role in fomenting JMB was unmasked, Haque had became a master of hiding At first, Prime Minister Khaleda Zia and other BNP leaders denied the existence of Bangla Bhai and JMB, dismissing them as fabrications of the media. But when JMB's suicide bombers struck in November 2005, killing eleven people and wounding a hundred—the first suicide attacks in the country's history—the government was forced to act.[25] A nationwide police dragnet captured Bangla Bhai and five other JMB leaders in March 2006. A year later, when the military took power, all six were hanged.

For years, Mohsin Ali, Monwar's father, had lived in fear, but with the extremist group seemingly neutralized, he filed a lawsuit against Haque in Rajshahi, holding him responsible for his son's death. Other victims of JMB reported that Bangla Bhai was often on the phone with Aminul Haque, who sometimes directed their torture.[26] The police also filed a case against Haque at the same time, so the two cases were merged.

Based on eyewitness testimony, Judge Rezaul Islam of the Second Additional Sessions Judge's Court in Rajshahi convicted the former minister and seventeen other JMB supporters of attempted murder, kidnapping, and abetting militancy—the first such judgment in Bangladesh's history. Islam accused Haque of personally orchestrating many of JMB's attacks and condemned the violence as a distortion of Islam. In July 2007, Haque was sentenced in absentia to thirty-one and half years in prison. At the sentencing, Nurul Islam, the public prosecutor, said, "Aminul and other politicians directly and indirectly financed and patronized the JMB."[27]

Neither Islam nor anyone else involved in the case was aware then that part of that funding may have come from Siemens's bribes. I first reported that in 2009, in a series of stories for *PBS Frontline/World,* the *Christian Science Monitor*, and *Der Spiegel*.[28] In response to my stories, the Bangladeshi government announced it was forming a parliamentary committee to probe whether money from Siemens had been used to fund JMB.[29] The committee, however, never released its findings, and the role of Siemens bribes has remained a mystery.

For his part, Saleh was convinced that "some of the money definitely went to terrorism. Terrorists raise money in different ways. But the bribery money is one source, categorically. Corporations are funding religiously motivated, terrorist violence." He noted that Haque received more than the $1.7 million that Siemens wired to Mizanur Rahman. Siemens's consultants also paid Haque in large amounts of untraceable cash, as they had Tarique Rahman. "Huawei also bribed Aminul," he added, referring to the Chinese company that partnered with Siemens on the deal. (The FBI has never investigated Huawei's alleged bribes, and the company has never been accused of any wrongdoing.)

Saleh's allegations have been confirmed by a Bangladeshi intelligence officer assigned to the country's internal security wing. In that role he personally questioned leaders of both JMB and an affiliated group called Harakat-ul-Jihad-Islami (HUJI), which is known to have links to Al Qaeda. "When we interrogated leaders of JMB and HUJI, we came to know about the role of corruption. The same money is moving around. Sometimes it goes into the banks of the terrorists; sometimes in the hands of the people behind the terrorists," the intelligence officer explained.[30] "Categorically they mentioned the name of Aminul Haque and Tarique. [Haque] supported them morally and financially." Neither Saleh nor the intelligence officer have evidence directly establishing that

Haque gave portions of the Siemens bribes directly to JMB, but any money he might have passed to them would almost certainly have been delivered in cash.

Both Saleh and the intelligence officer said that JMB had not been defeated but had merely gone underground. The group had metastasized and become better trained and more lethal. Its membership no longer consisted of the poorly educated madrassah students who formed its core when the group began, as a recent counterterrorism operation revealed. "In one night, we apprehended seven members of JMB," the intelligence officer described. "Out of the seven, six were educated from private universities. One guy was from North-South University," which is considered one of the most liberal universities in Bangladesh. "They were highly radicalized," the intelligence officer continued. "They were ready to die. They were ready to go to Pakistan and then to Syria. They wanted to fight with the Islamic State."

\* \* \*

In January 2009, the Justice Department filed a forfeiture action in Washington, D.C., against $2 million held in Koko Rahman's Singapore account (in addition to the $180,000 from Siemens, the balance was a bribe that had been paid by a Chinese construction company for a port infrastructure project), as well as the combined $1 million that remained in Ali and Selim's Singapore accounts. The DOJ, claiming jurisdiction on the grounds the bribes had been paid in dollars and routed through American banks, hoped that once the combined $3 million was seized, it would be given to Bangladesh and earmarked as funds to support the Anti-Corruption Commission.

To do so, however, they needed Singapore's consent and assistance, and Singapore was resisting cooperating. "The Singaporeans were basically worried about the precedent of people going after slimy money through their legal system because they get a lot of play," a former State Department official with long experience in the region explained.[31] "So they were faced with this conundrum of what's more important: being a good international player, or is it protecting the funds of, frankly, slime bags? And ultimately they came along."

When the Singaporean authorities finally froze Koko's Zasz Trading account, and he responded through his lawyers that the account did not belong to him, LaPrevotte produced a copy of Zasz's bank records, including a passport photo, obtained through international law enforcement contacts, that he had used to open the account. Koko continued to disavow his ownership, which ultimately worked in the DOJ's favor. With no one coming forward to claim the money, the DOJ was granted a default judgment. Both the U.S. and Singapore waived rights to the funds, and the $2 million was given to Bangladesh's ACC.

It was a small but important victory. LaPrevotte and Saleh, Samuel and Ahmad had established the foundation for a model of international cooperation. "What we have created is nascent, but if there's any hope, we have to keep it running," Saleh said.

The disastrous outcome of the Teletalk project underscored why fighting this kind of bribery was so vital. In 2009, a task force formed to examine the project found that Aminul Haque's poor management, coupled with corruption and delays, had led to losses of $30 million. The project was stalled for years, the probe report found, because Haque was working behind the scenes to ensure that Siemens won the bid. Teletalk never succeeded in building a subscriber base, and today accounts for only 1 percent of Bangladesh's 95 million mobile phone subscribers.[32] "Today Teletalk is so small as to be almost irrelevant," a 2012 market study of corruption in Bangladesh's telecom industry states.

LaPrevotte's team went after more. They were not able to trace Aminul Haque's money, but in 2011 they filed a tax evasion case against Mizanur Rahman, who'd acted as Haque's agent.

Then it set its sights on an even bigger target: Tarique Rahman. The Bangladeshi government did not yet have the evidence to charge Rahman with money laundering—or any of the sixteen charges, including murder, that were pending against him—and they could not seize his money because they did not know where it had been hidden. "He was known to have taken so much, and had set up a parallel government for giving out contracts. Here is the guy who is the most corrupt but we can't touch him," Ahmad said. "Bringing him to justice had symbolic value."

But at around the same time that LaPrevotte had been interviewing informants, a businesswoman named Khadiza Islam came forward to the police. Islam was the local agent of Harbin Energy, a Chinese firm pursuing a government contract for a power plant in Tongi, a town about two hours from Dhaka. After Harbin won the tender, the company paid a $750,000 bribe into an account that Tarique controlled in Singapore. Through official requests to Singapore, LaPrevotte obtained his Citibank records and traced how he'd been using portions of the Harbin bribe to make purchases around the world. It was the most direct evidence they had tying Tarique to money laundering.

Because it was LaPrevotte who had discovered the evidence, it was she who would have to testify in person in Bangladesh if its authorities wanted to use it. An FBI agent had never before given testimony in a Bangladeshi court.

On November 16, 2011, LaPrevotte and Samuel boarded a plane east. Days before they left, Samuel had taken LaPrevotte aside. "I just want you to know I have breast cancer," she told her, "so I might have to leave early." LaPrevotte, taken aback, told her, "You do whatever you need to do. Don't go if you don't need to go." But Samuel insisted on accompanying her.

LaPrevotte provided an hour and a half of testimony about Tarique's money laundering and submitted nearly three hundred pages of evidence.[33] "There was extreme resistance from Tarique's lawyers. People who were in charge said that under the law it could not be done, that an FBI agent cannot come testify," Saleh said. "But we did it."

*　*　*

On June 21, 2016, Bangladesh's High Court issued a landmark decision, finding Tarique Rahman guilty of money laundering and sentencing him in absentia to seven years imprisonment. The verdict was the first time in a decade-long legal battle that Tarique was convicted of a crime.[34] According to Bangladeshi law, the conviction means he might be barred from ever participating in politics again. Although the court's verdict was not directly tied to the Siemens case, it was an important offshoot of that investigation, and possible only because of the unique and sustained cooperation between the FBI and the Bangladeshi government.

Tragically, Linda Samuel did not live to see the result of her efforts. She died of cancer on September 13, 2013.[35] But the court's decision in Bangladesh marked a fitting end to Debra LaPrevotte's FBI career. She had retired only months earlier, though she now works as a corruption investigator for the Sentry, a nonprofit organization formed by George Clooney and John Prendergast. Still traveling the world, LaPrevotte investigates how political leaders in countries like Somalia and the Congo use the proceeds of corruption to fund conflict and civil war.

Two weeks after Tarique Rahman was convicted, five armed militants stormed a Western-style café popular among foreign expatriates in Dhaka. After hurling grenades, they took hostages and began separating the non-Muslim customers from the Muslims. As the siege continued overnight, JMB took credit for the attack, announcing that it had aligned itself with ISIS, the international terrorist group based in Syria. By morning, the police had killed all seven militants, but not before the JMB members had killed eighteen foreigners, the worst such attack in Bangladesh's history.[36] Tarique's conviction and the incident were not directly related, but they crystallized how long Bangladesh had been battling corruption and terrorism—and how both tie back to Aminul Haque, the bribes Siemens paid him, and Monwar's murder.

Haque remains a fugitive. He has appeared in public just once, in 2009, when he unexpectedly turned himself in on charges related to amassing illegal wealth.[37] He spent only four months behind bars before securing bail, then vanished again.[38] Since then, he has used a battery of lawyers and his own influence at the courts to stay, halt, and overturn at least thirteen cases filed against him for extortion, bribery, corruption, and money laundering. In April 2011, Haque successfully appealed his conviction for supporting

JMB.[39] At the hearing, the presiding judges criticized the prosecution for bringing a case on what they called flimsy evidence. The prosecution, however, has filed an appeal, which is now pending before the Supreme Court.

In 2012, the ACC filed a new case against Haque and Mizanur Rahman for laundering the $1.7 million the former minister allegedly received in bribes from Siemens. Haque is currently fighting the charge.[40] The outcome of Haque's terrorism and corruption cases will prove one of the most important tests in Bangladesh's ongoing struggle for justice.

"What is going to happen if this corruption and violence goes unchecked, and BNP comes back to power?" Saleh asked. "Aminul Haque will become a bigger minister. When Aminul comes back to power, these people killing people, they will become part of his government. They will say to him, 'I worked for you, to come to power; you should reward me.' That same violent entourage will became part of the police force, the administration," he said. "This would be scary not only for Bangladesh, but the whole region."

The cycle of violence is a genuine threat to people like Mohsin Ali. Even more than a decade after Monwar's execution, they are still living in fear. "Because they killed my son already, they will not delay to kill us," Tahura said about JMB operatives in the area. "The only protection we have is Allah, nothing else."

"The local JMB operatives, they live around this village and they sit together in the tea stall, in the bazaar. They often tell me that they will kill me when the Awami League government is not in power," Ali said. He had received such a threat only two weeks earlier, when JMB supporters told him, "We will kill all the people who accused us."

* * *

When the Justice Department announced its settlement with Siemens, government representatives at the subsequent news conference alluded to damage, though they tended to speak in broad terms about corruption and not discuss the actual impact of Siemens's bribes. "International corruption weakens good governance," Joseph Persichini said in public remarks at the time. "It inhibits social and economic development, and it tears at the very fabric of the public trust in corporations, government and the ideals of fundamental fairness." More generally, though, officials from Justice, the FBI, and the IRS discussed how bribery undermines competition and distorts the free market system.

By reinforcing the idea that these bribes, while bad for the free market, have no impact in the countries where they are paid, the companies responsible are simply allowed to pay a fine—again, a fine for a white-collar crime—with no acknowledgment of the harm they may have done to local communities. But as the framers of the FCPA recognized from its inception, bribery does have a terrible impact—socially, politically, economically and otherwise—which is why a law was enacted to prohibit it in the first place.

Likewise, nearly two thousand stories about Siemens have been published in American and English-language newspapers, magazines, legal journals, and web-based publications. It is one of the most widely discussed corruption cases, particularly as regards its legal implications and the sheer amount of money involved. Yet there does not appear to be a single story among them that has explored the effect the bribes may have had in any of the dozens of countries where they were paid.

It is only by tracing the consequences of these payments, by uncovering the stories of its victims, that we can begin to comprehend the full extent of the damage caused by foreign corporate bribery.

# Chapter 9

# Flash Bang

By January 18, 2010, Richard Bistrong had spent nearly three years cobbling together the most significant deal of his life. After more than a thousand days of negotiations, and twenty thousand text messages typed out on his phone, his anxiety over it had been inescapable, and not even his punishing runs through the park could calm him. When he caught sight of a convoy of SUVs approaching where he waited at a remote meeting point outside the city, he finally began to feel a sense of relief.

Bistrong is tall and fit at fifty-five, with a scholarly air. He had hoped to be a professor of foreign policy but for twenty years had been a prosperous arms salesman, having been born into the business, a family venture that sold body armor. Later he became vice president of international sales for Armor Holdings, one of the largest weapons brokers in the world, whose clients included regimes across the Middle East and Latin America.[1] He sold them grenades and outfitted their presidential guard in crooked backroom deals.

Bistrong had long since lost his way in life. Although his salary was at an all-time high and he had luxury cars and a condo in Florida, he was frequenting prostitutes and had a fifteen-thousand-dollar-a-month cocaine habit. He lied and cheated, led double and triple lives, and had a secret Swiss bank account. Bribery was the easy part: Lie on a regulatory form here, concoct a fake receipt there. Nobody got hurt. His company didn't care; law enforcement didn't care. He was a veteran now, traveling from one foreign capital to another, paying the kickbacks, getting the sales, booking the bonuses to Zurich.

But this deal would be different, for Bistrong was wearing a wire. He'd been indicted and was now the covert informant in one of the longest-running undercover white-collar stings in U.S. history. When his government had given him a choice—either help it or go to jail—he'd answered the call. The DOJ wanted to apprehend the individuals who bribed, and not merely fine the corporations that employed them.

* * *

Washington, D.C.'s Bond Building was constructed in 1901 at the corner of Fourteenth and New York Avenue, a Gilded-Age icon in the heart of the capital's eastern district. Its facade, squat and heavily articulated in the Beaux-Arts style, has been said to reflect a "sort of highfalutin street-wise charm."[2] That description might also suit the building's main tenants: the Fraud Section of the Criminal Division of the Justice Department. The Fraud Section then occupied the fourth floor, Asset Forfeiture the tenth. In early 2010, the Justice Department's newly formulated FCPA Unit took over the entire eleventh floor. On moving in, Charles "Chuck" Duross, the FCPA Unit's chief, felt "we've arrived."[3] From their perch overlooking the financial district, Duross and a small handful of attorneys set out to change the course of international commerce.

Tall and portly with an avuncular demeanor, Chuck Duross began his career in Miami, where federal prosecutors typically work drug cases and organized crime. They build cases that put people in jail and learn to be quick on their feet in the courtroom. In his new position, Duross had upwards of twenty prosecutors reporting to him. Energized and a bit overwhelmed, he sat down with his team and began, as he recalled it, "cleaning out files."

The Fraud Section's FCPA caseload had recently ballooned, and in the past four years its prosecutors had collected a record $4 billion in fines from some of the largest corporations in the world, including Baker Hughes, Lucent, and Volvo. Their investigations had made headlines and changed perceptions in international law enforcement, not to mention business circles, about what the FCPA could accomplish. With greater success came more resources. Lanny Breuer, assistant attorney general for the Criminal Division, lobbied for funding to hire more FCPA prosecutors to "institution-alize the unit," as he would later recall.[4] The eleventh floor soon became a hive of activity, staffed with paralegals and a team of translators who pored over evidence in a range of languages. The unit also hired contractors skilled in the forensic accounting of complex criminal bribery transactions. These additional resources increased the number of leads to beyond what Duross and his team could possibly follow.

"I remember being increasingly intimidated by the cases that were pending," Duross remembered. "Publicly the DOJ said a hun-dred and fifty cases—but there were even more than that. You need to make tough calls about what was worth pursuing."

Many former FCPA prosecutors described the process as triage. Given their constraints, a resolution ending in a settlement rather than a lengthy trial was often in their best interest—not to mention in the best interests of the companies themselves. FCPA prosecu-tors settled a majority of these cases through what are known as deferred prosecution agreements, or DPAs. First implemented in corporate cases in the 1990s, DPAs are a novel legal instrument.[5] In the past, the Justice Department either brought criminal charges against a corporation and tried to win a conviction, or it did not.[6] But corporate convictions were not only difficult for Justice to prove; they could also be catastrophic for the corporation in question, leading to debarment from government contracts, for example, and potential bankruptcy.

A DPA is a compromise for both sides, a legal gray zone. The federal government extracts a fine from the guilty company relative to the scope and severity of its bribery, and often seizes the amount of profit it generated from the kickbacks. The agreement also provides that the company agrees to address its problems, including by terminating employees deemed responsible for engaging in bribery; instituting tighter internal controls, such as better and more accurate records of transactions; and implementing a robust anti-bribery compliance program, such as training employees. If after a period of time designated by the Justice Department—usually three years—the company successfully demonstrates that is has reformed, Justice agrees to drop the charges. As part of a deferred prosecution agreement, a company also typically publicly admits to the criminal wrongdoing alleged by Justice, which is not the same as pleading guilty. Companies that settle civil charges with the SEC, however, neither "admit nor deny" their misconduct.

As the FCPA focus of the Fraud Section expanded, so too did the number of DPAs it issued (as did nonprosecution agreements (NPAs), where the department extracts a fine but, because of a company's proactive cooperation, declines to prosecute altogether). In 2009, only 24 percent of FCPA cases were settled through DPAs or NPAs, according to one analysis. By 2010, it had risen to 40 percent.[7] These continued to result in hundreds of millions in fines and penalties, and while they led to a dramatic change in corporate behavior, many people within the Justice Department wondered: Where was the justice? Few of those directly responsible for millions of dollars in bribery were going to jail. Many wanted that leniency to change.

Paul Pelletier, a twenty-five-year DOJ veteran who was then principal deputy chief of the Fraud Section, was one of them. "My belief, in the corporate environment, is that if you don't do executive prosecutions that you're not going to have an impact," he said.[8] "Otherwise the company's just going to pay the speeding ticket. You're not going to have the culture change that you need to make this whole endeavor worthwhile."

Half a mile away, at an office complex on H Street, at the edge of Chinatown, is the home of the FBI's FCPA squad, officially known as the International Corruption Unit (ICU). Agents from the ICU conduct investigations in tandem with the DOJ, often traveling repeatedly to foreign countries to gather evidence and interview witnesses. Like the DOJ's FCPA Unit, by 2010 the FBI's squad had dramatically grown in size and resources, to as many as 15 investigators. They, too, wanted to see executives behind bars.

"They got into this to put hands on bodies," a former senior FBI official said of his agents. "They wanted to be unleashed. At the end of the day, we're all about holding the individual responsible."[9]

"I'm a big believer that you have to hold institutions accountable, but you have to hold the individuals accountable," agreed Lanny Breuer, who oversaw all FCPA prosecution policy between 2009 and 2013. "But candidly, at that point, not a single executive had been prosecuted. And to me that was a problem."

In fact, Breuer had been traveling around the country, and often the world, making this very point.

Breuer, Pelletier, and Duross determined that to accomplish that they had to have attorneys who could argue the cases. "The prosecutors who came on from law firms were all bright and hard-working. But they had little trial experience," Duross explained. "You need to know how to prove a case." Duross reached out to federal prosecutors in Miami and convinced several to join the unit. Breuer, meanwhile, recruited hard-nosed litigators like Jeffrey Knox, a former terrorism prosecutor from New York.

In January 2010, in Las Vegas, the FBI arrested twenty-two executives from sixteen international arms companies and charged them with intent to pay bribes to high-ranking officials in the African nation of Gabon. It was to be single the largest bribery prosecution of individuals ever undertaken by the DOJ—a landmark in the enforcement of the FCPA. The operation was made possible by a secret ace that the DOJ and the FBI had been hiding up their sleeve: a former high-flying arms executive named Richard Bistrong.

*  *  *

By the time the Justice Department got its hands on Bistrong, he had broken nearly a dozen laws in the United States and around the world. Among other criminal activities, he had bribed government officials in several countries, embezzled from his own company, lied on his taxes, laundered money, carried unlawful amounts of currency across international borders, and transported illicit substances. He could be convicted for twenty years on the money laundering charges alone—unless he cooperated with Justice.

Sometime in 2007, a whistleblower at Armor Holdings discovered that Bistrong had bribed officials at the United Nations in order to win a contract, and that he been laundering money. Management investigated and fired Bistrong in May; a month later his wife filed for divorce. His drug habit, meanwhile, had gotten out of control. Just when he thought his situation couldn't get any worse, in June 2007 his lawyer received a phone call notifying him that Armor Holdings had reported Bistrong's bribery to the Justice Department. "We'd like for him to come in and talk to us," Bistrong remembers a federal prosecutor telling his lawyer.

Bistrong's descent into bribery had begun around 2000, as he began to do more and more business in underdeveloped countries like Bolivia and Nigeria. "I started to hear the talk of: I have to 'take care of' a foreign end user to win the contract. I have to 'take care' of this person," Bistrong recalled. He added that in a large multimillion-dollar arms sale, the actual act of bribery often begins with just one sales executive negotiating with a middle-man, an agent who represents a foreign government. At times an official of that government might be present as well, and the trans-action might take place over a simple dinner. Whatever the case, few words are involved, and "bribe" is certainly not one of them. "You're witness to something that is going on in front of you in a language that is not your own," Bistrong described. "You don't understand it. The agent's not telling you, 'By the way, I just paid the guy a bribe.' That's never directly articulated." But as Bistrong explained, intuition told him that something was wrong. "It's red flags you can see. You clearly know that you should be calling your company, walking away, but at the same time I've deceived myself it's necessary for getting the tender."

Bribery, he continued, is also driven by an individual sales executive's fears, as "it can be catastrophic to think about what happens if you don't make your numbers." Elaborating on his own case, he recalled: "At the time, I'm traveling two hundred and fifty days a year overseas. I would fly to England over a Sunday night, go to work Monday, take the next flight out on Friday. I'm now responsible for $100 million in sales. There was a constant anxiety about this."

When the Justice Department contacted him, Bistrong was apprehensive, but he was also ready to cooperate. "I had lived a life that was very off the tracks—I lost the closeness of my family, my friends, my religion," he explained. "Going into the government gave me an introspective chance to think about what I had been doing—to come clean, not just with the government, but with the way I had been living." In a conference room at Main Justice, in the Robert F. Kennedy Building on Constitution Avenue, Bistrong spoke with Joey Lipton, a DOJ attorney, and two FBI agents. "It's a line in the sand," Lipton told Bistrong. "No matter what you did in the past, now you're here."

As a crime, international corporate bribery is nearly impossible to uncover. Federal law enforcement, by its own admission, is often at a loss as to how to identify it. "Most of our crime problems are easy to detect. You know how many banks were robbed last year. But how do we keep a handle on this?" one FBI agent explained.[10] Investigators often fumble in the dark to uncover leads. "We've got no great technology," Duross said. "It's all smoke and mirrors." The DOJ often has to wait for someone to come forward to crack open a bribery case. Sometimes it is a whistleblower who believes his company has committed a crime; sometimes it is the company itself after discovering that its employees have committed bribery overseas, because they usually receive lower fines in return for their assistance. Still, because most do not self-report their criminal activity, federal prosecutors are often forced to react to bribery, rather than proactively exposing it. "And in this business you have to be proactive to be effective," Pelletier explains.

Bistrong presented an opportunity to change this dynamic. He revealed a great deal at that first session, not only about how bribery works, but how it feels, psychologically. He talked about what goes on in the mind of the executives who bribe. He was effectively an encyclopedia of bribery, not only of what he himself had committed, but of a global culture of kickbacks in the $50 billion arms industry, stretching from Ecuador to Turkey, from Amsterdam to Nigeria. He personally knew dozens of crooked arms dealers, agents, and distributors, including many based in the United States. "I talked a lot about what I had witnessed," Bistrong said. "You're giving them a window into the defense export business—a window onto an industry."

At their second meeting, several weeks later in July, Agent Chris Forvour asked Bistrong whether he would be willing to wear a wire. "We'd like you to meet with some of your business acquaintances, agree to record them, and discuss with these individuals what you shared with us," Bistrong remembers the FBI saying. He immediately said yes.

In their escalating war on foreign bribery, the DOJ and FBI had stumbled upon the ultimate insider. Through him they would have an informer in the clandestine world of corruption in the arms industry, or at least a small corner of it. They were certainly taking a risk, as Bistrong was a wild card—a recovering drug addict with a history of lying, and a criminal. But as one former FBI official said, "You're not going to get the devil by dealing only with angels. Every source is going to have some bag of shit." Still, many were uneasy, most of all Bistrong. "Just remember," Forvour reassured him, "the FBI always wins eventually, and you are on the right team."[11]

*  *  *

The federal rules of evidence stipulate that, to validate a conviction, a federal prosecutor must prove his or her version of events beyond a reasonable doubt. He or she must prove every element of a crime in a way that a jury can reach no logical conclusion other than that a defendant is guilty. The burden of proof required in "beyond a reasonable doubt" is intentionally high because the consequences of a criminal conviction are often so severe—the potential loss of personal liberty being foremost.

In FCPA cases, the Justice Department has the burden of proving the intent to bribe. It is not necessary to establish that a bribe was actually paid; proving that a promise was made to pay a bribe is sufficient. The question is: Within a large corporation, whom does a prosecutor hold responsible for the intent to pay a bribe, and how can it be proven beyond a reasonable doubt?

In any criminal case, proving individual intent is challenging. But foreign bribery cases add an additional layer of complexity. In a sprawling bribery scheme, where money has been funneled among several countries, it could take prosecutors months just to determine where to look for evidence, such as bank records, and then several months more to obtain those records through requests for mutual legal assistance. "You figure out the first country, you send the MLAT, it takes months," Duross explained. "You get the bank records after months and you realize that the money stayed there for a day." If the money was sent elsewhere and then disappeared, a prosecutor has to begin the process all over again.

FBI agents on the ground in foreign countries do not necessarily fare better. They are often out of their depth, working without dependable allies. "You can't trust anybody. You're in a world where you not sure what to believe. There are health concerns. The travel concerns," Joseph Persichini said. The Bureau and the State Department have spent years building bridges to foreign law enforcement in developing countries like Bangladesh and Nigeria. But those bridges, which are supposed to make the gathering of evidence easier, are often sacrificed to shield those in power. "You're really not going to get much help if you're in, say, a fictitious African country and you're investigating bribery that links to the president," a high-ranking official from the FBI's Corruption Squad said.

More than a dozen former and current federal law enforcement officials, including from the Justice Department and the FBI, were unanimous is stating that even when evidence is obtained—bank records, internal company emails, documents—it is still exceedingly difficult to prove that any given individual had the intent to bribe. The people who commit bribery obviously try to hide it, so evidence is seldom definitive. "It's very rare that you have the smoking gun document," as one former prosecutor explained. Moreover, to establish that a bank record or an email demonstrates individual intent, prosecutors need live witnesses willing to testify in court to make the case to a jury. Like the evidence, however, relevant witnesses tend to be thousands of miles away. Merely locating them is difficult enough, but securing their cooperation is often impossible. "The main person may be in Brazil, and Brazil doesn't extradite its own citizens. If that person says I'm not going to come, that's it," another former prosecutor described. "How are you going to get a witness statement out of Nigeria?" Duross asked. There is also the matter of the statute of limitations for individual prosecutions, which is five years after the bribes were allegedly paid.

If establishing intent for any individual is challenging enough, establishing it for high-level executives—CEOS and CFOs, for example—is often impossible, particularly in large corporations, law enforcement officials also stressed. "A lot of times you can establish acts from individuals at the transaction level. But it's almost like organized crime levels. How do you get to the boss? Even when you suspect they're knowledgeable, it's very difficult," a former FBI official said.

The greater the FBI and DOJ grew in size and resources, the more intently they were able to focus on targeting individuals—only to discover, however, that they lacked adequate means, because individual prosecutions require the collection of sufficient evidence. "It's a resource issue," Duross explained. "If you're going to bring a case against one of the largest companies in the world, you need to have more than two people working on it." In the early days of the FCPA Unit, two dozen prosecutors each had, on average, more than six complex cases to handle,

Smoking-gun evidence, a credible witness to testify before a jury, accessible defendants, and sufficient resources were all available in the Richard Bistrong sting.

Wiretap surveillance would record telephone and in-person conversations, and emails and text messages would be monitored. The suspects were all based in the United States, or traveled frequently there, so there would be no difficulty in securing their arrest and trial. Finally, the operation would be well-staffed. At its height, nearly a dozen FBI agents and three prosecutors would run the sting, one of the largest undercover surveillance operations the Fraud Section ever mounted. The operation was codenamed Alternate Breach.

A lot was riding on Alternate Breach, for if successful, it would demonstrate not only that the Justice Department was serious and capable of bringing individual prosecutions, but that it was proactively pursuing such a course, rather than simply being reactive. As the sting was set into motion, Lanny Breuer was especially tense. "Don't lose this case." he told the FCPA Unit, according to one former prosecutor, "because I'm going around the world talking about it."[12]

*  *  *

After gathering in Las Vegas to attend an annual arms trade show, twenty-one arms executives headed out to the desert in six SUVs to close a $15 million arms sale that Richard Bistrong brokered between their companies and the government of Gabon. The group included wealthy international businessmen, independent weapons distributors, and senior managers from large companies like Smith & Wesson. Some were even men of considerable national prestige, like R. Patrick Caldwell, a former deputy assistant director of the Secret Service who was now the CEO of the body armor company PPI. Bistrong would greet them, demo some of the equipment— the contract provided for weapons, ammunition, and armored vehicles for Gabon's presidential guard—and then introduce them to the Gabonese defense minister—or so they had been told.

As the vehicles traveled down road to the destination, the drivers simultaneously veered off in different directions all of a sudden, and then came to an abrupt stop. The doors of the SUVs were flung open by FBI agents in full tactical gear, assault rifles drawn. Amid the panic and confusion, agents dragged the men from the vehicles, handcuffed them, and then whisked them into a prefabricated building set up to conduct interrogations. To keep up the charade, Bistrong was handcuffed and taken with them.

At the secure location, a long table had been set up with twenty-two boxes lined up atop it. Each had a photograph of one of the defendants, with his name, date of birth, and the words "Armed and Dangerous" written on it. One of the men arrested that day remembers feeling sickened when he saw his box. "It [was] crushing seeing that," he recalled, as he was a businessman, not a criminal.[13] Equally crushing, he added, was noticing that the FBI agents led Bistrong off in a different direction. Later, the executive realized that everyone arrested had been moved to the same holding pen, but not Bistrong. He was gone. It finally dawned on the man that Bistrong had set them up; he had been working with the government, and lying for years (Another defendant was arrested the same day in Florida, bringing the total number to twenty-two).

It was only several hours later, when they were formally interviewed, that the executives learned why they had been arrested: According to the FBI, they had intended to collectively pay a bribe of $1.5 million to the defense minister of Gabon in order to win their share of the $15 million arms sale. The FBI had 615 audio and video recordings of more than 150 meetings, and logs of more than 5,000 phone calls, in which the executives, over the course of two years, had allegedly discussed the kickback.[14]

The following afternoon the Justice Department heralded the arrests as the "largest action ever undertaken by the Justice Department against individuals for FCPA violations." R. Patrick Caldwell's alleged involvement, as well as that of companies like

Smith & Wesson, attracted media attention. Lanny Breuer, speaking at a press conference, announced: "The fight to erase foreign bribery from the corporate playbook will not be won overnight, but these actions are a turning point."[15] He added wryly, "This is one case where what happens in Vegas doesn't stay in Vegas."

In a sense, Breuer was right: Operation Alternate Breach *was* a turning point, but not in the way the DOJ and the FBI had expected.

During the long months of the undercover operation, Bistrong and his FBI handlers developed more than a normal informant-handler association. They had a bantering rapport, and Bistrong enjoyed an unusually close relationship with Chris Forvour, the agent who convinced him to go undercover. They spoke almost every day for nearly three years. ("I talked to him more than I did my wife, frankly," Forvour would later testify.)[16] They even gave each other nicknames: Forvour called Bistrong "Flash Bang," which referred to a stun grenade that emits a large flash of light and then a deafening sound but has no effect beyond disorienting the enemy. The label was a nod to one of Bistrong's numerous talents: his ability to beguile and charm people, to catch them off guard.

The Justice Department's prosecution theory was that, during their hours of conversations, Bistrong openly informed the twenty-two defendants that they would all have to consent to paying a "commission" to win the Gabonese deal—money that would be shared with the defense minister of Gabon. Bistrong never actually used the terms "bribe" or "kickback," but he did state unequivocally that the defense minister had to be "taken care of." In the FBI's interpretation, all the defendants had been recorded as agreeing to "take care" of the official. That evidence was supposed to constitute the smoking gun.

This tidy argument, however, fell apart at trial. Before the hearing even began, an initial ruling by the judge, Richard Leon, preempted the Justice Department from ever winning its case, former law enforcement officials believed. DOJ prosecutors had intended to submit evidence allegedly showing that many of the defendants had participated in earlier bribery schemes. This is known as alleged evidence of prior bad acts, the purpose of which was to establish that the defendants were aware of how bribery worked and how a corrupt deal was arranged—in other words, what Bistrong meant when he said they would have to "take care" of the Defense Minister. Judge Leon ruled, however, that the alleged evidence of prior bad acts in the Alternate Breach case was inadmissible. "We couldn't win," Paul Pelletier concluded.

More troubles arose at trial. Bistrong was supposed to be the perfect witness. He was directly at the center of the bribery scheme; he had seen it unfold; he could clearly explain it to the jury. But on the stand, after he admitted to his former cocaine use and penchant for prostitutes, the defense repeatedly discredited him as an unreliable witness. "He's a liar, and this man began to believe him," one of the defense lawyers charged during his closing argument, pointing at Forvour.[17] The defense also seized upon Bistrong's chummy relationship with the FBI, citing the hundreds of text messages in which they joked about sex, women, and football. The defense argued that the sting was effectively an ego trip for Bistrong, a matter he didn't take seriously, and that he would do anything, including setting up innocent people, if it led to his receiving a reduced sentence.

Perhaps the biggest stumbling block at trial was a semantic one: the fact that Bistrong had never actually used the words "bribe" or "kickback" on tape, nor had any of the defendants. In real bribery schemes, Bistrong and former prosecutors insisted, no one uses such terms; participants employ more innocuous language, as a code. "Drug dealers don't sit around and say, 'I've got seven kilos of cocaine I imported from Colombia.' They say, 'The little girls have arrived.'" James Koukios, assistant chief of the FCPA Unit until 2014, said. "[Bribery] is not different than that." The lead federal prosecutor, Laura Perkins, had a difficult time convincing the jury of this nuance. As a result, the hours and hours of undercover recordings, far from being a smoking gun, were viewed by the jury as conversations that had nothing to do with corruption.

In the end, three of the defendants pled guilty before trial and were sentenced. The remaining nineteen fought the charges. The case was prosecuted in four separate trials. The first, involving four of the defendants, ended in a hung jury. The second ended in an acquittal for two defendants, including R. Patrick Caldwell, and a hung jury for three others. By the time the third trial was set to begin in early 2012, many in the Justice Department believed they could not possibly win, given Judge Leon's prior rulings.

In February 2012, Lanny Breuer announced that the Justice Department was withdrawing the cases. "I made the decision that after two times, our resources needed to go somewhere else," he explained. "I didn't think there was going to be a different outcome a third time."

The government's decision to dismiss the charges prompted a scathing rebuke from Judge Leon. He reprimanded the prosecution's "very, very aggressive conspiracy theory that was pushing its already generous elasticity to its outer limits." Leon also presciently told the court: "This appears to be the end of a long and sad chapter of white-collar criminal enforcement."[18] The sting was deemed a disaster by many, including a collection of lawyers, former U.S. officials, and corporate lobbyists, who argued that FCPA's prosecution policy was vague at best, and overly aggressive at worst. Alberto Gonzales, the former attorney general under President George W. Bush, told an audience in Washington: "Losses at trial are uncommon, but not rare. What is virtually unheard of is for the government to abandon a case in such a comprehensive fashion. This underscores what a tremendous failure this was for the government."[19]

At roughly the same time, the Justice Department lost an important FCPA trial in Los Angeles. Three defendants who were charged with bribery violations succeeded in having their convictions overturned on the grounds of prosecutorial misconduct. The judge in that case dismissed the government's indictment with prejudice.

\* \* \*

After the sting debacle, a pall spread over the eleventh floor of the Bond Building. At Lanny Breuer's direction, FCPA cases were subjected to greater internal oversight and review. He put more layers of bureaucracy into place, measures that seemed intended to clip prosecutors' wings. He called for frequent meetings to discuss the progress of cases. Prosecutors faced more questions about their decisions from supervisors. The effort was viewed as second-guessing, a lack of support. As a former high-ranking Justice Department official recalled: "It's an environment you can't work in. There's eighteen layers of no-value-added review just so people can say, 'You didn't tell me that. I have my notes of our meeting.'"

Breuer, who was born in Queens, New York, had already enjoyed an illustrious career in law before joining the Justice Department. He began as an assistant district attorney in Manhattan and then

spent several decades rotating between private practice and public service, with Covington & Burling, the prestigious Washington
law firm, as his base. After practicing there for almost a decade,
he was appointed as special counsel to President Clinton in 1997,
defending him during the impeachment proceedings. He returned
to private practice until 2009, when President Obama named him
to run the Criminal Division.

Breuer is widely credited with dramatically expanding the scope
of the Justice Department's FCPA investigations. Corporate resolu-
tions during his tenure resulted in unprecedented fines—fines that
helped bring about a significant reform in business culture both in
the United States and Europe.

Yet Breuer remains a controversial figure, whose legacy of
white-collar crime enforcement remains contested by both the
public and his former colleagues. It is the impression of some
former Justice officials that from the beginning of his appointment at Justice, Breuer treaded too carefully because he was more
focused on burnishing his credentials than tackling difficult cases.
He was viewed as being overly concerned with how the press
would portray an FCPA investigation, and by extension, how that
would affect his reputation. "[Lanny] cared deeply about what the
New York Times said. And that was it," a former prosecutor said.
Although the Bistrong sting operation had already been launched
by the time he joined Justice, he took the loss personally, and
some claimed that his subsequent bureaucratic oversight was in
part another effort to protect himself from bad press. "We're going
to lose this case. Why are we doing that one?" a former senior
Justice Department official described the new official mind-set,
adding, "The message was: Lanny can't look bad. And I would
say: I don't work for Lanny. I work for the Department of Justice.

I don't lose one minute of sleep as to whether Lanny will look bad."

Some FBI officials also felt that the Justice Department began to become too passive, to the point that resentment arose in the FBI's FCPA squad. "In FCPA [cases], they were ridiculously cautious. Some of my guys would say, 'Why do we do these cases? No one goes to jail.' They weren't clear on the motives—they weren't convinced there was purity of heart," as one official recalled. The bureau's own FCPA squad wanted to continue with a proactive approach, but Justice wanted them on a tighter leash. The Justice Department seemed to become less willing to charge individual executives, retreating to a position of settling for corporate convictions instead. The FBI official described their attitude as being, "If we can get a [corporate] conviction, why beat our heads against the wall? Do you really want to muck up the works and spend two years trying to prove that the vice president knew?"

Perhaps the most scathing criticism of Breuer came in the *Pbs Frontline* documentary "The Untouchables," which cast him as the central villain in a systemic Justice Department failure to take on Wall Street.[20] His interview in the segment was widely panned, with critics saying he spent far too much time giving reasons the DOJ should not act against individuals, rather than reasons it should.[21] Breuer resigned shortly after the program aired but said publicly that it had nothing to do with his decision to leave.

In a recent interview, Breuer stated that under his leadership the FCPA had launched an unprecedentedly aggressive campaign to charge executives who bribe. "We prosecuted more individuals than anyone ever," he said, adding that the work of the Department in those four years was "somewhat breathtaking." When asked why, despite an industrywide crackdown against pharma-

ceutical bribery, no executives were ever charged, Breuer declined
to comment, citing the fact that some of Covington's clients were
pharmaceutical companies. When questioned whether there had
been concerns within the Justice Department about how overseas
bribery in the pharmaceutical industry might have affected patients
overseas, Breuer again declined to comment.

Speaking more generally, he asserted that the decision whether
or not to bring an FCPA case was always based on the available
evidence, and nothing else. "If you were convinced beyond a reasonable doubt that someone committed a crime, and you thought
we could prove the elements beyond a reasonable doubt, then we
brought the case. If you didn't think we could do it, then we didn't
bring the case." As the discussion came to a close, Breuer said there
were a myriad of reasons for why charges might not be brought
against an individual, highlighting one in particular—namely, that
the decision to do so was not one to be taken lightly: "You can
never for a moment not be cognizant that bringing criminal charges
is probably, in my mind, the most significant decision the government can make against an individual. And so you have, I think, an
ethical and a moral obligation to do it very thoughtfully."

Many former prosecutors confirmed Breuer's account, and
agreed that he had in fact not shied away from individual prosecutions. "I don't think it equates to Lanny took a pass, or he's soft
on crime," Chuck Duross said. "If Lanny had been able to string
up Wall Street bankers with good cases, he would have." Duross
reiterated that individual prosecutions are simply much harder to
win than the public is willing to believe.

A closer look at the overall numbers suggests that the Justice
Department's record of prosecuting individuals is certainly mixed,
but that blaming Breuer is misguided. Between 2000 and 2009,

the period before Breuer took office, Justice charged forty-eight individuals with criminal offenses under the FCPA, according to one statistical analysis. Between 2009 and up until 2013, the years Breuer was in charge, the Department charged sixty-one individuals. Forty-two were charged in 2009 alone, including twenty-two in the Gabon sting. But given how long FCPA investigations take to assemble, it is likely that Breuer had little direct responsibility for launching the Bistrong sting operation. During his actual tenure, nineteen individuals were charged, of whom nine were related to the massive Siemens case, another matter that predated him. It appears that in three years, the FCPA Unit under Breuer brought charges against only ten individuals—slightly more than three individuals per year. After he left office, the number of individual prosecutions appears to have increased, with thirty-eight cases brought between 2013 and 2016, some of which he certainly helped launch. Examining individual prosecutions under Breuer's tenure alone, however, misses the greater point.

Mike Koehler, an associate professor of law at Southern Illinois University, is an outspoken critic of U.S. efforts to enforce the FCPA. He writes, "77 percent of DOJ corporate enforcement actions since 2006 have not (at least yet) resulted in any related DOJ FCPA charges against company employees."[22] The same is true of the SEC's enforcement record. Koehler has found that of the 68 enforcements the SEC has brought between 2008 and 2014, 82 percent resulted in no action being taken against a company employee. His analysis underscores the fact that, whereas one can quibble about the number of individual prosecutions brought under whose leadership, most FCPA-related criminal investigations, as well as civil actions by the SEC, are resolved with no company executives ever being charged.

* * *

Given these findings, it comes as no surprise that not a single employee from any of the large pharmaceutical companies investigated for bribery in China—Pfizer, Eli Lilly, Bristol Myers-Squibb,
GlaxoSmithKline, AstraZeneca, Novartis and SciClone—was
ever held responsible for a crime. The Justice Department initially opened an investigation into most of these cases, but declined
to bring proceedings against any of them, for reasons it did not
make clear. As of late 2016, the Justice Department has publicly
disclosed its reasons for declining to bring charges in a particular
case. James Koukious explained that in cases where bribes have
been paid by only the foreign subsidiary of a larger parent company in the United States, and there is no evidence directly tying the bribery back to it, the Justice Department does not have
jurisdiction to bring a charge. The SEC, however, can prosecute
the parent company for violating the books and records provision
of the FCPA—in other words, for failing to supervise its foreign
subsidiary—and did bring civil charges against the parent pharmaceutical companies.

The federal rules of evidence make it much easier to bring a
charge against a corporation than an individual. In the latter case,
a prosecutor is limited by the quality of the evidence he or she
has against that defendant, and a judge may rule, on a variety of
grounds, that that evidence is inadmissible (as was the case in the
Gabon sting trial). But the legal standards are much lower for holding a corporation criminally liable for the conduct of its employees.
The rules of evidence for corporate cases are also much more in the
prosecution's favor. If five different individuals are being investigated for bribery, and the evidence against any one of them is

not particularly strong, the allegations against them can be combined and the corporation be held vicariously liable. A jury hearing allegations that five people within a single company conspired in a bribery scheme is likely to believe that the crime occurred and return a conviction. (In reality most companies settle FCPA charges out of court rather than risk going to trial.)

Current U.S. prosecution policy toward corporate bribery is that sending the message to corporations that they will be held criminally liable, when possible, is more of a priority than taking a risk and expending resources on a case that could ultimately be lost. The same resources could be more effectively deployed in the safer strategy of reaching corporate settlements.

This mind-set has become enough of a concern within the Justice Department itself that in September 2015 its leadership felt compelled to issue a curious memo. "Individual Accountability for Corporate Wrongdoing" was authored by Sally Yates, then deputy attorney general of the United States. The document addresses not only FCPA cases but corporate cases more broadly and states: "One of the most effective ways to combat corporate misconduct is by seeking accountability from the individuals who perpetrated the wrongdoing."[23] It speaks volumes that the DOJ felt the need to issue a "new" policy guideline in order to underscore so fundamental a tenet of justice as this. Yates clarified elements of the policy in a speech to the New York City Bar Association White Collar Institute on May 10, 2016: "We cannot have a different system of justice—or the perception of a different system of justice—for corporate executives than we do for everyone else." But she added: "These cases do have a special set of challenges, challenges that can impede our ability to identify the responsible parties and to bring them to justice. It is not easy to disentangle who did what within a huge corporate structure—to discern whether anyone had the requisite knowledge and intent."[24]

Regardless of these challenges, Yates explained, the Department had issued new rules regarding individual accountability: Justice attorneys "may not release individuals from civil or criminal liability except under the rarest of circumstances," and they would now have to obtain approval to do so. If corporations expected to receive credit for cooperating with Justice—resulting in reduced penalties and fines—they would be required to provide meaningful information about the misconduct of their employees. (Yates added that this had in fact been a principle of federal prosecution of corporations for years but seemed to be suggesting, without irony, that the Justice Department was now serious about enforcing it.) Under a new pilot program, the Justice Department might, at its discretion, also offer a reduction in fines, according to federal sentencing guidelines, of up to 50 percent if corporations did provide meaningful information.

As Yates recounted, in the past, Justice Department prosecutors had not pushed back on corporations when they failed to provide information about individual misconduct, but gave them credit for cooperating anyway. With the individual accountability project, she seemed to be reassuring the public that the Justice Department, after a long and hard look in the mirror, was finally going to do its job.

\* \* \*

In 2015, the Justice Department's FCPA Unit once again used an undercover informant wearing a wire to prosecute an executive for bribery: the CEO of an oil services company called PetroTiger, a small, private business. When the defendant chose to fight the charges, the trial once again did not go in Justice's favor. The undercover informant, who was in fact the former general counsel of PetroTiger, provided false testimony on the stand, which sunk the case. Justice hurriedly negotiated a deal with the indicted executive, who pleaded guilty to one count of conspiring to violate the FCPA; he served no jail time but was put on probation for three years and paid a one-hundred-thousand-dollar fine.

In 2015, Justice hired at least ten more prosecutors for the eleventh floor of the Bond Building, bringing the total to more than thirty. The FBI, meanwhile, created three dedicated international FCPA squads, in Washington, Los Angeles, and New York. Since the Yates memo, as Koehler points out, the percentage of Justice Department settlements resulting in individual prosecutions—0 percent in 2016 and 33 percent in 2017—actually dropped below levels not seen since 2004, when the FCPA was barely enforced at all. Of course, trends are not a dependable barometer of DOJ action and policy, as Justice might currently be working on a large FCPA case against several individuals that will not be made public until the investigation in complete. Only time will tell.

# Part IV

# Redress

# Chapter 10

# Givebacks

In 2004, Gilberth Calderón Alvarado, a public prosecutor in Costa Rica, filed a legal motion virtually unheard of in his country's court system—or anywhere in the world, for that matter. Alvarado argued that Alcatel-Lucent, the French telecommunications giant, had caused extensive "social harm" in Costa Rica by paying millions in bribes to win state contracts—and that the country was therefore entitled to compensation. Alvarado's claim advanced a new theory in the resolution of bribery cases: Alcatel's crime should be penalized not only because the practice of bribery itself is technically illegal and, morally speaking, bad—but because the *results* of bribery are harmful to society as well.[1]

Alvarado, then the director of the Office of Public Ethics, filed the motion in the aftermath of yet another record-setting bribery scandal. Multiple international law enforcement agencies, including the U.S. Justice Department, accused Alcatel of using bribes to win contracts in several countries around the world, including Bangladesh, Kenya, Nigeria, and Honduras. Alcatel's alleged corruption in Costa Rica had been particularly egregious: It was accused of paying as much as $18 million in bribes to win more than $419 million in contracts. Company managers offered kickbacks to numerous high-level government officials, including nearly half the board of Costa Rica's state-run telecommunications company, as well as at least one legislator in the national assembly.[2] It also allegedly bribed two of Costa Rica's presidents, who received nearly $1 million each while in office. (In 2011, a Costa Rican court sentenced Miguel Ángel Rodríguez, who served as president between 1998 and 2002, to five years in prison for accepting the bribes.)[3] The scandal is still playing out in Costa Rica's courts and roiling the country's political landscape.

In 2011, Alcatel pleaded guilty to the bribery charges and paid fines of $137 million. This penalty, however, was paid to the U.S. Treasury, not to the countries where Alcatel had actually made the bribes. Alvarado hoped to change that. Although the legal theory that supported his attempt is complicated, as were the events that followed, it is worth examining how Costa Rica attempted to employ existing laws to highlight bribery's wider impact.

Under Costa Rica's criminal procedure code, the Attorney General's Office is entitled to file civil actions seeking damages when criminal offenses affect "collective interests." In his claim, Alvarado cited a definition promulgated by Costa Rica's Constitutional Court that "collective interests" means, among other things, that citizens in Costa Rica have a right to sound financial public management. Bribery by a corporation directly undermines those rights.

Alvarado argued that Alcatel's bribes resulted not only in the form of losses to the public treasury, but in harm to the country's national reputation, as Costa Rica was repeatedly labeled a corrupt nation in the international press. There were collateral economic losses as well, given that investors likely began to question the fairness of the Costa Rican market. Perhaps most novel of all, Alvarado argued that Alcatel's bribery likely had direct political consequences: Because the public lost faith in politicians and political parties following the scandal, many voters might have decided to abstain from voting in Costa Rica's 2006 elections, which likely affected their outcome. Alvarado eventually attempted to quantify the fallout and hired a consultant. Using a methodology that relied in part on surveys of public confidence in the political system, he tabulated an economic loss to Costa Rica of $34.5 million. That, combined with the nearly $18 million in kickbacks that Alcatel paid, led Alvarado to file a claim seeking $52 million in social damages.

But Alvarado's case never made it to court. According to many observers, it would have been difficult to defend on many accounts, not least of which would have been proving that Alcatel's bribes led to quantifiable economic losses and political damage. The Attorney General's Office had only once before pursued such a claim, suing a medical equipment company that bribed officials in the country's Social Security system for $89 million in social damages. In that case the court accepted the claim but awarded damages of just $600,000, which is now under appeal. When Alcatel offered to settle Alvarado's claim out of court, he therefore agreed—but for a record-setting amount. In return for the Attorney General's Office dropping the social damages claim, Alcatel paid $10 million as part of a formal settlement, signed in January 2010. "The settlement marked the first time in Costa Rica's history that a foreign corporation agreed to pay the government damages for corruption," the U.S. Justice Department noted.[4] Portions of Alcatel's $10 million payment were subsequently allocated to the budget of Costa Rica's Anti-Corruption police.[*]

---

[*] In 2015, the Costa Rican government negotiated another settlement with Alcatel, this time on behalf of the state-run telecommunications company whose officials Alcatel had bribed. The state-run company, known by the acronym ICE, had claimed millions in commercial damages because after paying the bribes and winning the contract, it alleged that Alcatel failed to deliver on a promised four hundred thousand mobile telephone lines. Alcatel paid an additional $10 million in damages to ICE.

Juanita Olaya, a Colombian lawyer and former member of Transparency International, has written extensively about the Costa Rican case.[5] She has argued that other states, with the example of Costa Rica in mind, should explore the concept of social damage even if their national legislations do not have an obvious legal basis for doing so. Such suits, Olaya argues, would better ensure that bribery's total impact is addressed. As it stands, the United States' paradigm of prosecuting foreign bribery does not acknowledge that impact. "The sanctions that the SEC imposes are collected entirely by the SEC and remain in the U.S. But the actual harm produced in the country of origin, or where the bribery actually happens is absolutely ignored. The impact of that is that bribery has no consequences."[6] She believes that social damage claims, like those pursued by Costa Rica, would have an important symbolic effect, as they would make public the damage caused by corporate bribery to communities, to citizens, and to collective interests. Identifying social damage, Olaya says, is the equivalent of acknowledging: "Look, there's a hole. There's a crater here created by this act of bribery, and we need to fill it up again."

In recent years, a small number of states have successfully won damages from companies for bribery, though the settlements have received little publicity or have been negotiated in secret. In Nigeria, government-appointed attorneys have reached settlements with Shell Oil, Halliburton, Siemens, and several other companies, collecting a total of $180 million, all of it paid to the Nigerian government. A lawyer in Abuja who spearheaded the settlements on behalf of Nigeria, Godwin Obla, described the process as "legalized extortion," given that Nigeria's laws have not been updated to actually make provisions for such settlements. "We used the legal process to force them into a settlement that, if you check the laws . . . our legal architecture cannot support," Obla said, highlighting the legal challenge that many countries face in reaching settlements.[7]

What is surprising is that more states have *not* attempted to sue for social damages, given that an entire science, developed over the last two decades by many of the world's leading economists, has shown empirically that bribery directly undermines a nation's development and health as a functioning state.

In the 1990s a World Bank economist, the Chilean Daniel Kaufmann, set out to prove that corruption could be measured. To do so, he and his colleagues pioneered a method of correlating raw economic data from more than 150 countries—data that captures a country's economic growth over decades, its income inequality, its life expectancy and so on—with public perception surveys about the prevalence of corruption, including foreign corporate bribery, within that country. Kaufmann surveyed thousands of corporations around the world, directly asking their managers whether companies like theirs were paying bribes. Because the resulting data is based on perception, it is subject to error, but because it is highly informed, candid perception, it represents the best gauge of bribe-related activity to which economists are likely to have access.

Kaufmann's results revealed striking patterns: The higher a country's perceived levels of corruption—including the prevalence of corporate bribery—the lower its economic growth, its health standards, its levels of education, and its income equality. Conversely, countries with less corruption, including lower levels of bribery, were healthier and had better governance and better-functioning economies. Since then, economists and social scientists have applied this method of inquiry to a data set of some two hundred countries and have produced dozens of studies examining bribery's effects.

Among their findings has been that corporate bribery undermines sound governance—for example, by influencing how officials allot public funds. One pioneering study, involving more than one hundred nations, found that in those countries where corporations are perceived to pay relatively more bribes, government officials spend less on education as a percentage of overall GDP, because they may be receiving kickbacks to invest in projects such as telecom instead of schools.[8] When bribes incentivize lower spending on education—which boosts growth potential through investment in "human capital"—they depress attainment levels, thereby impeding economic development and increasing income inequality. Bribes, in other words, contribute to poverty by diminishing a state's capacity to reduce that poverty. A similar study has found that where bribery is higher, governments spend less on maintaining existing infrastructure. When roads are broken and bridges are crumbling, the pace of economic growth, the delivery of services, and the very functioning of government is impeded.[9]

These studies of corruption have at times raised more questions than answers. Economists disagree, for example, as to whether corruption has a completely negative correlation with economic growth. Many countries in East Asia have actually experienced extraordinary levels of growth despite relatively high levels of corruption. As one OECD study emphasizes, strong correlation does not prove a direct causal relationship.[10] Still, the majority of experts believe that this strong connection does provides evidence of the costs of corruption. Big data now supports what Burgoyne and Paine believed intuitively.

This is not to say, of course, that the collateral damage caused by bribery can be easily assessed. How does one quantify the loss of citizen trust in political leadership or the state system itself? As the Alcatel case demonstrates, bribery scandals erode public confidence, preoccupy courts, and divert the limited resources of police agencies even a decade after they are discovered. How much does this cost the state not only in dollars but in political and social capital? When a Canadian company allegedly pays bribes to gain control of a lucrative gas field, and then accidentally blows it up, forcing the nearby rural village to evacuate (as actually happened in Bangladesh), what is the impact to health, to the environment, and to the quality of life in that village? How do courts explore causality, culpability, and adequate compensation? How should the victims be identified?

Courts around the world are already exploring such difficult issues. As Juanita Olaya writes, "The experience of measuring immaterial or moral damage is not new. Courts in different jurisdictions have already assumed standards for this knowing that there are certain types of damages that can hardly be reduced to a financial measure, or measured for integral reparation, or where the resulting situation can't be reinstated as it was before. These same principles, techniques and standards could be applied to reparation of social damage."[11]

In fact, American courts already have experience with assessing social damage, identifying victims, and devising mechanisms to award reparations. Restorative justice, a legal theory that emerged in the 1970s, is based on the notion that crimes not only break the law but cause injury to victims and communities. The goal of restorative justice, is not just preventing and penalizing crime, but healing its social wounds. Andrew Spalding has done some of the most innovative thinking in this area. Echoing Olaya, he believes American jurisprudence already has the tools in place to make this approach feasible. "By involving the perpetrator, victim, and community in the sentencing process," he writes, "restorative justice does not merely punish the wrongdoer, but remedies the harm caused by the crime, prevents future harm, and reintegrates the defendant into the very community it violated."[12]

Spalding points out that the Department of Justice has actually been applying the concept of restorative justice to white-collar criminal cases for more than two decades for violations of environmental law. In these cases, corporate actors are not only penalized for breaking the law, but are required to pay reparations to the communities they harm. In 2009, when a gas company was sentenced for illegally storing mercury in Rhode Island, it was fined $6 million but also had to pay $12 million to various local community initiatives, with a view toward environmental remediation. In 2013, after Walmart pleaded guilty to six violations of the Clean Air Act, it received a $40 million fine but also was required to pay $20 million to various community service projects as reparations. These settlements, significant as they are, pale in comparison to the settlement that British Petroleum (BP) faced in the wake of its catastrophic oil spill in the Gulf of Mexico. Of nearly $4 billion in criminal fines that the court mandated, it designated more than $2 billion of that amount to be earmarked to restore the communities that had been affected.[13] Spalding contends that this mechanism can easily be transferred to corporate bribery settlements, and that legal scholars and former prosecutors are already exploring ways to do so. "What we really want the DOJ to do, the antibribery enforcement folks," he explains, "is walk down the hallway to their colleagues in environmental enforcement, and say, 'Hey— tell us how you do this.'[14] And the environmental lawyers will say,

'Well you know what? It's easy. It's not controversial. It's fully legal under existing laws.' "

It remains to be seen how courts will navigate the new frontier of assessing social damage in bribery settlements. Perhaps states, following Costa Rica's example, can hire consultants to assess the specific economic losses incurred in each case. Future research on the economics of corruption will likely provide more robust data. In the meantime, there are other solutions if individual victims and direct damage cannot be identified. Spalding points out that U.S. federal sentencing statutes take into account the fact that victims may not always be easily discernible. In that case, courts can mandate "an order of probation requiring community service," which is intended to "repair the harm caused." In the BP case, for example, the company paid reparations to organizations dedicated to cleaning up and protecting the wetlands polluted by the oil spill, rather than to specific victims, a symbolical measure intended to restore that community.

While applying restorative justice is far more challenging when the community to be restored is located in another country, the Justice Department already has experience in doing so, though not often enough. In one well-publicized example, in 2003 Justice seized $84 million that James Giffen, a prominent American businessman, allegedly paid in bribes to the president of Kazakhstan on behalf of large oil companies, including ExxonMobil.[15] In 2007, the Justice Department consulted with World Bank officials, civil society organizations, and government officials in Switzerland and Kazakhstan to create BOTA, "the first foundation in the world which used recovered bribes to benefit victims of corruption—the poor," as its former director has written. BOTA was established in Kazakhstan in 2008 and administered a number of educational and social service programs for vulnerable children and mothers. An American-based nonprofit was chosen to run it, ensuring the proper use of its funds. BOTA's finances were audited every year by an international accounting firm and reviewed by the World Bank. For five and a half years, BOTA provided services to roughly 200,000 people. [16]

Following the Oil-for-Food scandal in Iraq, the Justice Department provided portions of those settlements "as restitution for the benefit of the people of Iraq," as its press release stated. Pursuant to its settlement with the Justice Department and the SEC, Chevron agreed to pay $20 million toward the Development Fund for Iraq, which, administered by the United Nations, assists in Iraq's reconstruction. U.S. courts also ordered subsidiaries of Oscar Wyatt's firms to collectively pay $25 million to the Development Fund for Iraq, while Vitol, a Swiss oil company, was ordered to pay $13 million. Other jurisdictions, notably the United Kingdom, have begun implementing similar arrangements. In 2009, a British court ordered the company Mabey to pay reparations to the countries where it had allegedly paid bribes, including £658,000 to Ghana, £139,000 to Jamaica, and £618,000 to Iraq.

Still, these examples remain very much exceptions to the rule. According to one tally, the United States has collected more than $11 billion in bribery-related fines since 2006.[17] Of that sum, only $142 million has been paid in reparations of any kind (to Iraq and Kazakhstan)—slightly more than 1.29 percent. Those arrangements, moreover, were made in 2007, and no similar compensation has been made since then, while the bribery-related fines remain with the U.S. Treasury. "In the majority of settlements, the countries whose officials were allegedly bribed have not been involved in the settlements and have not found any other means to obtain redress," a World Bank study points out.[18] The foreign countries directly harmed by bribery, specifically the citizens of those countries, neither receive any of the fines nor even have a voice in the settlements. The damage they suffered is not even acknowledged.

There may be good reasons why the U.S. government does not repatriate more bribery money, particularly because doing so would be putting money back into the hands of the corrupt government that solicited or accepted bribes in the first place. This is certainly a legitimate concern, but as has already demonstrated, especially in the case of the BOTA Foundation in Kazakhstan, provisions can be made to ensure that reparations are safely, transparently, and efficiently managed, using direct community involvement and outside monitoring.

\* \* \*

Leaving aside the question of whether restorative justice is the best approach for bribery settlements, would requiring offending corporations to fund such measures result in an effective deterrence of bribery? It may be instructive to look more closely at the penalties levied in such settlements and specifically at the impact these fines have on corporations and their behavior.

In 2009, Jonathan Karpoff, an economist at the University of Washington, began closely analyzing FCPA fines in order to assess the efficacy of antibribery deterrence. Since then, he and his colleagues have used data from 143 actual bribery settlements, ranging from 1978 to 2013, to produce several significant studies. Their evidence has shown that bribe payers are rarely apprehended and that bribe penalties are too low. In effect, bribery's value to a company is worth a great deal, even when that company is caught and obliged to pay what may seem like extraordinary fines.

It is, of course, impossible to determine how many companies in the world actually pay bribes. Most law enforcement officials and observers believe that the cases that have been discovered represent only a fraction of the actual total. Karpoff's work provides evidence, using statistical modeling, that supports this belief. Examining a sample size of 6,857 corporations that have foreign sales—including such companies as IBM and General Electric—he estimates that roughly 22 percent of them have likely engaged in foreign bribery. But of those 1,566 companies that have paid bribes, only 100 were actually charged. The likelihood of getting caught, in other words, is just 6.4 percent. Part of how Karpoff calculates the value of a bribe is to take this very low probability into account. Bribery is attractive as an investment because companies know that they will almost never pay a fine for it.

Karpoff estimates that for every $1.00 in bribes a company spends, it receives $5.60 in benefit—even accounting for any possible fines the company would have to pay if it were caught.[19] The Justice Department itself has calculated that firms receive $10.00 in benefit for every $1.00 in bribes they spend, while another study estimates $11 in benefit for every $1.00 in bribes. (These latter figures do not account for the penalties and other costs a guilty firm might incur.)

His studies also reveal that bribery is a worthwhile risk not only because it generates revenue or profits, but because it increases a company's overall value, as measured in its market capitalization (a value derived by taking the total number of a company's shares outstanding and multiplying it by the share price). When a company publicly announces the winning of a new contract that it has actually secured via bribery, its market capitalization increases, on average, by 3.15 percent.[20] Karpoff arrived at this figure by tracking how much the company's market shares increased after it was later revealed to have paid kickbacks. Even when companies are made to pay penalties and fines—including surrendering the profits they derived from bribes—and even after they incur the costs of internal investigations and monitoring fees related to a settlement, Karpoff has found that the value of the bribe-related activity is still, on average, worth +0.4 percent of the company's market capitalization.[21]

As one example: Alcatel's bribery generated profits of at least $45 million for the company between 2001 and 2006. After it was charged, it paid fines and penalties of $137 million. Because this figure included releasing the roughly $45 million the company made in profits from the kickbacks, the fines imposed on the company actually amounted to $92 million. That is certainly not an insignificant sum, but the size is relative, and relativity matters in deterrence. At the time that it paid those sums, Alcatel had a market capitalization of roughly $5 billion. The fines, in other words, represented less than 2 percent of the company's value, and that figure is actually higher than in most cases. According to Karpoff's overall estimate, the mean total monetary penalties that the Justice Department imposes in U.S. bribery settlements (excluding the cost of internal investigations and the costs of monitoring) is equivalent to 1.06 percent of a company's market capitalization.[22] Even in Siemens's record-setting criminal settlement—$1.8 billion paid to U.S. and German authorities—nearly $1 billion of the fines it paid actually represented a forfeit of the profit it had already derived from bribery. The actual fines the DOJ imposed, $800 million, were equivalent to less than 1 percent of Siemens's market capitalization of roughly $100 billion.[23]

Karpoff's studies have also concluded that corporations charged with bribery face little reputational risk. After settlements are announced, they may see their market value drop, but not because investors are reacting to the bribery itself. Rather, Karpoff has found, it is only when bribery charges include claims of financial fraud or financial manipulation of some kind that investors lose confidence. This evidence refutes the notion—often put forward by critics of the FCPA—that firms subjected to bribery investigations and prosecutions face large reputational losses. In other words, the reputational loss associated with a bribery charge is so low that it does not act as an effective deterrent.

Given the evidence, Karpoff's studies reach the conclusion that the Justice Department and SEC impose "insufficient expected penalties to offset firms' economic incentive to bribe."[24] "To deter bribery effectively, the chance of getting caught times the amount you pay if you get caught has to be at least as large as the benefits. So for deterrence to work better, you've got to have higher penalties," Karpoff explains.[25] He estimates, in fact, that in order to negate the value gained from the average bribery-related contract, more firms that indulge in bribery need to be identified and charged. That probability would have to go up by 52.8 percent in order for fines to have more of an impact. However, given that so few firms are charged, the fines they pay when they are would have to be significantly larger to serve as a deterrent.

Karpoff suggests that if the probability of getting caught does not change Justice Department and SEC fines would have to be increased by 8.3 times in order to negate the value a company derives from bribery. Stated differently, in order for FCPA deterrence to be effective, the Justice Department would have to levy fines that equal, on average, 38.5 percent of a firm's market capitalization. In the case of Alcatel, for example, the penalty would have been $1.92 billion.

This is, of course, the conclusion of one academic study, albeit one evidently grounded in firm analysis. It does, however, add empirical support to the argument that FCPA fines, however record setting, are still not high enough to deter the crime. As one law professor at the University of Texas has written: "The fines imposed for engaging in foreign corrupt practices comprise a tiny fraction of the potential revenue generated by lucrative contracts . . . [W]hen discounted by the low probability of detection, these sanctions are far too low to deter unlawful activity."[26] A recent OECD study calls attention to the fact that fines globally are also not sufficiently punitive to discourage bribery.[27] The OECD's Secretary-General, Ángel Gurría, recently told an antibribery conference: "Sometimes sanctions are so light that even if people have a one hundred percent chance of getting caught they would still choose to pay the fine and get the benefit of the act of bribery."[28] Bribery has not only been standard operating procedure for corporations doing business abroad; paying FCPA fines is part of the cost of their business—effectively a tax that companies can accommodate.

Under ideal circumstances, more corporate executives responsible for bribery would face criminal charges, and FCPA fines would be drastically increased to constitute such a financial burden that corporations would avoid paying bribes. Given that neither of these measures is likely to take place anytime soon, a more realistic way to make fines heavier and more punitive is for the Justice Department to push for reparations payments, returning some portion of their illegally earned profits to the citizens of the countries where the bribes were paid—a mechanism to transform kickbacks into givebacks.

Such reparations would not only result in heavier fines but would also levy meaningful reputational penalty. Corporations carefully safeguard their reputations, and for good reason: According to one study, 25 percent of a company's market value is based on its reputation. A 2013 survey by Deloitte found that reputational damage was the number-one risk concern of 300 executives from major corporations around the world. [29]

As Karpoff's study found, however, companies that pay bribes face little reputational risk. That is in part because they are required to pay only what amounts to a regulatory fine. They have no other consequences to fear, no harm to answer for, no victims to be held accountable to. To date, though more than 150 FCPA cases have been adjudicated or settled in the United States alone since 2004—representing dozens of countries and hundreds of millions in bribes—not a single company involved has ever made a public statement acknowledging the broader consequences of their bribery. Financial settlements effectively buy silence on the issue of bribery's impact.

The current FCPA enforcement regime—including the fines themselves, the manner in which these cases are privately settled, and the manner in which they are publicly announced—only reinforces this pattern. When it settles an investigation, the Justice Department rarely discusses how a particular bribery case may have resulted in specific harm to individuals or communities, but focuses instead on its effect on free markets and fair competition.

This approach only undermines the Justice Department's own stated deterrence goals. Officials at the FBI and the Justice Department's FCPA Unit have stated that they want to publicly emphasize the idea that bribery is not just a market transgression, but a crime with consequences that reverberate around the world. "That's the message we're trying to convey . . . the corruption is very much feeding corrupt regimes, and the knock-off effects of that are that those corrupt regimes are stealing money blindly from the treasury so that country cannot build up the infrastructure it needs to survive the drought or survive the floods or survive the storms," a high-level Justice Department official said.[30] Particularly after the Arab Spring, FBI officials said in an interview, there was greater concern within the Bureau about how corruption foments popular backlash, and how bribery is tied to political instability in regions of the world where the United States wants to support poverty alleviation and democracy, or otherwise has national security interests. The Justice Department can reinforce this message and change the perception about bribery's fallout—thereby achieving better deterrence—by mandating an acknowledgment, both public and financial, from corporate offenders that their bribes cause damage.

Advocates like Spalding and Olaya have proposed that, in the course of bribery settlements, corporate actors be made to formally recognize the harm their actions have caused—or even that they caused harm at all—and the Justice Department itself could explain to the public the repercussions of a particular act of bribery. Such acknowledgments would amplify the impact of penalties because they would damage a company's reputation, Olaya argues, "By making it visible you simply enlarge the consequences. Because it's social shame."

Andrew Spalding explained how this process might work: As it already does in bribery settlements, the Justice Department could offer companies a reduced fine in return for greater cooperation, except in this case, such cooperation would entail volunteering to fund community service projects that address the harm caused by the bribery. This could involve a company's consulting with outside experts, government officials, and civil society organizations in a particular country—as in the example of BOTA—to devise a project that, first, identifies and documents any possible harm caused by bribery, including what communities were affected; and second, publicly recognizes that harm and makes amends. What is significant in this plan is that the various stakeholders and parties affected by the bribery would have a voice in the settlement. Spalding even suggests that, as part of a settlement, a company could agree to write a comprehensive report about its bribery, "conced[ing] no further facts than were already made public in [its] deferred prosecution agreement" with the Justice Department. The report would not only serve as a sort of confession, but would edify local communities, local government, and local law enforcement about how to better prevent such crimes in the future.

For its bribery in Bangladesh, Siemens's subsidiary there paid a criminal fine of five hundred thousand dollars,[31] never acknowledging that by paying bribes to the Rahman brothers and Aminul Haque it had financially supported a political regime that flagrantly disregarded the rule of law, employed violence as a tool of political control, and likely supported Islamist extremism. The company could have worked with the Bangladeshi government, as well as local community organizations, to trace the kickbacks' impact, and to make reparations that could, even if only symbolically, remediate the damage. The company could have worked with international and local experts to establish an organization (or to identity an existing organization) that would assist poor families, or families that are victims of terrorist violence. Not just in Bangladesh, but in countries around the world where it paid bribes, Siemens could have made reparations and publicized its efforts. Even if Siemens had earmarked as much as $500 million for reparations in addition to the $800 million in fines it paid, that total ($1.3 billion) would have been both more punitive and also restorative—while still constituting less than 2 percent of the company's overall market capitalization, a sum the company could certainly afford.

A corporation that is willing to acknowledge its wrongdoing and address the harm it caused could become a paragon of corporate social responsibility in the twenty-first century.

# Chapter 11

# A New Standard

The new era of FCPA enforcement has already affected how corporations behave in the world, change that is particularly noteworthy given how quickly it has transpired. More effectively levied fines, including reparations, could certainly lead to even greater bribery deterrence and public understanding of bribery's consequences. Certainly more needs to be done globally, given the poor record of antibribery enforcement in the forty-two nations other than the United States that are signatories to the antibribery convention. To date, twenty-two of those forty-two countries have never imposed a single sanction for foreign bribery, according to a 2017 OECD analysis.[1] Corporate actors themselves have a responsibility to lead in this effort by changing their cultures from within.

Certainly, cultural change is already under way within the business community. Just a decade ago, companies thought little about FCPA compliance—having in place a suite of tools, safeguards, and best practices to help avoid or detect corrupt business dealings, ranging from conducting due diligence on third parties to training staff on the basics of anti-money laundering and bribery. "Until 2008, we couldn't spell FCPA. No one could. It was one of those things, if you get unlucky, then you get nailed for it," says Kent Kedl, Greater China and North Asia senior partner at Control

Risks, a compliance advisory firm. Today, however "[FCPA compliance] is part of the fabric right now—it's not an option," Kedl observed.[2] "There are levels of compliance and risk tolerance that companies are willing to take. But the do or don't we—that binary choice—is no longer there." By the time of a 2015 survey of businesses conducted by Deloitte, 59 percent of respondents reported having a chief compliance officer, a managerial position dedicated to reducing risk and addressing corruption, up from 37 percent in 2013.[3] Some companies have even made compliance a core of their business. In the wake of its bribery scandal, Siemens expanded it compliance department to at least four hundred people, up from only a reported handful earlier. Similar changes have taken place at Walmart. In 2012, a Pulitzer Prize–winning investigative news story in the *New York Times* exposed alleged corruption within the company's business practices in Mexico. Walmart, which is still under investigation by the Justice Department, has spent nearly half a billion dollars in legal fees and other costs investigating that charge, as well as alleged unethical practices in India and other countries. Today, Walmart says it has a team of one hundred "anticorruption associates" stationed around the world, who all report to a global anticorruption officer. The company has also provided anticorruption training to more than thirteen hundred third parties with whom it does business.[4] More important, Walmart has innovated by proactively employing a team of external experts to conduct random audits of third parties in high-risk regions to verify that they are adhering to sound practices.

Still, Walmart and Siemens remain outliers. Deloitte's 2016 compliance survey of nearly six hundred companies found that 73 percent had fewer than twenty full-time compliance staff. A majority (59 percent) had compliance budgets of less than $5 million. Even among companies with revenues of $1 billion or more, 35 percent reported having compliance budgets of $1 million or less.[5]

But FCPA compliance and bigger budgets allocated to it alone will not necessarily result in more ethical practices. Even some firms that dedicate more time, money, and personnel to compliance—or at least make the promise to—continue to engage in bribery. Jed S. Rakoff, a federal judge for the Southern District of New York, highlights the case of Pfizer in an article for the *New York Review of Books*.[6] Between 2002 and 2007, Pfizer entered into no less than three deferred prosecution agreements with the Justice Department after the company was investigated for paying bribes domestically in the United States and also illegally marketing its products. In each case, to avoid prosecution Pfizer agreed to implement better compliance protocols. Yet its employees continued to break the law, and only after the three DPAS were negotiated was Pfizer investigated again by the Justice Department and the SEC, this time for its foreign bribery. In 2012, Pfizer entered into its fourth deferred prosecution agreement, promising yet again that it would implement better compliance protocols.

In 2012, Biomet, an American manufacturer of medical devices, paid $17 million in fines and entered into a DPA with the Justice Department to avoid being prosecuted for alleged bribery in China, Brazil, and Argentina. In 2015, however, when new allegations surfaced that the company had paid bribes in Brazil and Mexico, Justice extended the time period of the company's DPA. In early 2017, it found that Biomet had again breached the terms of its DPA by continuing to pay bribes in Mexico and Brazil, from which it derived more than $5 million in profits. The Justice Department levied a criminal fine of $17 million for the breach and ordered that Biomet disgorge the $5 million in profits,[7] but then granted the company another DPA. Judge Rakoff has justifiably referred to these reforms as "often little more than window-dressing."[8]

Eradicating global corporate bribery will require more than strengthening compliance. What is also needed is a sea change in the fundamental corporate ethos of profit and the mind-set of sales.

Richard Bistrong, who spent a good part of his career engaging in bribery, believes that corporations that do business in foreign markets should restructure how their sales forces are paid. "If you're paying someone for whom 60 percent of his compensation is personal financial performance . . . [when you're] operating in countries that are low on the corruption index, you're going to have a problem," Bistrong says. "That individual may end up in a conflict of interest between compensation and corruption."

Sales executives, Bistrong argues, should be rewarded for turning down corrupt deals: "Compliance has to be achieved through a cultural ingraining of ethics, and a compensation plan that rewards proper legal and ethical behavior. You want it to be that there's no conflict—they see something, they walk away. They do not risk 60 percent of their compensation. They know that in no way will they be penalized." Compensation packages should prioritize the overall value that salespeople contribute to the company—and the concept of value should take into account ethical behavior. Some companies, including Eli Lilly and GSK, have restructured their compensation plans so that their sales forces do not work on commissions, but it remains unclear how many other firms are adopting this practice.

Bistrong also believes that companies need to revise not only *how* they make their profit, but *when* they do so. Refusing to pay bribes may result in lost deals, and a dip in sales in the short term, but the priority should be focusing on the long term: the value of building a better, more innovative, competitive business that derives its profit ethically. At a minimum, Bistrong argues, the consequences of losing sales in the short term are still better than the costs—not only in dollars, but also in reputation—that would be incurred in being fined for bribery: "You may be losing a sale, but you may *not* be getting a hundred- million-dollar fine down the road."

Undertaking such fundamental institutional changes also has to be explained and justified to investors, which is likely to be a harder sell. "You're just resetting your base," Bistrong says, adding: "I think there's a sales argument that says over the long haul, business which is done on the quality of the product and the competitiveness of the price is going to be better for business than business done through corruption."

Could a strong antibribery commitment prove to be its own value catalyst, translating into higher profits—even if it initially leads to lower sales? Pioneering academic research suggests that it can. In 2011, George Serafeim and Paul Healy of Harvard Business School sought to determine whether avoiding bribery came at a price to profitability. They analyzed data from a survey that Transparency International conducted in 2007 of businesses around the world, and focused on 250 of the world's largest corporations, 25 percent of which are American. The survey had asked those firms to disclose details about their anticorruption compliance programs, including their strategy, policies, and management systems. Transparency International then used that data to give each firm a rating that reflected its commitment to rejecting bribery. Healy and Serafeim took those ratings and cross-referenced them with each firm's sales growth in the three years after the survey was conducted. They found a dynamic that might, at first, appear dispiriting to investors: Those firms with a strong commitment to anticorruption experienced slower growth in high-corruption regions—in fact, they had only *half* the growth of companies with very low anticorruption commitments. The authors hypothesized that companies with a strong anticorruption commitment "are unable to compete effectively against local incumbents or multinationals with lower anticorruption standards."[9] When Healy and Serafeim looked more closely at the companies' profits, however, they found a different story: Firms that are more willing to bribe experience much higher growth in high-risk countries, but have lower profits, as expressed in return on sales and return on equity. Through bribes, these firms secure contracts and drive up sales—but those contracts, over the long term, often do not have healthy profit margins. (After winning a contract through bribery, firms sometimes experience delays in payments, or cost overruns for which they are never reimbursed.) Conversely, firms with a high commitment to anticorruption in high-risk countries "are able to defend their margins and [return on equity] on incremental sales in these markets." The takeaway is that shunning bribery may actually make for healthier profit over the long term.

Of course, a business maintains profitability not only by strong sales but by fostering a healthy culture that employees—not to mention consumers and investors—can buy into. Serafeim has begun researching how corporate bribery affects morale. In a recent study, he examined survey data from 244 companies that anonymously reported having engaged in bribery overseas. He found that, in the perception of corporate managers, the greatest fallout from the bribery incident was not necessarily its effect on the firm's stock price (which Jonathan Karpoff also found), or in the company's relationship with other firms. The greatest effect was on employee morale: Firms that engage in bribery produce disaffected workers, which ultimately makes the business less competitive. "High employee morale is related to high productivity, creativity and innovation, all significantly affecting the growth of a company," Serafeim writes.[10] This was certainly the experience of Edward Chen, the retired pharmaceutical executive. For more than a decade working in numerous companies, Chen witnessed how the use of bribery pitted a company's sales department against its own compliance team, a conflict that resulted in a drain on both morale and efficiency.

Ultimately, as countless studies, books, and observers have noted, innovation is the foundation for truly successful companies. By that measure, corporations that bribe are failing. For literally hundreds of years, businesses have used kickbacks for competitive advantage, however much they ultimately cause damage to their efficiency, their reputation, and their company morale—all the while sowing political instability and social discord around the globe. "Everyone else is doing it" has been the inevitable rationale, but engaging in inefficient—not to mention morally unacceptable and economically disruptive—behavior to follow the bad example of your competitors is distracting you only from your own ability to innovate.

Corporations in the world's most advanced nations should make antibribery innovation, and not just compliance, one of their top priorities. New sales practices, a novel kind of sales force, and a reconceived compensation structure should be among the key areas for business innovation in the twenty-first century. A genuinely innovative company would be one that not only develops cutting-edge drugs, but also cutting-edge methods to sell them.

This hardly seems an unreasonable proposition, not only because it would lead to larger returns on investment, increase competitiveness, boost employee morale, and enhance corporate reputation, but because it is the right thing to do, and what is right is also sustainable—the ultimate dividend in today's world.

Economists have yet to quantify how many corporate executives have the courage to refuse to engage in bribery. In the absence of empirical studies, we can rely only on anecdote for inspiration. A good example comes from an unlikely source—the Trump administration itself. In an article for the *New Yorker*, the reporter Dexter Filkins describes a meeting that took place in February 2017 between President Trump and then Secretary of State Rex Tillerson. Trump, the article describes, began "fulminating" about the FCPA and how it unfairly penalizes American companies. Tillerson interjected to disagree, and then related a personal story to the president. Tillerson described how, when he was the CEO of ExxonMobil, he met with government officials in Yemen to discuss a business deal. During the talks, Yemen's oil minister handed Tillerson a business card, on the back of which was written a Swiss bank account. "Five million dollars," the oil minister told Tillerson, implying that if Exxon wanted to close the deal, it would have to pay a bribe. Tillerson refused, and explained to Trump, "I don't do that. Exxon doesn't do that." If the Yemenis wanted to do business with Exxon, Tillerson told him, they'd have to do it cleanly. The Yemenis eventually agreed. "Tillerson told Trump that America didn't need to pay bribes—that we could bring the world up to our own standards."[11]

*  *  *

From its founding, the United States of America was intended to stand as an exception to the rule of corruption prevalent in the world. Thomas Paine imagined it as a corrective to economic tyranny, a nation that would not become the kind of abusive power from which it had had to violently separate itself. Through the implementation of the FCPA, Stanley Sporkin and William Proxmire had hoped to achieve a similar goal: that corporations operating on American soil, or benefiting from American stock exchanges, would work to promote democratic and liberal institutions abroad. Today, some forty years after the enactment of the FCPA, thanks to greater international cooperation and a new generation of political will, the United States is doing more than ever before to accomplish that.

But the struggle to halt bribery is also at a point of great uncertainty, threatened by a president not only openly hostile to these efforts, but possibly tainted himself by the crime. It remains to be seen whether Special Counsel Robert Mueller's investigation of Trump, his family, and his associates will uncover corrupt practices. What we are witnessing in the Trump presidency should be reason enough to convince us that efforts to eradicate commercial kickbacks need to be redoubled, not rolled back.

But for countless countries around the world, any change will likely come too little, and too late. Billions of dollars in corporate bribes have already exacted so heavy a price, and for so long a period, that freedom, prosperity, national wealth, and even public health are at risk. As we now know with greater clarity, kickbacks paid in the past have dramatically altered the world we live in today, so we can safely infer that the bribery taking place in the present will dramatically shape the future, potentially sowing conflict and wreaking havoc for generations to come. As Charles Duelfer has observed, corporations that engage in bribery may believe they are making microdecisions that will do no harm, but those choices add up to macro events that determine history. Funding Saddam Hussein's insurgency gave rise to the Islamic State in the Middle East, and whereas corporate bribery cannot be held accountable for ISIS, whose genesis was a highly complex event spawned by many dynamic elements, the bribes paid to Saddam were a critical part of that dynamic.

The consequences of bribery are not often this dramatic, of course, nor this visible. The crises it spawns more often unwind over the course of years, undermining public trust and fracturing political will. Alcatel paid bribes in Costa Rica almost fifteen years ago, yet the investigation still generates headlines on an almost daily basis in San José, the capital, and trials are now only just beginning.

Costa Rica, at least, is beginning to take a reckoning of the damage it suffered. Nigeria cannot say the same. Its own massive bribery scandal involving Kellogg Brown & Root, a subsidiary of Halliburton, has left the country in a kind of paralysis—one all too typical of these cases. Although American court proceedings based on credible evidence implicated at least three of Nigeria's former presidents in the bribery, along with several other prominent officials, no charges have ever been brought against any of them. The Halliburton case (as Nigerians call it) has become the single greatest test of whether the nation's political elite is willing to confront its high-level corruption. The failure to address this situation has become one of the single most important factors in perpetuating a culture of impunity that allows bribery to thrive. "When Nigeria refuses to bring bribe takers to book, it's just like an official sanctioning of bribery and corruption," Musikilu Mojeed, the managing editor of Nigeria's *Premium Times* newspaper in Abuja, says of the Halliburton case.[12] "And that's what the coming, young generation of Nigerians will learn from: that you can steal this money, you can take bribes, and nothing will happen."

The United States can only do so much to penalize these crimes, because, as we've seen, the FCPA provides jurisdiction just over the companies that pay the bribes, not the officials who receive them. But because of mounting criminal and civil actions brought by U.S. and European law enforcement, "Halliburton scandals" are now being uncovered regularly around the world. In Brazil, prosecutors are untangling the massive, and growing, web of bribery involving Petrobras, the state oil company, which appears to have received kickbacks that it allegedly funneled to Brazil's former president and members of the country's intelligence agencies. In Greece, the political system is ruptured by allegations, advanced by a parliamentary committee, that Novartis paid off dozens of public servants, as well as a former prime minister. In Israel, prosecutors have recommended charges against Prime Minister Benjamin Netanyahu for allegedly receiving bribes from foreign companies. Similar cases are being brought in Honduras, Kazakhstan, and South Korea.

The list of reforms needed to prosecute bribe takers is long and daunting. It will require, at a minimum, greater transparency in public spending, especially including more open tendering; more oversight and distributed authority in government, so that a single minister cannot have sole responsibility for a public contract; better pay for civil servants; more funding for anticorruption agencies; stronger antibribery laws; and more independent, better-resourced judiciaries to enforce those laws. These will require technical capacity, legislative reform, financial resources, and most important, political will. Whatever efforts countries like Nigeria and Greece make will be undermined if jurisdictions at the center of offshore company registration and banking—such as the United Kingdom, Cyprus, and increasingly the United States—do not enact more strategic oversight by closing the loopholes that allow foreign officials to hide and launder their bribes.

No country can fight the global kickback system alone, as each has a stake in seeing this crime rendered a practice of the past. Because bribery is fundamentally a system of power, how we regard, regulate, and prosecute it reflects our values with respect to what we are willing to tolerate as free and democratic societies, and what we deem acceptable as human behavior. Recall the words of Senator Charles Percy, speaking in the aftermath of Watergate about the dangers of kickbacks: "The means we use to achieve our objectives in this world define the type of world we are going to live in."

# Acknowledgments TK

# Notes

### Chapter 1: Introduction

1   Organisation for Economic Co-operation and Development, "OECD Principles for Integrity in Public Procurement," (Paris: OECD Publishing, 2009), www.oecd.org/gov/ethics/48994520.pdf.

2   Telephone interview with Michael Won, June 21, 2018.

3   Anne D'Souza and Daniel Kaufmann, "Who Bribes in Public Contracting and Why: Worldwide Evidence from Firms," *Economics of Governance* 14 (2013): 333–67.

4   Richard Brooks, "London's Dirty Laundry," *Private Eye*, August 2012.

5   U.S. Justice Department, "Siemens AG and Three Subsidiaries Plead Guilty to Foreign Corrupt Practices Act Violations and Agree to Pay $450 Million in Combined Criminal Fines," December 15, 2008.

6   Donald Trump, "Trump: Dimon's Woes & Zuckerberg's Prenuptial," CNBC, May 15, 2012, www.cnbc.com/video/2012/05/15/trump-dimons-woes-zuckerbergs-prenuptial.html.

7   Dexter Filkins, "Rex Tillerson at the Breaking Point," *New Yorker*, October 16, 2017.

8   "One of the US's Greatest Gifts to the Global Economy Is Under Threat from Trump, Quartz Media, March 13, 2017, https://qz.com/927217/one-of-the-worlds-best-weapons-against-bribery-and-corruption-is-under-threat-from-trump.

9   Dominic Rushe, "Donald Trump Lifts Anti-Corruption Rules in 'Gift to the American Oil Lobby'" *Guardian*, February 14, 2017, www.guardian.com/us/-news/2017/feb/14/donald-trump-anti-corruption-rules-dodd-frank-oil-companies.

### Chapter 2: "Foul Corruption"

1   Sir Eyre Coote's testimony in Parliament, April 27, 1772, *The Minutes of the Select Committee Appointed by the House of Commons to Enquire into East-India Affairs*, April 27, 1772 (London: T. Evans, 1772), 8. Sir Coote, who was present at the Battle of Plassey, stated: "Our army consisted of 750 men in

battalion, including 100 topazes, 2100 sepoys, 150 artillery, including sailors."

2    Sir Coote, during his interrogation in Parliament, read from his journal the following account of the Battle of Plassey: "Colonel Clive retired to Plassey House and ordered the troops to follow under cover of the wood. . . . The Colonel, being much fatigued both in body and mind, lay down to take a little rest." *The Minutes of the Select Committee Appointed by the House of Commons to Enquire into East-India Affairs*, 39.

3    William Nicholls, an agent of the company in Indonesia, was so vexed about the prevalence of bribery that, in a letter dated January 15, 1615, he wrote: "One toy or two in the beginning would have served; now so many have been so liberally offered to like idols, and to no purpose, and every business done by bribes, that I, that have nothing to give, am enforced to alter the whole course, lest it appear poverty." *The Original Correspondence Section of the East India Company's Records* vol. 4, 1616, reprinted (London: Sampson, Low, Matiston & Company, 1900), 11.

4    William Cobbett, "1695—Bribery and Corruption," *Cobbett's Parliamentary History of England*, vol. 5 (London: R. Bagshaw, 1809), 933–41.

5    Andrew Robinson, *India: A Short History*, (London: Thames & Hudson, 2014), 142.

6    Robert Clive's testimony in Parliament, May 3, 1773. *The History, Debates and Proceedings of Both Houses of Parliament of Great Britain From the Year 1743 to 1774*, vol. 6 (London: J. Debrett, 1792), 491. Accessible online at babel.hathitrust.org/cgi/pt?id=nyp.33433035254840.

7    William Dalrymple, "The East India Company: The Original Corporate Raiders," *Guardian*, March 4, 2015, www.theguardian.com/world/2015/mar/04/east-india-company-original-corporate-raiders.

8    Robert Clive's testimony in Parliament, March 30, 1772, *The History, Debates and Proceedings of Both Houses of Parliament of Great Britain From the Year 1743 to 1774*, vol. 6 (London: J. Debrett, 1792), 255.

9    John Burgoyne's testimony in Parliament, April 13, 1772, *The History, Debates, and Proceedings of Both Houses of Parliament of Great Britain from the Year 1743 to the Year 1774*, 255.

10   John Burgoyne's Parliamentary testimony, May 3, 1773, *The History, Debates, and Proceedings of Both Houses of Parliament of Great Britain from the Year 1743 to the Year 1774*, 503.

11   *A Collection of Treaties and Engagements with the Native Princes and States of Asia Concluded on Behalf of the British East India Company* (London: United East-India Company, 1812), 8.

12  John Walsh's testimony in Parliament, April 29, 1772, *The Genuine Minutes dated 27 April–25 May 1772 of the Select Committee* (London: T. Evans, 1772), 30.

13  Dalrymple, "The East India Company," *Guardian,* March 4, 2015.

14  John Burgoyne's testimony in Parliament, April 13, 1772, *The History, Debates, and Proceedings of Both Houses of Parliament of Great Britain from the Year 1743 to the Year 1774,* 252.

15  John Burgoyne's testimony in Parliament, April 13, 1772, *The History, Debates, and Proceedings of Both Houses of Parliament of Great Britain from the Year 1743 to the Year 1774,* 253.

16  Sir William Meredith's testimony in Parliament, April 21, 1773, *The History, Debates, and Proceedings of Both Houses of Parliament of Great Britain from the Year 1743 to the Year 1774,* 484.

17  John Burgoyne's testimony in Parliament, May 3, 1773, *The History, Debates, and Proceedings of Both Houses of Parliament of Great Britain from the Year 1743 to the Year 1774,* 486.

18  "Report from the Select Committee on East India affairs, and Debate," *The History, Debates, and Proceedings of Both Houses of Parliament of Great Britain from the Year 1743 to the Year 1774,* 493.

19  M. P. Jain, *Indian Legal History 2006* (Morrisville, NC: Lulu Press, 2014).

20  Thomas Paine, "The Life and Death of Lord Clive," *The Writings of Thomas Paine*, ed. Moncure Daniel Conway (New York: AMS Press, 1967), 31.

21  Daniel O'Neill, *Edmund Burke and the Conservative Logic of Empire* (Oakland: University of California Press, 2016), 35.

22  Thomas Paine, "A Serious Thought," October 18, 1775, in *The Writings of Thomas Paine,* 65–66.

23  Daniel O'Neill, *Edmund Burke and the Conservative Logic of Empire* (Oakland: University of California Press, 2016), 34–35.

24  Interview with Peter Clark, Washington, D.C., April 22, 2015.

25  Michael Ruby, "How Clean Is Business?," *Newsweek,* September 1, 1975.

26  Statement of Senator Charles Percy, Multinational Corporations and United States Foreign Policy, Hearings before the Subcommittee on Multinational Corporations, Committee on Foreign Relations, U.S. Senate, 94th Congress, May 16–19; June 9–10; July 16–17; September 12, 1975, (Washington, D.C.: U.S. Government Printing Office, 1976), 14.

27   Statement of Robert Dorsey, Subcommittee on Multinational Corporations, 24.

28   David Pauly, "A Head That Rolled," *Newsweek,* January 26, 1976.

29   Interview with Stanley Sporkin, Washington, D.C., November 9, 2015.

30   Sporkin interview.

31   Statement of Roderick M. Hills, Chairman, Securities and Exchange Commission, Foreign Payments Disclosure, Hearings before the Subcommittee on Consumer Protection and Finance of the Committee on Interstate and Foreign Commerce, House of Representatives, 94th Congress, September 21–22, 1976 (Washington, D.C.: U.S. Government Printing Office, 1977), 17.

32   Statement of Jerome Levinson, Counsel to the Subcommittee on Multinational Corporations, 125. See also Robert E. Smith, "Northrop Apologizes on Saudi Bribes; Senator Church Urges Sales Refiorms," *New York Times*, June 10, 1975, www.nytimes.com/1975/06/10/archives/northrop-apologizes-on-saudi-bribes-senator-church-urges-sales.html.

33   Statement of Representative John E. Moss, Subcommittee on Consumer Protection and Finance, 153.

34   Tom Nicholson et al., "A Question of Bribery," *Newsweek*, April 28, 1975.

35   Untitled, *Associated Press*, September 27, 1977. [full citation needed]

36   John F. Berry, "Extend Report Deadline, Lockheed Panel Urges; Lockheed Panel Asks Extended Report Deadline," *Washington Post*, March 30, 1977.

37   Statement of Senator Charles Percy, Subcommittee on Multinational Corporations,119.

38   David Pauly, "The Great Banana Bribe," *Newsweek*, April 21, 1975.

39   Sporkin interview.

40   Michael Ruby, "How Clean Is Business?"

41   Stanley Sporkin, "The Worldwide Banning of Schmiergeld: A Look at the Foreign Corrupt Practices Act on Its Twentieth Birthday," *Northwestern Journal of International Law & Business* 18, no. 2 (Winter): 273.

42   Peter Clark interview.

43   In 1975 the SEC tabulated $300 million in bribes, according to Sporkin, "The Worldwide Banning of Schmiergeld," 272. Adjusted to today's rates, that is roughly $1.385 billion.

44   Statement of Senator Frank Church, Subcommittee on Multinational Corporations, 341.

45  Statement of Senator William Proxmire, Foreign and Corporate Bribes, Hearings before the Committee on Banking, Housing and Urban Affairs, United States Senate, 94th Congress, April 5, 7, 8, 1976, (Washington, D.C.: U.S. Government Printing Office, 1976), 1.

46  Statement of Robert Dorsey, Subcommittee on Multinational Corporations, 13.

47  Statement of Senator Joseph Biden, Hearings before the Committee on Banking, Housing and Urban Affairs, 44.

48  Alvin Shuster, "Communists Gain 49 Crucial Seats in Italy Contest," *New York Times,* June 23, 1976, www.nytimes.com/1976/06/23/archives/communists-gain-49-crucial-seats-in-italy-contest-christian.html.

49  Statement of Representative Stephen Solarz, Unlawful Corporate Payments Act of 1977, Hearings before the Subcommittee on Consumer Protection and Finance of the Committee on Interstate and Foreign Commerce, House of Representatives, 95th Congress, April 20, 21, 1977 (Washington, D.C.: U.S. Government Printing Office, 1977), 172–73.

50  Statement of Senator Frank Church, Subcommittee on Multinational Corporations, 374–75.

51  Statement of Senator Dick Clark, Subcommittee on Multinational Corporations, 35.

52  Statement of Representative John E. Moss, Subcommittee on Consumer Protection and Finance, 152.

53  Statement of Senator Charles Percy, Subcommittee on Multinational Corporations, 264.

54  Andrew Spalding, "Corruption, Corporations, and the New Human Right," *Washington University Law Review* 91, no. 6 (2014): 1369.

55  Statement of Senator Frank Church, Subcommittee on Multinational Corporations, 240.

56  Andrew Spalding, "Restorative Justice for Multinational Corporations," Ohio State Law Journal 76, no. 2 (2015), 24.

57  John T. Noonan Jr., *Bribe: The Intellectual History of a Moral Idea* (Berkeley and Los Angeles: University of California Press, 1987), 680.

58  Statement of Senator William Proxmire, Hearings before the Committee on Banking, Housing and Urban Affairs, 76.

59  Statement of Senator William Proxmire, Hearings before the Committee on Banking, Housing and Urban Affairs, 15.

60 Statement of Roderick M. Hills, Subcommittee on Consumer Protection and Finance, 23.

61 Barbara Black, "SEC and the Foreign Corrupt Practices Act: Fighting Global Corruption Is Not Part of the SEC's Mission," University of Cincinnati College of Law Scholarships and Publications, 2012, 1115.

62 According to case information listed on the Department of Justice's website, under Foreign Corrupt Practices Act, Related Enforcement Action, Chronological List, www.justice.gov/criminal-fraud/chronological-list.

63 Andrew Spalding, "Corruption, Corporations, and the New Human Right," 1370.

64 Statement of Andrew Pincus, The International Anti-Bribery and Fair Competition Act of 1998, Hearing before the Subcommittee on Finance and Hazardous Materials of the Committee on Commerce, House of Representatives, 104th Congress, September 10, 1998 (Washington, D.C.: U.S. Government Printing Office, 1999), 6.

## Chapter 3: Money Boxes

1 Telephone interview with Kenneth Buff, May 18, 2013.

2 David Zucchino, "Cashiered Over Cache in Baghdad," *Los Angeles Times*, May 28, 2004.

3 Simon Romero and Eric Lipton, "Inquiry Into U.N. Program Puts Focus on Texas Deal Maker," *New York Times*, October 19, 2004.

4 Youssef M. Ibrahim, "Oil Executives Work the Room at OPEC Meeting," *New York Times,* March 23, 1999.

5 Telephone interview with Steve Wyatt, April 3, 2018.

6 Jan Jarboe Russell, "Meaner Than a Junkyard Dog," *Texas Monthly*, April 1991.

7 According to courtroom testimony that a former SOMO official, Mubdir Al-Khudhair, provided at Oscar Wyatt's criminal trial, as reported by David Ivanovich, "Ex-Iraqi Oil Company Officials Links Wyatt to Firms," *Houston Chronicle*, September 25, 2007, www.chron.com/business/energy/article/EWx-Iraqi-oil-company-official-links-Wyatt-to-firms-1600392.php.

8 CNN, "Dr. Germ in U.S. Custody," CNN.com, May 12, 2003, www.cnn.com/2003/WORLD/meast/05/12/sprj.nitop.drgerm.custody.

9 Telephone interview with Rehan Mullick, May 9, 2018.

10  Interview with Rehan Mullick. Many journalistic accounts capture the dire conditions in Baghdad at the time. See Scott Taylor, "Iraq's Decade of Despair," *Ottawa Citizen*, August 19, 2000.

11  According to statements made by UNICEF and cited in, among others, John Pilger, "Collateral Damage; Ten Years of Sanctions in Iraq," *In These Times*, May 15, 2000. In recent years, several studies have cast doubt on the rates of child mortality in Iraq during the sanctions period. See Liz Sly, "Saddam Hussein Said Sanctions killed 500,000 children. That Was 'Spectacular Lie,' " *Washington Post*, August 4, 2017.

12  Charles Duelfer, *Hide and Seek* (New York: Public Affairs, 2009), 385.

13  Telephone interview with Charles Duelfer, April 1, 2015. Unless otherwise specified, all subsequent quotes from Duelfer come from this interview.

14  Paul Volcker, "Manipulation of the Oil-For-Food Programme by the Iraqi Regime," Independent Inquiry Committee, October 27, 2005, 28.

15  Telephone interview with Steven Zidek, February 24, 2016.

16  Charles Duelfer, *Hide and Seek*, 453.

17  Telephone interview with Victor Comras, September 2013.

18  Simon Romero, "Inquiry Into UN Program Puts Focus on Texas Deal Maker," *New York Times,* October 19, 2004.

19  Benon V. Sevan, Biographical Note, United Nations, www.un.org/Depts/oip/ background/latest/sevancv.html.

20  Regime Finance and Procurement, DCI Special Advisor Report on Iraq's WMD, vol. 1, CIA, September 30, 2004, www.cia.gov/library/reports/general-reports-1/iraq_wmd_2004/chap2.html.

21  Regime Finance and Procurement, DCI Special Advisor Report on Iraq's WMD.

22  The Oil-for-Food Program: Tracking the Funds, Hearing Before the Committee on International Relations, House of Representatives, 108th Congress, November 17, 2004, http://commdocs.house.gov/committees/intlrel/ hfa96930.000/hfa96930_0f.htm.

23  Statement of Rehan Mullick, The United Nations Oil-for-Food Program: The Cotecna and Saybolt Inspection Firms, Hearing before the Subcommittee on Oversight and Investigations of the Committee on International Relations, House of Representatives, 109th Congress, March 17, 2005, (Washington, D.C.: U.S. Government Printing Office, 2005), 68.

24  Transparency International, "Transparency International Germany Files

Complaint Against 57 German Companies Over UN Oil for Food Scandal in Iraq," June 4, 2007, www.transparency.org/news/pressrelease/20070604_transparency_international_germany_files_complaint_against_57_comp.

25  Roughly 4,500 companies participated in the UN program, according to figures made public by the Volcker Commission. See Phil Hirschkom, "Report Finds Illicit Oil-for-Food Payments Widespread," *CNN.com*, August 14, 2005. www.cnn.com/2005/US/08/11/oil.for.food.

26  Statement of Steven Groves, Counsel, How Saddam Hussein Abused the United Nations Oil for Food Program, Hearing before the Permanent Subcommittee on Investigations, Committee on Governmental Affairs, U. S. Senate, 108th Congress, November 15, 2004 (Washington, D.C.: U.S. Government Printing Office, 2005), 46.

27  Testimony of Steven Groves, Hearing before the Permanent Subcommittee on Investigations, 45.

28  Regime Finance and Procurement, DCI Special Advisor Report on Iraq's WMD.

29  Iraq Survey Group, Comprehensive Report of the Special Advisor to the DCI on Iraq's WMD, September 30, 2004, 98.

30  Thom Shanker, "Hussein's Agents Behind Attacks, Pentagon Finds," *New York Times,* April 29, 2004.

31  Statement of Paul Wolfowitz, Iraq's Transition—The Way Ahead [Part I], Hearing before the Committee on Foreign Relations, United States Senate, 108th Congress, May 18, 2004 (Washington, D.C.: U.S. Government Printing Office, 2005), 7.

32  Paul Wolfowitz, Hearing before the Committee on Foreign Relations, 35.

33  Senator Norm Coleman, Hearing before the Permanent Subcommittee on Investigations, 2.

34  Statement of Juan Carlos Zarate, Hearing before the Permanent Subcommittee on Investigations, 99.

35  Charles Duelfer, *Hide and Seek,* (New York: Public Affairs, 2009), 380.

36  Dexter Filkins, "Bank Officials Say Hussein's Son Took $1 Billion in Cash," *New York Times,* May 5, 2003.

37  Duelfer, *Hide and Seek,* 380.

38  According to Charles Duelfer's report, most of the $1 billion robbed from the Central Bank was recovered, a claim echoed by U.S. officials who spoke with

ABC News. It seems that the money found by Sergeants Buff and Van Ess was the majority of the $1 billion stolen by Qusay.

39　"Saddam Hoard 'Funds Insurgency,' BBC News, December 3, 2003.

40　Claudia Rosett, "I Am Not Running Away," *Wall Street Journal*, April 1, 2006.

41　Mimi Swartz, "The Day Oscar Wyatt Caved," *Texas Monthly,* November, 1, 2007, www.texasmonthly.com/2007–11–01/feature3.php.

42　David Ivanovich, "Oilman Gets 12 Months in Iraq Scandal," *Houston Chronicle*, November 27, 2007.

43　David Ivanovich, "Oil-for-Food Figure Gets 2 Years; Houston Trader Schemed to Funnel Money to Saddam," *Houston Chronicle,* March 8, 2008.

44　"Saddam's UN Payroll," *Wall Street Journal*, October 28, 2004.

45　Duelfer interview.

46　Jamie Dettmer, "He Served Saddam. He Served ISIS. Now Al Douri May Be Dead," Daily Beast, April 17, 2015, www.thedailybeast.com/articles/2015/04/17/he-served-saddam-he-served-isis-now-al-douri-may-be-dead.html.

47　Yujin Jeong And Robert J. Weiner, "Who Bribes? Evidence from the United Nations' Oil-for-Food Program," *Strategic Management Journal* 33, no. 12 (2012): 1363–83.

48　Interview with Paul Pelletier, Washington, D.C., April 1, 2016.

49　Interview with Steven Tyrrell, Washington, D.C., March 26, 2015.

50　Peter Clark interview.

51　Interview with Joseph Persichini, Washington, D.C., November 6, 2013.

### Chapter 4: Happy Fools

1　Winne Chi-Man Yip et al., "Early Appraisal of China's Huge and complex health-care reforms," *Lancet* 379, no. 9818 (March 2012): 836.

2　Peter Carlson, "Potent Medicine: A Year Ago, Viagra Hit the Shelves and the Earth Moved, Well, Sort Of," *Washington Post*, March 26, 1999.

3　Novartis, Annual Report 2005, 120, www.novartis.com/sites/www.novartis.com/files/novartis-annual-report-2005-en.pdf.

4　Novartis, Annual Report 2008, 144, www.annualreports.com/HostedData/AnnualReportArchive/n/NYSE_NVS_2008.pdf.

5   Bristol-Myers Squibb, Annual Report 2005, s21.q4cdn.com/104148044/files/doc_financials/annual_reports/BMY_AR_05.pdf.

6   Marianne Barriaux, "Glaxo Cuts Jobs to Save £700m A Year After Profits Slide," *Guardian,* October 25, 2007.

7   Sara Sjolin, "Chinas Diabetes Boom Promises $23 Billion Pot for Drug Makers,"Market Watch, March 21, 2016, www.marketwatch.com/story/chinas-diabetes-boom-promises-23-billion-put-for-drug-makers-2016-01-15.

8   Ma Zhenhuan, "GSK May Shift Some Relenza Manufacturing to Mainland," *China Daily*, November 19, 2009, www.chinadaily.com.cn/business/2009-11/19/content_8999949.htm.

9   Arthur Daemmrich, "The Political Economy of Healthcare Reform in China: Negotiating Public and Private," Daemmrich, Arthur. "The Political Economy of Healthcare Reform in China: Negotiating Public and Private." *SpringerPlus* 2 (2013): 448, www.ncbi.nlm.nih.gov/pmc/articles/PMC3776089.

10  Winnie Yip and William C. Hsiao, "What Drove the Cycles of Chinese Health System Reforms?," *Health Systems & Reform* 1, no. 1 (2015): 52–61.

11  Telephone interview with Ping, October 10, 2015.

12  Meina Li et al., "The Problem of Unreasonably High Pharmaceutical Fees for Patients In Chinese Hospitals: A System Dynamics Simulation Model" *Computers in Biology and Medicine* 47 (2014): 58–65.

13  Conclave Report, Pharma Future Knowledge Conclave 2014, May 16, 2014, http://pharmafuture.org/pdf/new-commercial-models-to-create-customer-value/PharmaFuture2014EventSummary.pdf.

14  Rachel Cooper, "AstraZeneca Is Well Placed for the Chinese Boom," June6, 2010, *Telegragh,* www.telegraph.co.uk/finance/newsbysector/pharmaceuticalsandchemicals/7807002/AstraZeneca-is-well-placed-for-the-Chinese-boom.html.

15  Lizzy Li, "Eli Lilly Has Own Strategy to Extend Its Reach in China—CEO," China Pharmaceuticals and Health Technologies Weekly, April 2, 2008.

16  Nicholas Zamiska, "AstraZeneca Taps China's Hinterlands," *Wall Street Journal,* June 13, 2008.

17  Interview with Lijuan (not her real name), China, 2015 (date and place withheld). All subsequent quotes from Lijuan come from this interview.

18  Adam Jourdan and Ben Hirschler, "GSK in China: Escaping the Shadow of a Scandal," Reuters, November 25, 2015,

19  Xinhua, "China's Hospital Wards Haunted by Violence," XinhuaNet.com, May 11, 2016, www.xinhuanet.com/english/2016–05/11/c_135351592.htm.

20  Telephone interview with Yanzhong Huang, February 5, 2016.

21  U.S. Securities and Exchange Commission, In the Matter of GlaxoSmithKline PLC, Order Instituting Cease-and-Desist Proceedings, September 30, 2016, 3.

22  U.S. Securities and Exchange Commission, In the Matter of Bristol-Myers Squibb Company, Order Instituting Cease-and-Desist Proceedings, October 5, 2015, 5.

23  *U.S. Securities and Exchange Commission v. Pfizer Inc.,* 2012, 7

24  U.S. Securities and Exchange Commission, In the Matter of SciClone Pharmaceuticals, Inc., Order Instituting Cease-And-Desist Proceedings, February 4, 2016, 3.

25  *U.S. Securities and Exchange Commission v. Pfizer Inc.,* 2012, 7.

26  U.S. Securities and Exchange Commission, In the Matter of SciClone Pharmaceuticals, Inc., 3.

27  U.S. Securities and Exchange Commission, In the Matter of AstraZeneca PLC, Order Instituting Cease-And-Desist Proceedings, August 30, 2016, 3.

28  U.S. Securities and Exchange Commission, In the Matter of Novartis AG, Order Instituting Cease-and-Desist Proceedings, March 23, 2016, 4.

29  U.S. Securities and Exchange Commission, In the Matter of Eli Lilly and Company, Order Instituting Cease-And-Desist Proceedings, December 20, 2012, 8.

30  Interview with Edward Chen, Taipei, Taiwan, October 7–9, 2015. All subsequent quotes from Chen come from these interviews.

31  Novartis, *Annual Report 2011*, 11, www.novartis.com/sites/www.novartis.com/files/novartis-annual-report-2011-en.pdf.

32  Franck Le Deu et al., "Healthcare in China: Entering 'Uncharted Waters," McKinsey & Company, November 2012, www.mckinsey.com/industries/healthcare-systems-and-services/our-insights/health-care-in-china-entering-uncharted-waters.

33  Duff Wilson, "Drug Firms Face Billions in Losses in '11 as Patents End," *New York Times,* March 6, 2011, www.nytimes.com/2011/03/07/business/07drug.html?_r=0.

34  Bill Smith, "China Charges Top GlaxoSmithKline Executives with Bribery," *Deutsche Presse-Agentur,* May 14, 2014.

35  Craig Charney and Shehzad Qazi, "Corruption in China: What Companies Need to Know," Charney Research, White Paper No. 1, January 2015, www. charneyresearch.com/wp-content/uploads/2015/01/White-Paper-Corruption-in-China-FINAL-v10.pdf.

36  OECD Foreign Bribery Report: An Analysis of the Crime of Bribery of Foreign Public Officials, 2014, https://read.oecd-ilibrary.org/governance/oecd-foreign-bribery-report_9789264226616-en#page3.

37  Interview with Dr. Lee, China, September 21, 2015.

38  Xuan Yu et al., "Pharmaceutical Supply Chain in China: Current Issues and Implications for Health System Reform," *Health Policy* 97 no. 1 (2010): 8–15.

39  Interview with Dr. Ming, Ningbo, China. September 20, 2015.

40  J. Currie et al., "Patient Knowledge and Antibiotic Abuse: Evidence from an Audit Study In China," *Journal of Health Economics* 30, no. 5 (September 2011): 933–49.

41  Chengcheng Jiang, "When Penicillin Pays: Why China Loves Antibiotics a Little Too Much," *Time,* January 5, 2012, http://content.time.com/time/world/article/0,8599,2103733,00.html.

42  Zheng Wang et al., "Deadly Sins of Antibiotic Abuse in China," *Infection Control & Hospital Epidemiology* 38 no 6 (June 2017): 758–59.

43  U.S. Securities and Exchange Commission, In the Matter of Eli Lilly and Company, 17.

44  Prepared remarks by Lanny A. Breuer, Annual Pharmaceutical Regulatory and Compliance Congress and Best Practices Forum, Washington, D.C., November 12, 2009.

### Chapter 5: The Black Curtains

1  Telephone interview with Jeremy Nottingham, January 17, 2017.

2  Telephone interview with Sasi-Kanth Mallela, January 24, 2017.

3  The Victor Dahdaleh/Clinton Foundation Scholarships, as detailed here: www.clintonfoundation.org/clinton-global-initiative/commitments/victor-dahdalehclinton-foundation-scholarships.

4  Letters, *The Spectator,* May 26, 1961, archive.spectator.co.uk/article/26th-may-1961/15/sir-i-am-an-arab-palestinian-refugee-from-ramleh-i.

5  Wikileaks, "Business Inquiry from Jordanian Firm," March 21, 1979, wikileaks.org/plusd/cables/1979AMMAN01781_e.html.

6   *United States of America v. Alcoa World Alumina LLC,* Criminal Information, 10.

7   Rawmet Limited corporate filings retrieved from the Jersey Financial Services Commission, www.jerseyfsc.org/registry/#, copies with author.

8   David Armstrong and Alan Katz, "Billionaire Found in Middle of Bribery Case Avoids U.S. Probe," *Bloomberg*, August 14, 2014.

9   World Report 2011: Bahrain, Human Rights Watch, www.hrw.org/world-report/2011/country-chapters/Bahrain.

10  U.S. Securities and Exchange Commission, In the Matter of Alcoa Inc., Order Instituting Cease-and-Desist Proceedings, January 9, 2014, 5.

11  *United States of America v. Alcoa World Alumina LLC,* 11.

12  Telephone interview with former U.S. law enforcement official, February 28, 2017.

13  *United States of America v. Alcoa World Alumina LLC,* 11.

14  *Aluminum Bahrain B.S.C v. Alcoa Inc.,* First Amended Complaint, United States District Court, Western District of Pennsylvania, 32.

15  U.S. Securities and Exchange Commission, In the Matter of Alcoa Inc., 7.

16  Statement of Carl Kotchian, Subcommittee on Multinational Corporations, Committee on Foreign Relations, 94th Congress, February 4 and 6, May 4, 1976 (Washington, D.C.: U.S. Government Printing House, 1977), 367.

17  Central Intelligence Agency, Office of Central Reference, Biographical Register, "KODAMA, Yoshio," undated. Copy with author.

18  Central Intelligence Agency, Central Reference Service, "Yoshio KODAMA," January 29, 1976. Copy with author.

19  Central Intelligence Agency, "1948 Press Censorship Reports," September 15, 1953. Copy with author.

20  Central Intelligence Agency, Central Reference Service.

21  Figures cited by CIA documents range from 400 million yen to 3.2 billion yen, or several billion dollars in today's currency. Documents with author.

22  Richard Halloran, "5 Japanese Had Key Roles in Pushing Lockheed Bids," *New York Times*, March 1, 1976.

23  Richard Halloran, "Lockheed Ex-Official Says Initiative in Bribe Cases Came from Japanese," December 20, 1976, *New York Times,* www.nytimes.com/1976/12/20/archives/lockheed-exofficial-says-initiative-in-bribe-cases-came-from.html?_r=0.

24  "Japan Arrests 17th Official in the Lockheed Bribe Scandal," *New York Times,* August 21, 1976.

25  Statement of Senator Frank Church, Multinational Corporations and United States Foreign Policy, Hearings before the Subcommittee on Multinational Corporations, Committee on Foreign Relations, U.S. Senate, 94th Congress, May 16–19; June 9–10; July 16–17; September 12, 1975, (Washington, D.C.: U.S. Government Printing Office, 1976), 332.

26  Yomiuri Shimbun, "Top Court to Give Final Ruling In Lockheed Bribery Case," *Daily Yomiuri,* February 22, 1995.

27  Statement of Senator Charles Percy, Subcommittee on Multinational Corporations, 342.

28  Alistair Osborne, "Fresh Reversal for SFO as £40m Bribery Trial Collapses," *Telegraph*, December 10, 2013.

29  Telephone interview with William Rice, May 9, 2018.

30  *United States of America v. Alcoa World Alumina LLC,* 7.

31  Økokrim v. Cabu Chartering AS, Penalty Note, May 19, 2014, translated from the Norwegian.

32  Økokrim v. Cabu Chartering AS.

33  Bjorn  Segrov,  "Indicated  Payments  to  the  King  of  Bahrain," *Dagen    Naeringsliv,*    September    6,    2012,    www.dn.no/nyheter/ naringsliv/2012/09/06/-indikerte-utbetalinger-til-kongen-i-bahrain.

34  A U.S. State Department cable leaked by Wikileaks observes, "The Bahraini officials who stand to be embarrassed are most likely in the camp of the Prime Minister," wikileaks.org/plusd/cables/08MANAMA192_a.html.

35  Interview with Ala'a Shehabi, London, England, April 18, 2017.

36  In the Crown Court Southwark, *Victor Dahdaleh v. Mark MacDougall and Akin Gump,* Case No. T20117607 & T20117073, Judgement, March 21, 2014, 6.

37  Department of Justice, Office of Public Affairs, press release, "Alcoa World Alumina Agrees to Plead Guilty to Foreign Bribery and Pay $223 Million in Fines and Forfeiture," January 9, 2014, www.justice.gov/opa/pr/alcoa-world-alumina-agrees-plead-guilty-foreign-bribery-and-pay-223-million-fines-and.

38  *United States of America v. Siemens Aktien Gesellschaft,* U.S. District Court, Information,  December  12,  2008,  9,  www.justice.gov/sites/default/files/ criminal-fraud/legacy/2013/05/02/12–12–08siemensakt-info.pdf.

39  *U.S.Securities and Exchange Commission v. Siemens Aktien Gesellschaft,* .U.S. District Court, Complaint, December 12, 2008, 8–10, www.sec.gov/litigation/complaints/2008/comp20829.pdf.

40  Diego Cabot, "The Financier of the Julia Plane, in the Judicial Sight," *La Nacion,* January 13, 2011, www.lanacion.com.ar/1341128-el-financista-del-avion-de-los-julia-en-la-mira-judicial (Translated from the Spanish).

41  Peggy Hollinger and Catherine Belton, "Rolls-Royce Humbled by Long List of Corruption Offenses," *Financial Times,* January 18, 2017, www.ft.com/content/5c85eab6-dcd5–11e6–86ac-f253db7791c6.

42  Department of Justice, Office of Public Affairs, press release, "Rolls-Royce PLC Agrees to Pay $170 Million Criminal Penalty to Resolve Foreign Corrupt Practices Act Case," January 17, 2017, www.justice.gov/opa/pr/rolls-royce-plc-agrees-pay-170-million-criminal-penalty-resolve-foreign-corrupt-practices-act.

43  York University Media, "York U Establishes the Dahdaleh Institute for Global Health," Youtube.com, December 8, 2015, www.youtube.com/watch?v=A3BnOj0gqPY.

44  McGill Newsroom, "Victor Phillip Dahdaleh Supports Neuroscience Research," McGill Channels, May 26, 2016, www.mcgill.ca/channels/news/victor-phillip-dahdaleh-supports-neuroscience-research-261018.

45  British Lung Foundation, press release, "£5 Million for Life-Changing Mesothelioma Research," undated, www.blf.org.uk/your-stories/5-million-for-life-changing-mesothelioma-research.

46  York University, press release, "Philanthropist Victor Phillip Dahdaleh Urges Grads to Go Out and Make a Difference in the World," June 20, 2016, yfile.news.yorku.ca/2016/06/20/philanthropist-victor-phillip-dahdaleh-urges-grads-to-go-out-and-make-a-difference-in-the-world.

47  Author correspondence with Anthony Brovane, Communication Specialist, the Office of the Attorney General of Switzerland OAG, January 31, 2017.

48  European Commission, press release, "Commission Clears Merger Between Alcoa and Reynolds Metals, Under Conditions," May 3, 2000, europa.eu/rapid/press-release_IP-00–424_en.htm.

49  "Alcoa Completes Sale of Stade Alumina Refinery to Dadco Alumina and Chemicals, Ltd.," *Business Wire,* April 11, 2001.

50  Norsk Hydro ASA, public filings with U.S. Securities and Exchange Commission, Exhibit 99.1, June 30, 2004. Filings list the sale price at 750 million Norwegian Kroner, or roughly $110 million in 2004 rates.

51 Andrew Thomas, "Rio Tinto and Norsk Hydro Sell Boke Stakes," *Mining Journal,* July 2, 2004.

52 Ellis Island Honor Society, International Medal of Honor and Global Humanitarian Honorees, www.neco.org/medal-of-honor/international.

53 Top Donors to the William J. Clinton Presidential Foundation, *New York Sun,* November 22, 2004, www.nysun.com/national/top-donors-to-the-william-j-clinton-presidential/5152.

54 The Victor Dahdaleh/Clinton Foundation Scholarships, Clinton Global Initiative, Clinton Foundation,

www.clintonfoundation.org/clinton-global-initiative/commitments/victor-dahdalehclinton-foundation-scholarships.

55 Peggy Curran, "Clinton Picks Up Honorary Degree, Feels the Warmth," *Montreal Gazette,* October 17, 2009.

56 Alcoa Corp. Annual Report filing with the U.S. Securities and Exchange Commission, December 31, 2017.

## Chapter 6: A Houseboat in the Swamps

1 U.S. District Court for the District of Columbia, In Re Enforcement of Restraining Order Issued by the High Court of England and Wales, 1:12-mc-00289-RCL, May 16, 2012, 9.

2 U.S. District Court for the District of Columbia, In Re Enforcement of Restraining Order Issued by the High Court of England and Wales, 9.

3 Interview with Nuhu Ribadu, Abuja, Nigeria, February 18, 2016.

4 Telephone interview with Robert Palmer, June 2, 2016.

5 "The World's Largest Oil Reserves by Country," WorldAtlas, www.worldatlas.com/articles/the-world-s-largest-oil-reserves-by-country.html.

6 Ofeibea Quist-Arcton, "Ethnic Clashes Disrupt Nigeria Oil Production, World Markets Hit," allAfrica.com, March 26, 2003, allafrica.com/stories/200303260001.html.

7 "Nigeria; Ibori Inspects Vandalised Flow Stations, Weeps," *Africa News,* July 8, 2003.

8 Mike Oduniyi, "Nigeria: Siege on Chevron: 300 Oil Workers Released, 700 Still Held," *Africa News*, July 16, 2002.

9 Austin Ogwuda, "Nigeria: Ibori Dismisses Critics Over 13% Derivation," *Africa News,* August 31, 2000.

10  The cable leaked byWikileaks can be accessed at wikileaks.org/plusd/cables/08LAGOS41_a.html.

11  Malalchy Uzendu, "Chevron Denies Illegal Contract with Ibori," *Daily Champion* (Nigeria), February 22, 2008.

12  Interview with Bhadresh Gohil, London, England, April 20, 2017. All subsequent quotes from Gohil come from this interview.

13  Saharareporters, "V-Mobile $37 Million Shares Fraud—Bhadresh Gohil, Ibori's UK Lawyer Sentenced to 7 Years in Prison," Saharareporters.com, March 8, 2011, saharareporters.com/2011/03/08/v-mobile-37million-shares-fraud-bhadresh-gohil-ibori's-uk-lawyer-sentenced-7-years-prison.

14  Background interview with FBI agent, Washington, D.C., April 16, 2015.

15  Phone interview with Ryan Rohlfsen, Chicago, IL, April 21, 2016.

16  According to court remarks by Sasha Wass, lead prosecutor in the UK corruption case against Ibori.

17  According to a report published in the Nigerian newspaper *This Day,* which cites an official Request for Mutual Legal Assistance, the investigation began in March 2005. According to documents in the Panama Papers, leaked by ICIJ, the investigation began in April 2005.

18  U.S. District Court for the District of Columbia, In Re Enforcement of Restraining Order Issued by the High Court of England and Wales, 5.

19  Telephone interview with Andrew Warren, February 28, 2017.

20  *United States of America vs. Wojciech J. Chodan,* Statement of Wojciech Chodan, transcript of rearraignment, December 6, 2010, 3.

21  Interview with Paul Novak, Abuja, Nigeria, March 9, 2016.

22  *U.S. Securities and Exchange Commission v. Weatherford International Ltd.,* Complaint, November 26, 2013, 6–7.

23  Archived versions of the photos available with author.

24  M.E.R. Engineering incorporation documents obtained through the Corporate Affairs Commission, Abuja, by B. I. Dakum & Co., Barristers, Abuja, M.E.R. Engineering RC#192670. Documents with author.

25  Interview with James Koukious, Washington, D.C., March 31, 2016.

26  U.S. District Court for the District of Columbia, In Re Enforcement of Restraining Order Issued by the High Court of England and Wales, 5, 9.

27  Interview with Gary Walters, London, England, April 18 and 21, 2017; telephone interview, May 14, 2018.

28  Background interview with EFCC Investigator, Abuja, Nigeria, March 6, 2016.

29  In the Court of Appeal (Criminal Division) on Appeal from the Crown Court Sitting at Southwark, Royal Courts of Justice, *R v Bhadresh Babulal Gohil and Ellias Nimoh Preko, [2018] EWCA Crim 140, Judgement, February 15, 2018,* www.judiciary.gov.uk/wp-content/uploads/2018/02/r-v-gohil-and-r-v-preko. pdf.

30  Correspondence with former Metropolitan Police officer, April 21, 2017.

31  Estelle Shirbon, "Rags-to-Riches Nigerian Governor Faces UK Jail Term," Reuters, April 16, 2012, www.reuters.com/article/us-britain-nigeria-ibori/rags- to-riches-nigerian-governor-faces-uk-jail-term-idUSBRE831F14D20120416.

32  Transcript of court hearing at Southwark Crown Court, *Regina v. Mr. James Onanefe Ibori,* September 30, 2013, 66. Copy with author.

33  Background telephone interview with U.S. Justice Department prosecutor, FCPA Unit, August 6, 2015.

34  In the Court of Appeal (Criminal Division) on Appeal from the Crown Court Sitting at Southwark, Royal Courts of Justice, *R v Preko,* Court of Appeal, Criminal Division, [2015] All ER (D) 50 (Feb); [2015] EWCA Crim 42, 3 February 3, 2015.

35  Estelle Shirbon, "Ex-Goldman Sachs Banker Jailed in UK in Nigerian Corruption Case," Reuters, December 9, 2013, www.reuters.com/article/ us-britain-banker-corruption-idUSBRE9B80OE20131209.

36  Background telephone interview with U.S. Justice Department prosecutor, March 17, 2016.

37  "James Ibori," Offshore Leaks Database, offshoreleaks.icij.org/ nodes/15006801.

38  U.S. Justice Department, Office of Public Affairs, press release, "Hewlett- Packard Russia Agrees to Plead Guilty to Foreign Bribery," April 9, 2014, www. justice.gov/opa/pr/hewlett-packard-russia-agrees-plead-guilty-foreign-bribery.

39  "British Virgin Islands Business Company (BVI BC)," Fidelity Corporate Services, www.offshorebvi.com/bvi-offshore-companies.php.

40  Steve Reilly, "Dozens of Firms Creating Foreign-Based Shell Companies in Two U.S. States," May 26, 2016, www.usatoday.com/story/news/2016/05/26/ dozens-firms-creating-foreign-based-shell-companies-two-us-states/84222480.

41  "Tackling Corruption," Prime Minister David Cameron's speech, Lee Kuan Yew School of Public Policy, Singapore, July 28, 2015, www.gov.uk/ government/speeches/tackling-corruption-pm-speech-in-singapore.

42  Ana Swanson, "How Secretive Shell Companies Shape the U.S. Real Estate Market," Washington Post, April 12, 2016, www.washingtonpost.com/news/wonk/wp/2016/04/12/how-secretive-shell-companies-shape-the-u-s-real-estate-market/?utm_term=.cbd616f60eb1.

43  Transparency International UK, "National Risk Assessment of Money Laundering and Terrorist Financing," May 2014, 15, www.issuu.com/transparencyuk/docs/ti-uk_submission_to_the_hm_treasury.

44  Robert Booth, Helena Bengtsson, and David Pegg, "Revealed: 9% Rise in London Properties Owned by Offshore Firms," Guardian, May 26, 2016, www.theguardian.com/money/2016/may/26/revealed-9-rise-in-london-properties-owned-by-offshore-firms.

45  David Charter, "Labour Donor Laundered Abacha Money," Times (London), December 24. 2003.

46  Financial Services Authority, "FSA Publishes Results of Money Laundering Investigation," March 8, 2001, www.fsa.gov.uk/Pages/Library/Communication/PR/2001/029.shtml.

47  "International Thief Thief: How British Banks Are Complicit in Nigerian Corruption," Global Witness, October 2010.

48  Financial Conduct Authority, Final Notice: Barclays Bank PLC, November 25, 2016, www.fca.org.uk/static/documents/final-notices/barclays-bank-nov-2015.pdf. Outlines the FCA's investigation and findings about Barclay's controversial deal.

49  United States of America v. Mahmoud Thiam, Sealed Complaint, December 12, 2018, 13–14. Details the actions of two U.S. banks to perform due diligence on Thiam's accounts.

50  David Rose and Martin Beckford, "Met Police Chief Under Fire Again over Claims That Officers Were Bribed During into Nigerian Politician Jailed for Fraud," February 13, 2016, www.dailymail.co.uk/news/article-3446061/Met-police-chief-fire-claims-officers-bribed-investigation-Nigerian-politician-jailed-fraud.html.

51  According to a ruling on Gohil's appeal from the Royal Courts of Justice, February 15, 2018, www.judiciary.gov.uk/wp-content/uploads/2018/02/r-v-gohil-and-r-v-preko.pdf.

52  Fiona Hamilton and Michael Gillard, "Top QC Quits Cases in Row Over Police Bribery," Times (London), June 11, 2016.

53  Peter Marshall, "UK Aid Funded Firms 'Linked to Nigeria Fraudster Ibori,'" BBC Newsnight, April 16, 2012.

54  Interview with anonymous source, Abuja, Nigeria, March 9, 2016.

55  Interview with Victor (last name withheld), Port Harcourt, Nigeria, March 4, 2016.

## Chapter 7: *Miza*

1   Helena Smith, "Greek Suicide Seen as an Act of Fortitude as Much as One of Despair," *Guardian*, April 5, 2012, www.theguardian.com/world/2012/apr/05/greek-suicide-dimitris-christoulas-protest.

2   Interview with Thanassis (last name withheld), Athens, Greece, August 29, 2015.

3   Naina Bajekal, "The Next Greek Crisis Is Coming, *Newsweek,* April 29, 2016, www.newsweek.com/2016/04/29/next-greece-crisis-coming-449410.html.

4   "Timeline: The Unfolding Eurozone Crisis," BBC News, June 12, 2012, www.bbc.com/news/business-13856580.

5   "Greece Fallout: Italy and Spain Have Funded a Massive Backdoor Bailout of French Banks," Council on Foreign Relations, *Geo-Graphics* (Blog), post by Benn Steil and Dinah Walker, July 2, 2015, blogs.cfr.org/geographics/2015/07/02/greecefallout.

6   Background interview with public prosecutor, Athens, Greece, September 10, 2015.

7   "The House of Tsochatzopoulos in Areopagitou," *Kathimerini,* May 5, 2010, translated from the Greek, www.kathimerini.gr./394776/article/epikairothta/politikh/h-oikia-tsoxatzopoyloy-sthn-areopagitoy.

8   James Angelos, *The Full Catastrophe: Travels Among the New Greek Ruins* (New York: Broadway Books, 2016), 74.

9   Ara Tatevosyan, "New Alliances Centered on Caucasus," *Moscow News,* July 24, 1997.

10  Rupert Cornwell, "Greece Claims Turkey Buzzed Minister's Jet," *Independent,* October 17, 1997.

11  Figures come from SIPRI, quoted in Nikos Chrysogelos, europeangreens.eu/sites/europeangreens.eu/files/militaryexpencesses.pdf.

12  Background interview with Greek public prosecutor, Athens, Greece, August 29, 2015.

13  Reuters Staff, "Greece to Overhaul Arms Procurement after Scandal,"

Reuters, January 3, 2014, www.reuters.com/article/greece-bribes-idUSL6N0K D23B20140103.

14  "German Firm Tried to Reach Deal on Arms Bribes in July, May 9, 2015, *Kathimerini,* www.ekathimerini.com/201213/article/ekathimerini/news/ german-firm-tried-to-reach-deal-on-arms-bribes-in-july.

15  Niki Kitsantonis, "Greek Prosecutors Focus on Corruption at the Top," *New York Times,* January 18, 2014.

16  Interview with Constantinos P. Fraggos, Kiffissia, Greece, September 7, 2015.

17  Reuters Staff, "German Prosecutors Raid Offices of Tank Maker Krauss-Maffei," Reuters, November 15, 2014, http://uk.reuters.com/article/ uk-krauss-maffei-wegmann-corruption-idUKKCN0IZ0T420141115.

18  In the Crown Court at Southwark, *Regina v Robert Dougall,* Proceedings, April 14, 2010, 102. Copy of sentencing transcript with author.

19  *United States of America v. Depuy, Inc.,* U.S. District Court, Information, April 8, 2011, 12, www.justice.gov/sites/default/files/criminal-fraud/ legacy/2011/04/27/04–08–11depuy-info.pdf. Karagiannis is not openly named in these documents, but the UK's Serious Fraud Office, as well as prosecutors in Greece, identified him as the agent in question. See the following judgment in Dougall's appeal in criminal court at Southwark, openmedicineeu.blogactiv/ eu/files/2011/10/JJ-DOUGALL-Appeal-Judgement1.pdf.

20  In the Crown Court at Southwark, *Regina v Robert Dougall,* Proceedings, 50.

21  Interview with Panagiotis Nikoloudis, Athens, Greece, September 3, 2015. All subsequent quotes from Nikoloudis come from this interview.

22  *United States of America v. Smith & Nephew, Inc.* U.S. District Court, Information, February 6, 2012, 8.

23  In the Crown Court at Southwark, *Regina v Robert Dougall,* Proceedings, 31.

24  *U.S. Securities and Exchange Commission v. Johnson & Johnson,* U.S. District Court, Complaint, April 8, 2011, 5.

25  In the Crown Court at Southwark, *Regina v Robert Dougall,* Proceedings, 11.

26  Interview with Spyros Georgouleas, Athens, Greece, September 1, 2015.

27  *United States of America v. Smith & Nephew, Inc.,* U.S. District Court, Information, Information, February 6, 2012, 8.

28  From John Dougall's initial interview with police, transcript of Attendance Note Re: John Dougall, 3. Copy with author.

29  Marcus Walker, "Tragic Flaw: Graft Feeds Greek Crisis," *Wall Street Journal,*

April 15, 2010, www.wsj.com/articles/SB1000142405270230382830457517 9921909783864.

30  Menelaos Tzafalias, "Greek Crisis Fallout Is an Opportunity for Health," *Bulletin of the World Health Organization,* 2014, www.who.int/bulletin/ volumes/92/1/14–030114/en.

31  Charalampos Economou et al., "The Impact of the Financial Crisis on the Health System in Greece," World Health Organization, 2014, 10, www.euro. who.int/__data/assets/pdf_file/0007/266380/The-impact-of-the-financial-crisis-on-the-health-system-and-health-in-Greece.pdf.

32  Reuters Staff, "Greece Says to Pay Hospital Supplier Debt Mostly with Bonds," June 15, 2010, www.reuters.com/article/greece-debt-hospitals/greece-says-to-pay-hospital-supplier-debt-mostly-with-bonds-idUSLDE65E1MZ20100615.

33  Figures cited by Marty Makary, "Greece's Costly Health Care Craze," *New York Times*, July 20, 2015, www.nytimes.com/2015/07/21/opinion/greeces-costly-health-care-craze.html, citing the Organization for Econonic Co-Operation and Development.

34  Charalampos Economou et al., 16.

35  Alexander Kentikelenis,"Greece's Health Crisis: From Austerity to Denialism," *Lancet* 383, no. 9918 (February 22, 2014): 748–53.

36  Press release, Johnson & Johnson, "Johnson & Johnson Statement on Voluntary Disclosure," February 12, 2007, www.investor.jnj.com/releasedetail. cfm?releaseid=229695.

37  "Reaction Report: Raiko Forgot about Gianno and Liakunakos," Documento, March 24, 2017 (in Greek), www.documentonews.gr/article/ anaforasok-anakritrias-h-raikoy-xexase-stoixeia-gia-gianno-kai-liakoynako-sto-documento-poy-kykloforei-ektaktws-to-sabbato.

38  Novartis AG, filings with the U.S. Securities and Exchange Commission, Exhibit 99, "Additional Exhibits." filed January 25, 2017. See this report in *Politico,* Simon Marks, "Drugs Scandal Roils Greek Politics," *Politico,* May 30, 2018, www.politico.eu/article/ greece-politics-novartis-scandal-pharmaceutical-whistleblower.

## Chapter 8: Fueling the Fire

1  Interview with Mohsin Ali, Natore, Bangladesh, February 15, 2015.

2  "Foreign Operators Vie for Bangladesh Mobile Telephone Service," Agence France Presse, December 19, 2002.

3    *United States of America v. Siemens Bangladesh Limited,* U.S. District
     Court, Information, 10, www.justice.gov/sites/default/files/criminal-fraud/
     legacy/2013/05/02/12–12–08siemensbangla-info.pdf.

4    *United States of America v. Siemens Bangladesh Limited,* 10.

5    The account of LaPrevotte's investigation in Bangladesh is based on a
     background interview with an FBI investigator in Washington, D.C., April 16,
     2015; interviews with serving and former officials in Bangladesh; U.S. law
     enforcement court filings; U.S. diplomatic cables leaked by Wikileaks; and
     newspaper reports in the Bangladeshi press.

6    Telephone interview with Debra LaPrevotte, April 3, 2018.

7    Interview with Salahuddin Ahmad, Dhaka, Bangladesh, February 12, 2015.

8    International Crisis Group, "Bangladesh Today," Report No 121/Asia, October
     23, 2006, www.crisisgroup.org/asia/south-asia/bangladesh/bangladesh-today.

9    Interview with Anisul Huq, Dhaka, Bangladesh, February 10, 2015.

10   Background interview, Dhaka, Bangladesh, February 15, 2015.

11   The cable leaked by Wikileaks can be accessed at wikileaks.org/plusd/
     cables/08DHAKA1143_a.html.

12   According to a biographical account submitted as part of his money laundering
     case in Bangladesh. Copy with author.

13   Interview with Saleh, Dhaka, Bangladesh, February 7, 2015.

14   Background interview, former police official, Dhaka, Bangladesh, February 7,
     2015.

15   Julfikar Ali Manik, "Bangla Bhai Active for 6 Years," *Daily Star,* May 13,
     2004, archive.thedailystar.net/2004/05/13/d4051301022.htm.

16   Staff Correspondent, Rajshahi, "Police Escort JMJB in Rajshahi Showdown,"
     *Daily Star,* May 24, 2004. archive.thedailystar.net/2004/05/24/d4052401033.
     htm.

17   Background telephone interview with Western diplomat, February 2014.

18   Background interview with former criminal intelligence officer, Dhaka,
     Bangladesh, February 10, 2015.

19   Julfikar Ali Manik, "Evidence, Confessions Point at JMB HallMark," *Daily
     Star,* August 19, 2005, archive.thedailystar.net/2005/08/19/d5081901011.htm.

20   The cable leaked by Wikileaks can be accessed at wikileaks.org/plusd/
     cables/08DHAKA1143_a.html.

21  Background interview with FBI agent, Washington, D.C., April 16, 2015.

22  *United States of America v. All Assets Held in the Name of Zasz Trading and Consulting PTE Ltd, Account Number 1093101397, at United Overseas Bank, Singapore and Proceeds Traceable Thereto,* U.S. District Court, January 8, 2009, 7.

23  *United States of America v. All Assets Held in the Name of Zasz Trading and Consulting PTE Ltd, Account Number 1093101397, at United Overseas Bank, Singapore and Proceeds Traceable Thereto,* U.S. District Court, January 8, 2009, 6.

24  The cable leaked by Wikileaks can be accessed at wikileaks.org/plusd/cables/08DHAKA1143_a.html.

25  David Montero and Somini Sengupta, "Bangladesh Blast Kills One and Hurts 30," *New York Times,* December 2, 2005, www.nytimes.com/2005/12/02/world/asia/bangladesh-blast-kills-one-and-hurts-30.html?_r=0.

26  Telephone interview with Ekramul Haque, one of the public prosecutors in the case, Rajshahi, Bangladesh, February 15, 2018.

27  Anwar Ali, "JMB Patron Aminul Jailed," *Daily Star,* July 27, 2007, archive. thedailystar.net/2007/07/27/d7072701011.htm.

28  See David Montero, "Bangladesh: Bribery's Dangerous Beneficiary," *PBS Frontline/World,* May 11, 2009, www.pbs.org/frontlineworld/stories/bribe/2009/05/bangladesh.html; David Montero, "Bangladesh Fights Rampant Corporate Corruption," *Christian Science Monitor,* April 1, 2009, www.csmonitor.com/World/Asia-South-Central/2009/0401/p06s15-wosc.html; Jurgen Dahlkamp and David Montero, "KORRUPTION: Benzin ins Feuer," *Der Spiegel,* June 29, 2009, www.spiegel.de/spiegel/print/d-65872369.html.

29  "Watchdog Panel to Probe Siemens Bribe-JMB Funding Link," BDNews, May 24, 2009, bdnews24.com/bangladesh/2009/05/24/watchdog-panel-to-probe-siemens-bribe-jmb-funding-link.

30  Background interview with domestic intelligence officer, Dhaka, Bangladesh, February 8. 2015.

31  Background telephone interview with former State Department official, March 31, 2015.

32  Ewan Sutherland, "A Short Note on Corruption in Telecommunications in Bangladesh," September 3, 2012, http://ssrn.com/abstract=2052355.

33  Chaitanya Chandra Halder and Rizanuzzaman Laskar, "Tarique Laundered Money," Daily Star, November 17, 2011, www.thedailystar.net/news-detail-210437.

34  "Bangladesh: Tarique Rahman Jailed for Money Laundering," July 21, 2016, www.aljazeera.com/news/2016/07/bangladesh-tarique-rahman-jailed-money-laundering-160721073133821.html.

35  Linda M. Samuel, Obituary, September 22, 2013, www.legacy.com/obituaries/thetimes-tribune/obituary.aspx?pid=167109816.

36  Andrew Marszal, "20 Hostages killed in 'Isil' Attack on Dhaka Restaurant Popular with Foreigners," *Telegraph*, July 2, 2016, www.telegraph.co.uk/news/2016/07/01/gunmen-attack-restaurant-in-diplmatic-quarter-of-bangladeshi-ca.

37  Court Correspondent, "Aminul Sent to Jail on Surrender," *Daily Star*, July 7, 2009, www.thedailystar.net/news-detail-95894.

38  Staff Correspondent, "Aminul Freed from Rajshahi Jail," October 6, 2009, *Daily Star,* www.thedailystar.net/news-detail-108685.

39  Staff Correspondent, "HC Cancels Aminul Haq's Sentence," *New Age*, April 9, 2011.

40  Staff Correspondent, "HC Grants Bail to Aminul," *Daily Star,* June 13, 2012, www.thedailystar.net/news-detail-238082.

### Chapter 9: Flash Bang

1   Interview with Richard Bistrong, Rowayton, Connecticutt, April 25, 2014, and July 21, 2014. All subsequent quotes from Bistrong come from these interviews.

2   Benjamin Forgey, "Preservation with Personality; The Sensitive Restoration of the Southern and Bond Buildings," *Washington Post*, December 19, 1987.

3   Interview with Charles Duross, Washington, D.C., October 8, 2014; March 26, 2015.

4   Interview with Lanny Breuer, Washington, D.C., February 25, 2014.

5   Sharon Oded, "Deferred Prosecution Agreements: Prosecutorial Balance in Times of Economic Meltdown," *Law Journal for Social Justice* 2, (January 2011).

6   As Lanny Breuer once described, "Prosecutors faced a stark choice when they encountered a corporation that had engaged in misconduct—either indict, or walk away. . . . Companies now know that avoiding the disaster scenario of an indictment does not mean an escape from accountability." Lanny Breuer, prepared remarks, New York Bar Association, September 13, 2012, www.justice.gov/opa/speech/assistant-attorney-general-lanny-breuer-speaks-new-york-city-bar-association.

7   According to public remarks made by Denis McInerney, chief of the Justice Department's Fraud Section, and William Stuckwish, assistant chief of the Justice Department's Fraud Section, quoted in Morgan Lewis LawFlash, "DOJ and SEC Affirm Continued Commitment to Rigorous FCPA Enforcement," November 14, 2011, www.morganlewis.com/pubs/doj-and-sec-affirm-continued-committment-to-rigorous-fcpa-enforcement.

8   Pelletier interview.

9   Background interview, former FBI official, FCPA unit, September 23, 2015.

10  Interview with FBI official, FCPA Unit, Washington, D.C., April 11, 2014.

11  Testimony of FBI agent Chris Forvour in *United States of America v. Pankesh Patel et al.,* U.S. District Court, District of Columbia, June 13, 2011, A.M. Session, 26.

12  Background interview, former Justice Department prosecutor, Washington, D.C., 2016.

13  Background interview, business executive, October 2013.

14  As detailed in court documents filed in the case, see *United States of America v. Daniel Alvirez and Lee Allen Tolleson,* United States' Notice Regarding Discovery, U.S. District Court, District of Columbia, April 1, 2010, www.millerchevalier.com/sites/default/files/resources/StingDiscoveryNotice.pdf.

15  United States Department of Justice, Office of Public Affairs, press release, "Twenty-two Executives and Employees of Military and Law Enforcement Products Companies Charged in Foreign Bribery Scheme," January 19, 2010, archives.fbi.gov/archives/washingtondc/press-releases/2010/wfo011910.htm.

16  Testimony of FBI Agent Chris Forvour in *United States of America v. Pankesh Patel et al.,* U.S. District Court, District of Columbia, June 8, 2011, A.M. Session, 79.

17  Christopher Norton, "FBI's Tactics In Gabon FCPA Sting Come Under Fire," Law360, June 22, 2011, www.law360.com/articles/253246/fbi-s-tactics-in-gabon-fcpa-sting-come-under-fire.

18  As quoted in Mike Koehler, "Africa Sting—In the Words of Judge Leon, FCPAProfessor.com, February 23, 2012, www.fcpaprofessor.com/africa-sting-in-the-words-of-judge-leon.

19  Alberto R. Gonzales, "Prepared Remarks by Former Attorney General Alberto R. Gonzales, Lawyers for Civil Justice Meeting, Washington, DC, May 2012," www.wallerlaw.com/portalresource/lookup/wosid/cp-base-4-13102/media.name=/TAP%20-%20Speech%20to%20LCJ%20by%20Judge%20Gonzales%202012%2005.pdf.

20  "The Untouchables," *PBS Frontline,* Season 31, Ep. 4, www.pbs.org/wgbh/frontline/untouchables.

21  See Jed S. Rakoff, "The Financial Crisis: Why Have No High-Level Executives Been Prosecuted," *New York Review of Books*, January 9, 2014, www.nybooks.com/articles/2014/01/09/financial-crisis-why-no-executive-prosecutions.

22  "A Focus on DOJ FCPA Individual Prosecutions," FCPA Professor, January 20, 2015, fcpaprofessor.com/a-focus-on-doj-fcpa-individual-prosecutions-3.

23  Individual Accountability for Corporate Wrongdoing, Department of Justice, Office of the Deputy Attorney General, September 9, 2015, www.justice.gov/dag/file/769036/download.

24  U.S. Justice Department, Office of Public Affairs, press release, "Deputy Attorney General Sally Q. Yates Delivers Remarks at the New York City Bar Association White Collar Crime Conference," May 10, 2016, www.justice.gov/opa/speech/deputy-attorney-general-sally-q-yates-delivers-remarks-new-york-city-bar-association.

## Chapter 10: Givebacks

1  For background see "English Translation: Settlement Agreement Between Alcatel-Lucent France, and the Office of the Attorney General of the Republic, on Behalf of the Costa Rican State, Relating to the Civil Recovery Action Included in Criminal Case 04–6835–647-PE," available at star.worldbank.org/corruption-cases/sites/corruption-cases/files/settlement/ICE_US_Opposition_Exhibit_1_Costa_Rice_Settlement_SDFLA_May_23_2011.pdf.

2  *United States of America v. Alcatel-Lucent France, S.A. (as to Alcatel Centroamerica, S. A.),* U.S. District Court, District of Columbia, December 27, 2010 Plea Agreement, 7.

3  "Former Costa Rican President Sentenced to Prison over Alcatel Bribery," *Wall Street Journal,* April 28, 2011, star.worldbank.org/corruption-cases/sites/corruption-cases/files/documents/arw/Alcatel_Rodriguez_Conviction_Wall_Street_Journal_Apr_28_2011.pdf.

4  Department of Justice, Office of Public Affairs, press release, "Alcatel-Lucent S.A. and Three Subsidiaries Agree to Pay $92 Million to Resolve Foreign Corrupt Practices Act Investigation," December 27, 2010, www.justice.gov/opa/pr/alcatel-lucent-sa-and-three-subsidiaries-agree-pay-92-million-resolve-foreign-corrupt.

5  Juanita Olaya, "Repairing Social Damage Out of Corruption Cases: Opportunities and Challenges as Illustrated in the Alcatel Case in Costa Rica (December 6, 2010)," available at SSRN: https://ssrn.com/abstract=1779834;

"Corruption Causes Social Damage: Can It Be Repaired," January 31, 2011, juanitaolaya-impactools.com/tag/victims-of-corruption.

6    Telephone interview with Juanita Olaya, August 25, 2017.

7    Interview with Chief Godwin Obla, Abuja, Nigeria, February 27, 2017.

8    Paulo Mauro, "The Effects of Corruption on Growth, Investment, and Government Expenditure," International Monetary Fund, Policy Development and Review Department, September 1996, papers.ssrn.com/sol3/papers/cfm?abstract_id=882994.

9    Vito Tanzi and Hamid Davoodi, "Corruption, Public Investment and Growth," International Monetary Fund Working Paper, 1997, www.imf.org/external/pubs/ft/wp/wp97139.pdf.

10   "Issues Paper on Corruption and Economic Growth," Organisation for Economic Co-operation and Development, www.oecd.org/g20/topics/anti-corruption/Issue-Paper-Corruption-and-Economic-Growth.pdf.

11   Juanita Olaya, "Dealing with the Consequences: Repairing the Social Damage Caused by Corruption," draft paper 2016, available at impactools.files.wordpress.com/2015/10/repairing-the-public-good-v2-01_2016.pdf.

12   Andrew Spalding, "Restorative Justice for Multinational Corporations, 1.

13   Spalding, 32.

14   Telephone interview with Andrew Spalding, March 27, 2015.

15   ExxonMobil and the other companies denied that Giffen was acting on their behalf. Giffen was never convicted of bribery offenses and instead pleaded guilty to one count of tax evasion.

16   "The Bota Foundation Revisited—Part Two: BOTA—A Quick Recap," FCPA Blog, post by Aaron Bornstein, February 27, 2017, www.fcpablog.com/blog/2017/2/27/the-bota-foundation-revisited-part-two-bota-a-quick-recap.html.

17   According to statistics compiled by the author, the FCPA Blog (www.fcpablog.com) and information available on the FCPA enforcement section of the Justice Department's website, www.justice.gov/criminal-fraud/related-enforcement-actions.

18   Jacinta Anyango Oduor et al., "Left Out of the Bargain," Stolen Asset Recovery Initiative, World Bank, 2.

19   Jonathan Karpoff et al., "Foreign Bribery: Incentives and Enforcement," April 7, 2017, 10, papers.ssrn.com/sol3/papers.cfm?abstract_id=1573222.

20  Karpoff et al., "Foreign Bribery," 32.

21  Karpoff et al., "Foreign Bribery," 5.

22  Karpoff et al., "Foreign Bribery," 22.

23  In its annual report for 2008, Siemens lists its market capitalization for 2007 at €88 billion, or roughly $100 million. Siemens, Annual Report 2008, 12, www.siemens.com/investor/pool/en/investor_relations/e08_00_gb2008.pdf.

24  Karpoff et al., "Foreign Bribery, 40.

25  Telephone interview with Jonathan Karpoff, February 16, 2018.

26  Drury D. Stevenson and Nicholas J. Wagoner, "FCPA Sanctions: Too Big to Debar?," 80, Fordham Law Review 80, no. 2 (2011), 775 http://ir.lawnet.fordham.edu/flr/vol80/iss2/13.

27  Organisation for Economic Co-Operation and Development, "OECD Business and Finance Outlook 2016, Chapter 7: Is Foreign Bribery an Attractive Investment in Some Countries?, www.oecd.org/corruption/BFO-2016-Ch7-Bribery.pdf.

28  Reuters Staff, "Disparate Laws, Low Fines Mean Corporate Bribery Often Pays: OECD," Reuters, June 9, 2016, www.reuters.com/article/us-oecd-corruption/disparate-laws-low-fines-mean-corporate-bribery-often-pays-oecd-idUSKCN0YV1BR.

29  "2014 Global Survey on Reputation Risk, Deloitte, October 2014, www2.deloitte.com/content/dam/Deloitte/global/Documents/Governance-Risk-Compliance/gx_grc_Reputation@Risk%20survey%20report_FINAL.pdf.

30  Background telephone interview, Justice Department prosecutor, FCPA Unit, August 6, 2015.

31  U.S. Department of Justice, press release, "Siemens AG and Three Subsidiaries Plead Guilty to Foreign Corrupt Practices Act Violations and Agree to Pay $450 Million in Combined Criminal Fines," December 15, 2008, www.justice.gov/archive/opa/pr/2008/December/08-crm-1105.html.

### Chapter 11: A New Standard

1  OECD, "Data on Enforcemnt of the Anti-Bribery Convention," Organisation of Economic Co-operation and Development, November 14, 2017, www.oecd.org/corruption/data-on-enforcement-of-the-anti-bribery-convention.htm.

2  Telephone interview with Kent Kedl, February 4, 2016.

3  Deloitte, "In Focus: 2015 Compliance Trends Survey," www2.deloitte.com/

content/dam/Deloitte/global/Documents/Risk/gx-aers-reg-2015-compliance-trends-survey.pdf.

4    "Global Ethics & Compliance Program Report, April 20, 2016, Walmart, corporate.walmart.com/global-responsibility/global-compliance-program-report-on-fiscal-year-2016.

5    Deloitte, "In Focus: 2016 Compliance Trends Survey," www2.deloitte.com/content/dam/Deloitte/us/Documents/governance-risk-compliance/us-advisory-compliance-week-survey.pdf.

6    Jed S. Rakoff, "Justice Deferred Is Justice Denied," *New York Review of Books,* February 19, 2015, www.nybooks.com/articles/2015/02/19/justice-deferred-justice-denied.

7    *U.S. Department of Justice, Office of Public Affairs, press release, "Zimmer Biomet Holdings Inc. Agrees to Pay $17.4 Million to Resolve Foreign Corrupt Practices Act Charges,"* January 12, 2017, www.justice.gov/opa/pr/zimmer-biomet-holdings-inc-agrees-pay-174-million-resolve-foreign-corrupt-practices-act.

8    Rakoff, "Justice Deferred is Justice Denied."

9    Paul Healy and George Serafeim, "Causes and Consequences of Firm Disclosures of Anticorruption Efforts," Harvard Business School, 2011, 25.

10   George Serafeim, "Firm Competitiveness and Detection of Bribery," Working Paper 14–012, Harvard Business School, April 4, 2014,

11   Dexter Filkins, "Rex Tillerson at the Breaking Point," *New Yorker,* October 16, 2017, www.newyorker.com/magazine/2017/10/16/rex-tillerson-at-the-breaking-point.

12   Telephone interview with Musikilu Mojeed, March 31, 2016.

# Index TK

[hold 8–10 pages]